HOWARD'S GIFT

Howard's Gift

Uncommon Wisdom to Inspire Your Life's Work

Eric C. Sinoway

with Merrill Meadow

ST. MARTIN'S PRESS NEW YORK

To Howard H. Stevenson, a man of head and heart, of wisdom and warmth, of perspective and emotion—one who has given these gifts selflessly to thousands throughout his life, and who, despite initial trepidation and an endearing bit of shyness, permitted me to share them with the readers of this book.

To Frederika Stevenson and the Stevenson family.

To the men and women who collectively kept a heart-stopping moment from becoming a tragic one—including Jeff Sandefer and Linda Hill, Andrew O'Brien, William Kaden, Andrew MacMillan, Bruce Biller, and Debra Poaster from Harvard Business School; and Drs. Kim Saal, Robert Campbell, Vladimir Birjiniuk, Michael Kjelsberg, Michael Farmer, and the caring and skilled professionals at the Mt. Auburn Hospital Cardiac Unit.

In their honor, a portion of the proceeds from *Howard's Gift* will be donated to Mt. Auburn Hospital and Harvard University—supporting miracles yet to be performed.

HOWARD'S GIFT. Copyright © 2012 by Eric Sinoway. All rights reserved. Printed in the United States of America. For information, address St. Martin's Press, 175 Fifth Avenue, New York, NY 10010.

www.stmartins.com

Library of Congress Cataloging-in-Publication Data

Sinoway, Eric C.
    Howard's gift : uncommon wisdom to inspire your life's work / Eric C. Sinoway with Merrill Meadow.
        p. cm.
    ISBN 978-1-250-00424-6 (hardcover)
    ISBN 978-1-250-01562-4 (e-book)
    1. Business planning.   2. Strategic planning.   I. Meadow, Merrill.   II. Title.
    HD30.28.S477 2012
    650.1—dc23

2012028243

First Edition: October 2012

10 9 8 7 6 5 4 3 2 1

CONTENTS

HOWARD'S GIFT

CHAPTER ONE

Business Planning for Your Life's Work

W<small>E CAN ALL USE</small> a wise man or woman in our lives. Someone who helps us make sense of the challenges we face. Who guides us as we navigate times of change. Who counsels us as we move along life's path.

Who among us wouldn't want to call on a person with wisdom and experience when we have to make important decisions about our careers and our personal lives? Especially when those decisions are fraught with risk and uncertainty, and complicated by fundamental changes in the world around us.

And let's face it, wisdom is at a premium, as we've experienced an unbelievable amount of change over the last few years.

When I first had the idea of writing this book, the stock market was at an all-time high, prosperity was increasing all over the world, and megamillionaires were being created every other day. It looked like the economic good times would never end. Quite frankly, it was an environment in which many people who weren't getting rich—and that's most of us—were wondering why not, and whether we should be approaching our lives and careers in a very different way.

The assumption, of course, was that wealth equaled success and success equaled happiness. The initial concept for this book was to help people think through how to achieve happiness and meaning in their lives within that environment.

And then things changed, seemingly overnight.

In a breathtakingly short period of time, the economic world as we knew it imploded. A company that was once synonymous with American economic success, General Motors, went bankrupt. The disintegration of a single Wall Street icon, Lehman Brothers, threatened the entire global finance system. Average people—like you and me and the folks across the street—unwittingly helped overzealous lenders drive the nation's mortgage industry and housing market over a cliff.

As a society, we ran headfirst into an inflection point.

What is an inflection point? It is what Andy Grove, the founder and former CEO of Intel, defined as an event that fundamentally changes the way we think and act. Usually, an inflection point isn't a little change. It is a moment when—by choice or not—we pivot from the path down which we are traveling and head in an entirely different direction.

During the past dozen years, we've gone through several extraordinary inflection points. We have experienced a series of economic and political events that caused the future to look very different from what we'd expected it would.

Until not too long ago, a whole generation of college graduates believed they were destined to follow the path of the founders of Microsoft, Google, and Facebook and become multimillionaires before they were thirty. Investment banking was seen as the guaranteed path to becoming a "master of the universe." People were celebrated as heroes for running companies based on business models that, in any other time, would have been considered laughable. Policy makers in Washington, DC, were so confident that the stock market would keep rising—seemingly forever—that they considered privatizing Social Security, the economic safety net of the American working man and woman.

Beginning in 2007 and continuing to this day, we've been reminded of two rules that we'd apparently forgotten: (1) what goes up does eventually come down, and (2) businesses built on a foundation of smoke and mirrors will surely fail.

At breakneck speed, discussions about the stock market turned to preserving capital, not growing it. People with jobs were satisfied just to keep them—forget about promotions and raises. Homeowners went from visions of windfall profits to hopes of avoiding foreclosure. Folks with newly minted college and graduate degrees suddenly faced a frozen job market.

Even those people whose financial lives did not collapse had a tremendous scare. And we're all trying to guess if there's a new problem just over the horizon.

In times of extraordinary challenges and dizzying change—whether it's happening around us or to us—we can all use a wise guide. A person who helps us think through our basic assumptions about what we want and need in our lives, about what "success" means to us and how best to navigate our lives during unsettling times.

Wise men and women come in plenty of flavors and sizes, and with varying degrees of insight. Like beauty, wisdom is often in the eye of the beholder. And the wisdom you find depends a lot on the kind of wisdom you may benefit from at a particular moment. For some, the ideal wise person looks like Abraham Lincoln or Mother Teresa; for others it's Warren Buffett or Oprah Winfrey.

The wise man I've found is a mixture: he has the business acumen of Warren Buffett, and the warmth and spirit of Morrie Schwartz, Mitch Albom's professor in the book *Tuesdays with Morrie*. He also has a rather humorous resemblance to Yoda, the wise, skilled, and experienced Jedi knight of *Star Wars* fame.

Although my wise man looks a bit like Yoda, in place of a light saber he wields razor-sharp logic and scalpel-like insight. He is a real-life teacher, mentor, and guide through challenging, risky, and downright scary adventures. His name is Howard Stevenson.

Howard is an entrepreneur, an author, and a philanthropist. And for forty years, he has been one of the most important and respected professors at Harvard Business School. He possesses an amazing combination of business brilliance, keen psychological perception, energetic spirit, and long-term vision. He has an endearing perspective on life, something I didn't fully appreciate until it was almost gone.

Howard is exactly the kind of person that so many of us would like to be able to turn to when important decisions are to be made or challenges met. One whose wisdom and experience have guided thousands of men and women through the inflection points in their lives.

Over the course of four decades, Howard has taught, mentored, and counseled thousands of Harvard MBAs, graduate students, and global business leaders. His students have included world leaders, CEOs of major corporations, and entrepreneurs whose visions have changed our world.

Numbered among Howard's many students, friends, and confidants are some of the most successful businesspeople and philanthropists in the world. They have included people like Jorge Paolo Lemann, the Brazilian billionaire co-owner of the international beverage conglomerate Anheuser-Busch InBev, William Bowes, one of the creators of the U.S. bio tech industry; Hansjörg Wyss, the Swiss medical appliance industry pioneer and mega philanthropist; the late Frank Batten, who created the Weather Channel; and Arthur Rock, the legendary investor who helped launch Intel and Apple.

Why have business icons like Lemann, Bowes, Wyss, Batten, and Rock—people who have reached the pinnacle of professional success—continued to look to this remarkable man? For the same reason that I do: to benefit from the insight, wisdom, warmth, and pragmatic perspective that this rumpled Harvard Business School professor shares with everyone whose life he has touched.

This book is my way of introducing you to my friend and mentor Howard Stevenson.

Every book has a catalyst, something that makes an author believe, "It's essential that I tell people about this." For some authors that moment feels like an earthquake or a thunderclap; for others, it's a slowly dawning realization or a voice whispering in the mind's ear.

To me, that moment felt like a punch to the gut and the urge to vomit.

I was standing in the parking lot of Harvard Business School one mild winter day in Cambridge, Massachusetts, staring dumbly at a colleague who was telling me something I didn't want to believe. I heard his words, but I couldn't absorb their meaning. "Howard had a heart attack two hours ago. It's bad."

At age sixty-six, Howard Stevenson was a legend at Harvard Business School. An iconic teacher, he was an innovator who defined the academic field of entrepreneurial business. He was a successful businessman who'd made a fortune several times over, and a philanthropist and philanthropic adviser of the first rank. A towering figure among corporate leaders, he was a warm friend and a generous mentor.

Howard was considered the father of entrepreneurship at HBS, and he was like a second father to me.

We had first met when I was a thirty-something "mid-career" graduate student at Harvard's Kennedy School and he agreed to advise me on an independent study project. From our initial conversation, I found myself oddly connected to this Ivy League scholar with a quirky smile. His ruffled hair, piercing gaze, and slightly hunched posture were an amusing contrast to the interior man: brilliant, witty, playful, and endlessly curious. I came to adore his unique spirit.

And now . . . "They had to give him CPR. He might not make it."

Despite getting a clean bill of health from his doctor only weeks earlier, Howard had collapsed in cardiac arrest as he walked across campus after lunch. It had been an otherwise typical day until his ticker simply stopped ticking.

I was frantic at the news and spent the next several hours calling colleagues and rushing from one office to the next, vainly trying to get some update on Howard's condition. It was only days later that his assistant, Bobbie, could give me good news. Howard would be all right—but only because of amazing good luck: he had collapsed next to a building that had a portable defibrillator, and someone immediately brought the device to his side; plus the HBS campus is just two miles from a good hospital. (That evening, when I saw my friend Josh Silverman—a brilliant surgeon and scientist—I learned that the survival rate for "unattended cardiac arrest" is about 1 percent. So in any other circumstances, Howard likely would have died there on the manicured lawns of Harvard Business School.)

Even when I knew that he'd fully recover, my stomach clenched at the thought of Howard lying flat on his back, staring up at the clouds, wondering if he was headed to what he'd once called "the great business school in the sky." I realized that during the endless hours we'd spent joking, debating, and analyzing together, I hadn't stopped to tell him what he meant to me. Hadn't thanked him for making me think about things differently, for challenging my assumptions about business, about my career, about my life. I hadn't expressed my gratitude for the wisdom he showered on me each time we spoke. And I hadn't told him that I loved him.

Ironically, when I went to see Howard in the hospital, he was in remarkably good spirits. So good, in fact, that when I asked him what he'd been thinking when he first woke up after his heart attack, he gave me a deadpan answer that made me laugh out loud.

"Well, first I thought, 'Damn, I bet they ruined the favorite sportcoat I was wearing when I collapsed.' Then, seeing all the equipment they had me hooked up to, I thought, 'Gee, I'm glad I gave the hospital a nice-sized gift last year.'"

His humor was encouraging, but something in me wanted a more serious answer, so I asked, "Howard, when you were lying on the ground, knowing you might die right there in the middle of the campus, did you have any regrets?"

"You mean like regretting that piece of cheesecake I ate at lunch just before I collapsed? Or kicking myself for not ordering that expensive bottle of wine at the restaurant the night before?"

"I was thinking of something more significant," I said. "Like, 'Boy, there are sixty things I'd do differently about my life, if I could,' or 'If I survive, I'm going to change things in a major way.'"

He thought about it for a minute, then answered, "They tell me I was unconscious when I hit the ground, so—technically speaking—I had no time for regretting anything. But I understand what you're asking. And the answer is nope."

"And in the days since—any regrets?"

"Not a one."

"Really?" I asked.

"Look, Eric, a person has regrets when his life doesn't match up with his expectations, or when he has dreams he hasn't vigorously pursued," Howard said in his smooth growl. "I've lived the life I wanted, and accomplished more than I could have wished. I have an amazing wife and a loving family. I've been surrounded by wonderful friends. And I think I've left a little piece of the planet a bit better for animal and man."

"So you would have died happy and satisfied?"

"Well, not happy about dying. But satisfied with the life I've lived," he replied. "No one can say that he or she hasn't made mistakes or had faults—we're human, and you've got to accept that. But I would have gone with no major regrets over things I'd done or not done."

For a reason I didn't immediately understand, I left Howard's hospital room feeling worse than I think he did. He was upbeat, encouraged, joking. I was reflective, brooding, confused. I couldn't figure out why. Instead of heading home after that first hospital visit, I drove back to the Harvard campus and spent a few hours that evening wandering around, alone with my thoughts.

I remembered my first meeting with Howard several years earlier, and how he had challenged me—right off the bat—to think differently than I had been doing to that point. He'd done it in a way that was hard-nosed and stimulating, insightful, and warm and caring, all at the same time. As I continued to walk aimlessly around campus late into the evening, I realized that while I was incredibly grateful that Howard had survived and had lived his life with what he described as "no regrets," there was something eating at me. A thought sitting, annoyingly, just beyond my mind's reach. Then it came to me: Howard's experience had made me realize that I had a giant regret of my own.

For the last three years, Howard and I had been spending a few hours a week together—in his office, at his home, or simply walking around the Harvard campus. In that short time, he had evolved from my professor to a mentor to a dear friend. We had talked about many things, some frivolous, but most serious. Our conversations had touched on music and books and travels, on politics and economics, on family and philosophy, on business strategy and professional development, on the value of education versus experience, and on the many ways one could make a difference in the world. We talked about pursuing success and recovering from failure. About setting goals and setting out to achieve them.

If I had to sum up the topic of all those conversations in one sentence, it would be this: we talked about how to chart a satisfying path through career and life—about pursuing what Howard called your "life's work."

"Life's work" was a term I had heard in several different contexts. Most often for me it conjured images of deep and long devotion to great causes and difficult, admirable labors. The phrase brought to mind Mother Teresa and her work with India's poor and sick, or Paul Farmer and his efforts to heal and rebuild Haiti. Or it made me think of the anonymous struggling artist, or the inventor determined to bring her mind's vision to reality. When Howard talked about people pursuing their life's work, he was certainly referring to all the saints and visionaries, but not only to them. He was talking about everyone and anyone who got up each morning hoping to achieve something of substance with their lives. He was talking about accountants and engineers, teachers and Web designers, lawyers and social workers, business owners and nonprofit executives. He was talking about you and me and the folks living two doors down.

For Howard, describing one's life's work means the totality of who we are: the interwoven strands of our labors, our loves, our hopes, and our tangible needs and wants; the interdependent elements of our lives that we sometimes try to wall off into independent silos that we name "the job," "the family," and "the rest of my life."

In my many conversations with Howard, I had soaked up the seemingly endless ideas and sage advice that he offered on approaching my life's work. But I'd made no effort to capture exactly what he was giving me. At first, I hadn't even realized how much I was learning. I'd met many smart, even brilliant, people at Harvard. But Howard was different—he wasn't just smart, he was *wise*. And, eventually, I understood the cause of the energetic buzz in my brain after our conversations: it was from the tiny infusions of wisdom I'd been receiving. He was like no one else I had ever met.

Driving home on the night of my hospital visit with Howard, I recognized that I had more than regret on my mind. At the moment that I learned Howard had cheated death, I had made a subconscious decision that was only just becoming clear to me. The decision that was coming into focus was to capture some of the wisdom that Howard had been effortlessly dispensing—and to share that wisdom with people who'd never have the chance to learn from him directly.

That's why, visiting Howard again a few days later, I told him that I had his next project picked out. "Once you're done with all those tubes, wires, and probes you're wearing, I want us to write a book together. Actually, you'll talk, I'll write it down, and it'll be your next book."

"Really?" he asked with a wry smile.

I explained my idea for a book based on his experience and insight—on the things he'd learned directly and the lessons he'd gleaned from watching his students' careers and lives over the decades. "I want to capture some of the amazing things we've talked about. Give everyone a chance to learn from you like I've been doing these past few years."

Howard thought about it for a few minutes, then said, "Well, writing a book sounds fine. But I think we should do it a little differently. I don't want you to simply transcribe my words. I'm happy to do some talking, but you've got to talk, too."

"Talk about what?" I asked.

"I want you to add yourself to the mix, put your experiences in there. I'll be part of it—most if it, even—but it will be your book."

"But why?"

"For quite a few reasons, actually." And he went on to list them in the well-reasoned way he approached all his strategic decisions. "First, I've already got my name on more publications than anyone wants to read," he said, referring to the two hundred case studies, articles, and books he had written.

"Second, printing out what I say is all well and good. But I'll know that you really understand what I'm saying when you've put it in your own words.

"Third, when we sit down together, I don't do all the talking. I've been listening—and I've learned from you, too. You've got interesting things to say yourself. Having seen ten thousand masters of the universe pass through my door at Harvard, I know that your perspective on life isn't typical of a person your age. Your career decisions haven't been traditional. And Lord knows you've had some creative life experiences. I think you have some novel and instructive ideas to offer."

I had to laugh, because "creative, novel, and instructive" was a mild way to describe the not very traditional path I've taken in my career. Decisions that made perfect sense to me at the time have led to what an outside observer might consider a somewhat schizophrenic résumé: positions in the hospitality industry after graduating from the School of Hotel Administration at Cornell; a few years in corporate America; creating and promoting a national community education program; owning a couple of franchise businesses; grad school and fund-raising for Harvard; and, now, running a partnership development company that works with some of the world's leading brands and most innovative companies.

"And fourth, you're an entrepreneur at heart, just like I am," he said. "We both know how to pursue opportunities beyond the resources we currently control. Neither of us likes repeating what's already been done and proven. We want to take the essence of what's useful from the old and use it to create something new, better, more effective, more interesting."

"Howard Stevenson 2.0?" I joked.

"Sounds great—especially if a sleek new body comes with it," he said, laughing at the thought. "Eric, I'm really good at what

I do, and I've helped a lot of people become very successful. In business terms, you might consider me a franchise product—but I'm not perfect."

"But you're a wise man and I'm a wise ass."

He smiled and said, "Yeah, but a truly wise man knows he has no monopoly on wisdom. So for all those reasons, let's keep talking and listening to each other—and then you write the book, Mr. Wise Ass."

I still wasn't completely convinced about his approach, but, I told him, I was not going to argue with a guy recovering from cardiac arrest.

"A wise decision," he said. "And if you do a half-decent job, I may even buy a few copies for my seven kids, my dozen grand-kids, and a few of my students."

I remember a time when I was fifteen years old, playing Ping-Pong in the basement with my best childhood friend. As we knocked the ball back and forth, we had a conversation that now seems quite deep for two kids from rural New Jersey.

Vikram, whom I'd met on the first day of preschool, lived around the corner. Our weekend games of Ping-Pong had become a bit of a ritual. On this particular Saturday afternoon—as he was about to serve for match point—he asked me if I was worried about being successful when I grew up.

It was an odd question for a fifteen-year-old kid. But Vikram was mature for his age. The guy was born with the demeanor and outlook of a thirty-five-year-old. The son of immigrants from India, he was incredibly smart and—I now realize, looking back—a total entrepreneur. He was always inventing things, winning science contests, and otherwise impressing the adults around him. On this particular afternoon, he was obviously thinking about his future career.

"I actually don't really worry about being successful," I said in response to his question. "Somehow I figure that success will work itself out. What I worry about is whether or not I'll be happy."

Vikram thought about that for a minute, nodded, then proceeded to whip his serve just past my outstretched paddle. Then he smiled and said, "If you're happy about succeeding as a lousy Ping-Pong player, you're set for life."

I recount that conversation because the basic idea my fifteen-year-old self had stumbled on—"success doesn't always equal happiness"—is one that Howard repeatedly impresses on his students, colleagues, and friends. It is an idea that's been borne out in countless situations that I've seen and experienced.

My career has given me direct exposure to some amazingly accomplished men and women—university professors, deans, and presidents; corporate CEOs and self-made entrepreneurs of every type; and famous music industry and Broadway theatrical producers and the talent they work with. Traveling the globe on behalf of Harvard University for almost four years as a fundraiser, I got to know some of the world's most significant philanthropists. In my business career, I have worked with the corporate officers of a Fortune 500 company, with an amazingly successful hotel entrepreneur, and with an iconoclastic technology billionaire and professional sports-team owner. Today I am the president of a company whose clients provide me with the opportunity to work with some of the world's most successful people.

While many of the highly accomplished people I've interacted with are both successful and happy, I continue to be amazed by the enormous number who are at the top of their professions but feel unfulfilled. People who when faced with a moment of almost certain death, as Howard was, could not honestly claim they'd lived the life they had hoped to.

What I've seen over and over—in industry to industry, from country to country—is that all of us, regardless of our status in life, our career ambitions, our backgrounds, the size of our bank accounts, or our particular personal situations, are striving for a similar goal: professional accomplishment and *satisfaction*. This is what Howard has achieved better than anyone else I have ever known—and I hope to share some of his "secrets of satisfaction" in the pages that follow.

The goal of this book is to help you to maximize your career satisfaction as a cornerstone for a fulfilling life. Because if you're not happy with your work, then you're almost certainly not going to be fulfilled in your life.

Given that Howard is a greatly respected business-school professor, you might think this is a "business book." But it's much more than that. It's about life. Your life. So think of this book as focused on the business of your life. I have distilled from Howard's experience and wisdom a series of practical strategies for pursuing the goal of professional satisfaction. Drawn together and put into action, these strategies form an ongoing process that you could call "business planning for your life's work."

In describing my goal here, I've deliberately used the word *satisfaction* instead of the word *success*. Too often, success is automatically measured in terms of economic wealth, educational level, or one's place in an organizational structure. And too many benchmarks of success are set in relation to other people. But *satisfaction* encompasses more than just money and prestige and juxtaposition. The benchmarks for satisfaction—which certainly might include salary, title, and academic pedigree—are unique to each person. Each of us gets to define satisfaction for ourselves.

With that said, you should know up front that this book doesn't contain some A-to-Z prescription for a satisfying professional life. There can't be a single prescription when everyone's definition of satisfaction is different. Many of us are not even sure of what it is for ourselves.

"The first hurdle most of us face in pursuing a satisfying career is our intuitive assumption that what works for other folks—

co-workers, friends, family, even role models—*must* be right for us," Howard told me in one of our earliest conversations. "It's the disconnect between assumption and reality that causes false starts, professional disappointments, mid-career crises— and the directly related problems that spill over into our personal lives."

For that reason, what this book offers is not a specific path, but a clear framework. It introduces a way of thinking about your career, rather than providing a detailed action plan.

This framework is built on Howard's forty years of studying and teaching and advising the leaders of organizations of every imaginable type—from start-ups to conglomerates, schools to NGOs.

Howard told me once, "One reason I love being a professor of entrepreneurship is that I get to see endless ideas and plans for companies, products, and new approaches. While each idea is different, over time you recognize patterns. The good plans have certain consistent elements in the framework of thought behind the founders' motivating idea."

Like the frameworks he has observed for decades while evaluating businesses, the construct presented in this book can be applied by readers from all walks of life to their individual careers, desires, and goals. Howard's perspective will help you identify and define what success looks like *for you;* and it will provide "thought tools" that you can utilize in building the career and life you envision.

The process of business planning for life should occur throughout our careers. So this book is intended for people of many ages and for many stages of their lives. It is for the college sophomore who lines up a series of internships to test the career options she's considering, and the twenty-something professional taking a few extra days to consider if the big promotion he's been offered is actually right for him. It is for the thirty-five-year-old accounting manager deciding whether to take MBA courses or piano lessons, and the fifty-five-year-old who's been offered an early-retirement package and the option to begin a new career path.

Who will benefit most from this book? People who consider themselves smart and hardworking, who want to be proactive in setting the course of their careers—as opposed to simply reacting to what happens to them; people who want to be the entrepreneurial managers of their own lives, and build the life and career that they envision. This book is for people who, when they anticipate looking back on their lives, want to be able to say—as Howard did—they have no regrets.

None of the questions touched on in this book are simple ones. None of the answers are easy. This book is not intended for someone looking for a quick, one-night read on career success. In fact, you'll get the most out of *Howard's Gift* by reading a chapter, then pausing to consider the potent ideas and questions it offers, before continuing on to the next chapter.

Life is complex and sometimes hard. It's often confusing and uncertain. To make the most of yours, isn't it worth investing the same energy, enthusiasm, and reflection in it that you would if you were writing a plan for a grand new business venture? Because you are indeed exploring such a plan—a plan for the business of your life's work.

Before you read on, a few quick notes on conversations, chronology, and names in this book.

Howard's Gift is based on hundreds of hours of conversations with Howard over the course of more than six years. Many of those conversations occurred well before Howard's brush with death, and took place during leisurely walks around campus, in his office or at his house, or over a meal together. Another set of discussions took place during recorded interviews I conducted once we'd agreed that I should write this book; and still others took place as the book was evolving. Collectively, the ideas—the wisdom—that Howard shared with me in those conversations would fill several volumes. The conversations captured in this book are deliberately chosen, integrated, streamlined, and polished versions of the original discussions. The goal has been to convey the essence of Howard's wisdom in a manner that would be most effective for you, the reader.

The chapters in *Howard's Gift* have been organized in a manner that allows ideas to flow naturally and build on one another. Ultimately, I hope that you will use those ideas in a continuous cycle of thought and action that drives your life's work over the long term. Don't be confused by the fact that the events recounted in the book are not laid out chronologically from chapter to chapter.

In addition to sharing Howard's wisdom and that which I've picked up throughout my career, *Howard's Gift* features contributions from a wide variety of other remarkable men and women I interviewed while writing this book. In some instances, you'll meet these people in the pages that follow. In other cases, I felt it important to change a person's name, modify some details, or combine several individuals' similar experiences—especially where a factual retelling of their stories might have negative implications for the individuals or the people around them.

That said, you should know that every word of the book has been read, considered, and blessed by Howard. And every word of the individual profiles at the end of each chapter has been read and approved by those folks.

KIRK POSMANTUR

Kirk Posmantur is my longtime friend, mentor, and business partner. We've known each other since the early 1990s, when, as a hospitality-industry executive, he agreed to take on an energetic, overconfident, and utterly inexperienced intern from Cornell's School of Hotel Administration. Neither of us could have known then that we'd be linked professionally for almost twenty years and counting. We also couldn't have guessed how personally attuned we'd become—able to anticipate each other's ideas, instincts, and reactions with amazing accuracy. After all this time, we can almost literally read each other's minds. I tell people lovingly that he's like my older, taller, and balder brother; he says that he knows me better than my wife does—although I encourage him not to say it in *her* presence!

When I told Kirk that I was writing this book, he nodded and smiled, giving me a kind of "that's nice, have fun" response. He considered it my hobby and didn't take the project all that seriously—and, frankly, there was no reason he should have. I'd never written a book before or even suggested that it was a goal. But, as I continued to talk about the project over the following weeks, he came to understand that Howard's cardiac arrest was, indeed, an inflection point in my life; and as he saw how committed I was to the book, he paid more serious attention to my progress.

However, even though he never said anything specific, I also sensed some ambivalence on his part. So, when I was ready to show him a big chunk of the manuscript, I wasn't completely sure what his reaction would be.

At first, as is Kirk's style, he began skimming the pages as soon as I handed them to him, and started to comment on one facet or another. But as he got deeper into the manuscript, the pace of both his reading and his comments slowed. After just a dozen pages or so, he stopped reading, thought for a moment, and said, "Hey, no . . .

I'm going to take this stuff home tonight and go through it carefully. There's some stuff here I want think about. Can we talk about it tomorrow?"

Because of our hectic calendars and travel schedules, Kirk and I are in the habit of having an early phone call to check in each day. So, sitting in my kitchen at six-thirty the next morning, I picked up the phone to hear him say, without pleasantries or prelude, "I have to tell you, for a while I've been worried about how much energy you've been putting into this writing project. You're working your butt off at the office; traveling days on end to see clients; then spending dozens of hours a month writing this book."

"Well, it's important to me," I explained.

"That's been clear from the beginning. And from the start I've worried that you could end up really frustrated at the results, given how much energy you're investing," he replied. "But I'm not concerned anymore. Somehow, you've captured your relationship with this extraordinary guy, Howard, and then found a way to extend that relationship to include the rest of us. And that's got to feel really satisfying."

When Kirk said that, I realized that I'd been so focused on writing the book that I hadn't really been able to see the end product. (A classic "can't see the forest for the trees" perspective.) But his comments gave me a reason to stand back for a moment and appreciate that, at least for one person, I had achieved my goal of sharing Howard's wisdom and insight—of enabling a reader to establish a vicarious relationship with him. That this one person was my longtime friend and business partner was satisfying; but the fact that Kirk "got it" was meaningful for a wholly different reason, too.

Why? Because Kirk himself is the consummate relationship builder. Relationship building is part of his
DNA, something he inherited and learned from his father. His wife refers to him as Forrest Gump because of
his uncanny ability to develop friendships with people
from all walks of life, from the waiter at his local Italian
restaurant to some of the biggest names in business and
entertainment. Kirk remembers virtually every person
he's ever had a substantive interaction with and maintains
connections to lots of them—a unique ability that enables him to "connect the dots" with breathtaking reach.
Relationship building is also central to Kirk's philosophy
of life: if he could, he'd put the classic Coca-Cola ad into
action—he'd buy the world a Coke, introduce every
person to the next person, have them hold hands, and
get them to sing in perfect harmony. (No surprise, then,
that the company he and I run, Axcess Worldwide, is
based on a concept that he created, called "partnership
development." Axcess connects leaders of extraordinary
and iconic brands—helping them pursue opportunities
together that neither could achieve individually.)

Beyond that, as someone who found the formula for
pursuing career satisfaction relatively early in his working
life (a formula I call "Kirk's Triple Threat"—weaving
together extraordinary creativity, unparalleled capacity
for relationship-building, and uncanny instincts for bringing businesses together for their mutual benefit), he is
passionate about helping people develop their own for-
mulas for pursuing success and satisfaction. So, it was
doubly pleasing to hear him say, "Beyond the beauty of
your relationship with Howard, the timing of *Howard's
Gift* is almost prescient. This is a moment when many
people are looking for a spark of inspiration—an infusion
of energy and optimism about their careers. This is a

point when the economy might just be tilting in the right direction, and when women and men with dreams and ambitions are again asking themselves, 'Is now the time to go for it?'"

CHAPTER TWO

Slingshot Round the Moon

Inflection points come in all forms: positive, negative, easy, hard, obvious, and subtle. The way you respond—whether you grab hold of an inflection point and leverage it for all it's worth or just let it carry you along—is as important as the event itself.

ONE DAY NOT LONG AFTER I first started working at Harvard, Howard and I were walking across the campus toward the Charles River. It was the kind of early April day that, while still chilly, held the promise of frostless mornings and slowly budding trees. The weather seemed to be hanging on a pinpoint, waiting for a nudge that would push it from winter to spring.

I loved these "walking meetings," which we had begun when I was a grad student and continued through our years of working together at the university. While we sometimes had a specific piece of business to discuss, more often we had no agenda. We just talked about whatever was on our minds, from the psychological to the philosophical to the entrepreneurial. It became an escape from the everyday; a bit of intellectual therapy for both of us. Since Howard was then one of the most senior administrators at Harvard, I never had to explain to colleagues or bosses why I regularly took time to meet with him.

On this particular morning I was telling Howard about my

friend Michelle, whose boss had unexpectedly announced her retirement. Michelle is an extraordinarily creative and hard-working woman who was a few years behind me at college. Her boss, the head of their department, had been a mentor and champion throughout Michelle's time at the company. Michelle had worked for this boss for almost ten years and credited the woman's support and wise counsel for her own continuous career progress.

Despite Michelle's success, she felt that her future was uncertain now that her professional champion was departing. It was unclear whether her boss had retired of her own volition or had been forced out—or something in between. All Michelle knew was that on an otherwise unremarkable Friday morning, she had been told that her boss was leaving in a few weeks and that the company was "reconsidering the entire department's role and structure."

Normally decisive and confident, Michelle was caught off guard. She felt frozen, with no idea how long the organization's review process would take, how extensive it might be, or what it might lead to for her. For the first time in her career, she didn't know what to do.

As I shared the story with Howard, a bewildered look crept over his face.

Michelle's plan, I explained to him, was to keep her head down and wait to see how the department might be reshaped. After she learned what opportunities would be presented to her as part of the potential reorganization, she would decide what to do next. After all, at this point she didn't know if she'd be "downsized," "realigned" into a job with less authority, "morphed" into a different professional path at the company—or even "supersized" with a promotion. What she did know was that the economy was weak and she had invested ten years at the company, so she was hoping for the best.

When I finished the story, Howard shook his head, kicked a pinecone out of his path, and grumbled, "Wasting a good opportunity."

"Her problem is that no one has clarified what her options might be," I explained.

Howard stopped and gently poked me in the chest, "No. Her problem is that she doesn't recognize the opportunity staring her in the face."

It was classic Howard, looking at the world from a unique perspective: where almost everyone else would see a problem, he sensed an opportunity; where most people might have endorsed Michelle's "sit tight" approach, he saw reason for thoughtful action.

"She's waiting for someone to decide her fate for her," Howard remarked. "She doesn't realize that she's being given a gift."

"What kind of gift?"

"An inflection point," he said. "In Michelle's case, it's coming at a moment in time when the structures are removed and the rules are suspended. A moment in which she can reflect inwardly about what *she* wants, and then act to redefine the situation in such a way as to help her accomplish it."

Howard motioned for me to sit on a bench with him under a huge oak tree. "Inflection points change the way we think about things. They present an opportunity that only occurs periodically. And they possess a kind of latent motivational energy, which, when recognized and harnessed, can unleash potential that one wouldn't seize otherwise."

" 'Latent motivational energy'?" I'd teased Howard for years that he had a language all his own—"Howard-speak"—that people didn't always understand. "Latent motivational energy" was quintessential Howard-speak, and when I called him on it, he laughed.

"All right, all right," he said. "How's this? Latent motivational energy is another way of describing a situation's potential to spur you into action, when you wouldn't have acted before."

"In even plainer English," I suggested, "it's a much-needed kick in the ass."

Howard chuckled and said, "A kick that can provide a boost of career momentum." He paused, then gave me a wink as he thought of just the right way to illustrate his point. "You're too young to remember this," he began, "but in the early 1970s the Apollo 13 spacecraft was midway between Earth and the moon when an air tank exploded and almost wrecked the command module. There wasn't enough fuel to stop its momentum and turn back for Earth. So the crew decided to let the moon's gravity do the work for them. Moving faster and faster, they orbited the moon once, used a single powerful burst of the engine to add to the momentum gravity provided, and, like a stone in a slingshot, zoomed back to Earth. They got home because they used the lunar orbit as an inflection point to change their trajectory and add the energy boost they needed."

"I remember that scene in the movie *Apollo 13*," I said. "It was riveting because you knew the slightest mistake would send them out into deep space."

Howard smiled. "Here on Earth, the opportunity provided by an inflection point is a lot easier to overlook or ignore— until the window for action passes. As a result, most people are like Michelle: they won't realize they're at an inflection point until it has passed. And if they do realize it, they'll often just react to it without constructive thought. They see inflection points as something that *happens to them,* something they can only respond to defensively. Like passive observers in their own lives.

"Very few people see inflection points as the opportunities they often are: catalysts for changing their lives; moments when a person can modify the trajectory he or she is on and redirect it in a more desirable direction," he continued. "Whether it's a new job, a change in a relationship, or something else, an inflection point is one of those periodic windows of opportunity when a person can pause, reflect, and ask: 'Self, do I want to continue on this path or is now the moment to change direction?'"

I thought about the moments when I had made real change in my career, when I pivoted and began traveling in a totally new direction. Had I seen these moments as opportunities? Had I just been instinctively reacting, or were the changes the result of conscious introspection?

Howard continued, "I think it's human nature to get so caught up and focused on succeeding on the path we're currently traversing that most of us never pause and ask if, in fact, this is the road down which we want to continue. We look to move obstacles out of our way on that path. We try to find ways to go faster on that path. And in the process, we come to assume that our current path is the *only* appropriate path."

"So, in addition to being energy boosters, inflection points can be like on-ramps and off-ramps on the highway of life," I offered.

"Yeah, that's a good metaphor," he said. "Except that there are no maps or GPS to give you definitive guidance. So as these points come along, it takes some thinking to figure out whether this is the exit or entry point for something new." He let that sink in, then continued. "What's important for Michelle to understand is that despite the lack of certainty—the absence of a definitive career map—recognizing and seizing on the inflection point heading her way is a key to controlling the future trajectory of her career and her life."

As I glanced over at Howard, I caught a suddenly serious look on his face. "Are you speaking from experience?" I asked.

He didn't respond for a moment, just watched a squirrel scratching up an acorn buried the previous fall.

"Oh yeah, some good experiences and a few bad ones," Howard said, then paused to look out over the slow-moving water of the Charles River. "For me, my divorce from my first wife was one of my most important inflection points," he continued, almost to himself. "It was painful at the time, of course, but now, years and years later, I recognize that it was an opportunity to pivot, to move away from a situation that was not working, to build a life that would. That inflection point gave me an extra boost of energy to reflect on what I truly wanted, both personally and professionally." I was quiet, just accepting this very personal insight into Howard's life.

After a moment, he snapped back to our prior conversation. "I would tell Michelle," he said, his mind back on the here and now, "that in decades of studying companies, I have rarely seen one that announces a reexamination of an entire department unless it already thinks the status quo needs changing. Tell her that she doesn't need to wait to hear the details to know that her job is probably going to be affected. Like it or not, she's at an inflection point. One way or another, her future is going to be different than what she thought it would be. I learned early on that simply reacting to 'what happens'—or worse, not reacting at all—can undermine your ability to create a satisfying career or happy life.

"Guessing about your future is a poor substitute for making your future happen. And if Michelle is just sitting passively, she's missing the opportunity to do some advance thinking about the concrete possibilities and challenges she could face, and how she'd respond to each. She should be intellectually honest with herself and recognize that an inflection point—in this case, significant change in her work environment—seems to be barreling toward her like an oncoming train."

"So she should do some scenario planning," I said.

"Absolutely," Howard said. "Recognizing an inflection point is the first step. But, as you've heard me say endless times before, it's critical to live life forward, to learn from the past but focus on the future. She can bemoan the fact that her boss is leaving.

But that's water under the bridge," he said, pointing out at the water of the Charles that was, literally, flowing under the bridge in front of us. "Now she should imagine a variety of possible futures, choose the one she most wants, and figure out how to proactively shape this inflection point in a way that helps her move forward in the days and months ahead. We're talking about the difference between active management and passivity."

"Makes a lot of sense," I suggested. "People actively manage their investment portfolios to try to generate the best returns. They actively manage employees and tasks to influence the outcome of projects at work."

"So why should she sit still passively with something infinitely more valuable, which is her own career and future?" Howard responded just as his cell phone rang. He answered the call, listened, and motioned for us to start walking back to his office. As we did, I thought about his point. So many of us throw energy into the active management of our budgets, our staffs, our projects, our kids' schedules, even our hobbies. But how many people actively manage their own careers?

When the call ended, I picked up the conversation right where it had left off. "What you're suggesting," I said, "is that rather than wait for the company to shape her department around her, Michelle should try to play a part in the process— both generally and as it relates to her future role in it." I thought a bit before I continued. "It's a bit bold, perhaps, but she could proactively propose a concept for moving forward that serves both the company and her own career."

He stopped and put his hand on my shoulder. "I like that idea. She needs to become a part of the conversation, not a potential victim of it. At a minimum, she should make clear to whoever the decision maker is in this situation what her strengths are, where she'd like her career to head, and how these things can fit into a reshaped department."

I wondered if there was a risk that Michelle would be perceived as overstepping, as being the stereotypical "young hotshot," resented for her impatience to move up the career ladder.

As if reading my mind, Howard said, "There is no option here completely without risk. Doing nothing is also a decision—to be passive, to hope for a good outcome without trying to influence it. But I think that if Michelle is as smart as you say she is, she'll understand the organization's overall goals. She can offer an informed perspective on how the department should support those goals—and on how she could fit in most effectively. Her ideas don't have to be 'right.' There really is no definitive right and wrong on these kinds of things. They just need to be well thought out. And they have to be objective, not just a veiled pitch for a promotion or a raise."

"What if the response she gets is, 'Thanks, but we're not really interested in your ideas'?"

"Then she's got a whole lot of information about her future in that organization. Because either she doesn't know it as well as she thinks she does, or she's not valued by its leadership. In either case, she's gleaned key data points. She's learned."

Howard's observations made sense, as they always seemed to. Just getting a response—any response—to her ideas made more sense than waiting passively, with no new data coming in. Whether Michelle's recommendations elicited positive or negative feedback was, for the moment, almost irrelevant. Because whatever feedback she received would provide insight into her future with the company and dramatically change her ability to deal with the situation. She would get ahead of the inflection point wave, not get caught, tossed, and potentially drowned by it.

"Once Michelle acknowledges that the inflection point is coming," Howard observed, "she can make some educated guesses as to in which direction the wave may break. So tell her to get in the game. To act. The only losing move here is not to play. She needs to take advantage of the gift that she's been given."

I wondered aloud how I was going to explain all of this to Michelle. I was sure she would laugh at me if she heard the term *latent motivational energy* coming out of my mouth. "Just tell her!" Howard barked in response. "On a basic emotional level, Michelle is going to start feeling better immediately. Right now, she's just sitting in the dark, with no information, feeling powerless, dreading the memo that will determine her fate. But almost as soon as she decides to leverage this inflection point rather than just watch it pass by, she's going to feel a greater sense of control over her present situation—and her future. Tell her to stop hoping and start acting."

A few minutes later we were back at the door to his office. I chided him, "You know, Howard, back there you sounded a lot like Yoda, who, as you may recall, once quipped, 'Hope is not a plan.'"

He shot me a glare, as if offended by my comparison of him to the wrinkled *Star Wars* space amphibian. But as I turned to leave, I saw the glare turn into a knowing smile.

Just stop for a moment and reflect: When was the last time you faced a situation that had the potential to change the way you viewed your future career? What type of "latent motivational energy" did it pack? Enough to motivate you to change the way you work? Or to change your place of work? Or to change your entire line of work?

Whether that inflection point was good or bad, expected or not, with great or little motivating energy—how did you respond to it? At the time, did you even realize it was there?

In the years since that first conversation about Michelle's experience, Howard and I have talked often about inflection points. Sometimes our discussions related to specific experiences in my own life. More often, they arose in connection with a seemingly unrelated topic. Out of nowhere during a discussion about a particular situation we'd observed—whether with a major gift prospect, or a colleague, or an organization he was working with—Howard would stop, raise his finger ever so slightly, and ask, "Inflection point?" And if we agreed that it was, he'd then ask, "How can it be leveraged? How can this person or organization gain additional momentum from it?"

Over time, I came to recognize what an important role inflection points had played in my own career. I didn't call them inflection points at the time, of course. Heck, I usually didn't call them anything, because I hadn't even realized I'd experienced one. But as I reflected on the directions my career had taken, I began to understand the significance of inflection points—the ones that I'd recognized and addressed, and those that had passed unseen or ignored.

I also began to pay attention to how inflection points played out in the careers of people around me. Sometimes when I was having lunch with co-workers or catching up with old friends, I'd challenge them to identify the inflection points in their careers. After a while, I found that most people's inflection points fell into what I began to think of as one of three categories: Friend, Foe, or Silent.

Inflection points that are Friends are the ones we're grateful for. For example, the event that enables us to realize that we don't "*have to*" stay at a job we don't want, or stick to a career track that is unsatisfying. Or, conversely, the experience that validates our hopes and aspirations—that enables us to recognize that we do, indeed, have what it takes to succeed on the career path we've envisioned. A friendly inflection point could also come in the form of a subtle, even neutral, change in present circumstances that, if we choose to exploit it, might have major benefits down the line. (Your employer launches a tuition reimbursement program that enables you to pursue the master's degree you've always dreamed of, for example.) When we're tuned into it, the inflection point that is a Friend often feels like an awakening, the realization of a new possibility. We're lucky when one appears—and we should grab it with both arms outstretched.

Inflection points that are Foes are—at least initially—unwelcome. They typically come out of the blue, sneaking up to bite us in the ass. It's the event that catches its victim—and I purposely use the word *victim*—unprepared. A Foe inflection point hits, for example, when we get rejected from the only graduate program we're interested in, despite assurances that we're a shoo-in for admission. Or it nails us with the news that, as a streamlining move, our company has eliminated an entire layer of management—ours. Or that our spouse has been offered a great promotion, but it will require a move to Timbuktu.

Experiencing a Foe is like being sideswiped into a tailspin on our career highway. Because it can cause surprise and doubt, it often leads us to be defensive and passive. Rather than pursuing a well-thought-out response or figuring out how to mine positive future opportunities from a negative situation, we react out of fear, frustration, or confusion.

While inflection points that are Friends or Foes are generally sparked by external situations and events, the third kind of inflection point is rooted internally. While the first two may produce relatively strong reactions, the Silent inflection point is more subtle. We may not recognize it, and as a result, we may not respond at all—which is the problem. I call it the Silent inflection point because it involves discovering something about ourselves. It occurs when we realize that something is waiting for us to make it happen. It's the inflection point that *we create*. It occurs in the recognition of a connection between a situation that *is* and one that *might be*. Sometimes it arises as a little voice in the back of your mind—the one that tells you that the vague discontent you've had is because you're bored or you're uncomfortable with the path you're on. Other times, it's a spark of a question, like "What would happen if I turned my hobby into a career?" or "Is this the time to turn up the energy and prove what I can do?"

Of course, many inflection points are hybrids of these three categories: a Friend can have some negative elements to it; a Foe can give you a much-needed kick in the butt or lead to a subsequent Silent recognition of a better, different path; and a Silent inflection point might involve accepting short-term pain in return for a long-term benefit. But what I find most amazing when I think about the variety of inflection points in my life and in the lives of colleagues and friends is the number and significance of the opportunities that are missed in not actively responding to inflection points in any form.

So if you have any doubt about the value of a proactive approach, just remember Howard's bottom line on the subject: "Inflection points come in all forms: positive, negative, easy, hard, obvious, and subtle. The way you respond—whether you grab hold of an inflection point and leverage it for all it's worth or just let it carry you along—is as important as the event itself. And each individual inflection point has the potential for immeasurable impact on your satisfaction with your life and career."

WENDY KOPP & ARVIND RAGHUNATHAN

Some major inflection points come on with resounding thunder; others creep up, tap lightly on the shoulder, and only later is it clear how significant they were. Likewise, one person experiences a single, big inflection point early in her career, while another comes upon a diverging path well into his career.

Consider the experiences of Wendy Kopp, founder and CEO of Teach for America, and Arvind Raghunathan, founder and CEO of the investment firm Roc Capital Management. Wendy's career-defining inflection point occurred really early—before she even finished college—and she's still experiencing its latent energy, over twenty years later. On the other hand, Arvind spent years training for a scholarly career in computer sciences—until, one night, he read a book that changed the way he viewed his life's work.

Back in 1989, as a senior at Princeton University, Wendy Kopp had two problems. First, she had no idea what she wanted to do after college. "I was in an absolute funk," she told me when we spoke last summer, "and I didn't want to even *think* about looking for a job." Her second, more immediate, problem was that she needed a topic for her required senior thesis. Ironically, the solution to that problem also solved the "got-no-idea-what-to-do-with-my-life" concern.

One day, attending a conference on education reform, Wendy was pondering the plight of kids in poorly performing urban and rural schools, when she wondered, "Why can't talented college seniors be recruited as aggressively to spend two years teaching in high-poverty schools as they are recruited to spend two years on Wall Street?" That question became the catalyst for her senior thesis, in which she proposed the concept behind Teach For America: enabling and encouraging high-achieving college seniors to spend two years in the classroom as public school teachers, and to serve as education evangelists wherever their careers eventually took them. The initial reaction to her proposal was anything but positive; her thesis adviser told her, "My dear Ms. Kopp, you are quite evidently deranged." But Wendy, herself, felt a burst of energy and confidence.

Ignoring detractors and tapping her latent capacities for organization, strategic planning, and motivating other people, Wendy set off on a quest to improve education across the United States. She founded Teach For America shortly after graduating Princeton, and in 1990 a group of five hundred recent college grads signed up for the nascent program. Now, more than two decades later, tens of thousands of young people have participated in the program, connecting with—and becoming advocates for—millions of schoolchildren.

Teach For America's path has not always been completely smooth; as its creator and chief executive, Wendy had some lean times and major administrative challenges to navigate. But from the point she conceived of the fundamental idea, she's been driven by a passion, a mission. She's been determined to build her organization and extend its capacity to help improve public education. And, by many measures, she has done that exceedingly well: Teach For America is widely considered one of the best-run nonprofits; it has been listed on *Fortune* magazine's list of 100 Best Places to Work; and each year, more college seniors apply for the program than the year before. Wendy's vision is also going global, as social entrepreneurs in dozens of countries adapt her model—supported by Teach For All, the global network she leads.

Looking back at the beginnings of her career, Wendy observed, "Somehow I found my way directly and quickly to something I was uniquely suited to do. I'm lucky to have found my dream job, to be able to pursue my passion. More than lucky." She laughed. "Because to this day I don't know what else I'd be good at, what other career path could possibly have engaged me as completely as this."

By comparison, Arvind Raghunathan's path has been more winding and marked by multiple inflection points. Nevertheless, they were powerful inflections and their "latent motivational energy" fueled his journey from a childhood in Chennai, India, to his being a wildly successful entrepreneur and philanthropist.

Arvind graduated from one of the prestigious Indian Institutes of Technology, and earned a doctorate in computer science from the University of California, Berkeley. Then he worked as a professor for three years. But a single evening's reading led him to the major inflection point that has guided his life's work for more than a decade since.

"I was one of these nerdy kids in college who happened to excel at math," he told me as we sat in his office not long ago. "As a child growing up in India, I learned about America from watching TV—and I dreamed. There was one very obvious way out of the hierarchical Indian society: getting into one of the Indian Institutes of Technology, which are India's equivalent to MIT or Berkeley. At the time, for every three hundred thousand students that applied, two thousand were admitted. For months and months as a high school student, I locked myself in my room for ten hours a day and studied for the admissions test.

"When I learned that I'd been accepted, my life changed. Suddenly, opportunities that wouldn't have been available otherwise seemed possible—like going to graduate school in the United States. When I arrived at Berkeley in 1984, I had just one hundred dollars and had lost my passport during the two-day trip from India. But my life at Berkeley and, subsequently, as a professor was great. I did what professors do: I researched, I taught, and I thought. I believed that my scholarly work would, if I kept at it over many years, make useful, incremental contributions to the field of computer science.

"For a few years the idea of making small contributions in a large field was appealing. Of course, I'd always been focused on an academic career and had never considered doing anything else. But over time, I began to wonder—first subconsciously and then more concretely—'Is this it?'"

I mentioned to Arvind one of Howard's favorite warnings: "Beware the velvet-lined rut, because it's so easy and comfortable to stay there."

He nodded and said, "I could definitely feel its lure, but one day something interesting happened to yank me out of the rut. While dropping off a memo in a colleague's office, I glanced at his bookshelf and one title caught my eye—*Liar's Poker*. This classic is about the incredibly inefficient way that investors went about their business in the 1980s. I borrowed the book, brought it home that night, and read it in a single sitting. When I put it down, one thought crossed my mind: 'I know a better way to do this.'

"After a few days of deep thought, I decided to resign as a professor. I just knew it was the right thing to do. My decision was based on a simple but powerful inflection point: the recognition that the mathematics I knew and the advent of computing power that I was studying could be combined to replace the old-school hunches and intuition used by investors described in *Liar's Poker*.

"It was an inflection point that, when seized, took my life in an entirely new direction, one that has led me to places I never could have imagined going." And it's given him a capacity to help others that he never imagined possessing: he and his wife have become significant philanthropists, supporting education and cultural programs in the United States and India.

On the surface, Wendy's and Arvind's experiences appear unrelated. But when I look at them, I see two people who are both pursuing their life's work—wholeheartedly and with great success. I see two people benefiting society in complementary ways: she's engaged in a noble effort that depends hugely on philanthropic support and will have the long-term effect of changing lives and enhancing the country's economic capacities; he's making carefully chosen investments that underwrite new companies and new jobs, and in the process he has developed the resources to support education through his own philanthropic gifts.

And in both cases, they have fully leveraged inflection points to capitalize on what they do best and enjoy doing most.

CHAPTER THREE

Start at the End

"Starting at the end means investing time up front to develop an aspirational picture of your future—a guide for the decisions you make throughout your career and life."

IT WAS AN EARLY EVENING in May. I sat at the table in Howard's kitchen, drinking a beer and watching him make a couple of roast beef sandwiches.

"You know, I can just grab something later, on my way home," I said. "You don't have to cook for me."

"If you consider this 'cooking,' you've got more to learn than I thought," Howard replied. "Besides, we've got a lot of prep work to do, and I want you fully functional." We were meeting the next day with a former student of Howard's who was considering a huge philanthropic gift to the university, and we needed to finalize our strategy that night.

He put the plate of sandwiches in front of me and smiled when I practically attacked the food. "Hungrier than you thought, huh?"

"Missed lunch," I said, in between chews. "An interesting situation, actually. Can I get your take on it?"

"Go," he said, then sat back and listened as I told him about George, a former colleague of mine who was disciplined, smart, diligent, and—throughout the decade I'd known him—singularly focused on his career.

George had been in Boston for the day, and we'd planned to have lunch and catch up on our lives. But when we met in front of the restaurant, he was keyed up with anxious energy and not hungry. So instead of eating, we spent two hours walking throughout the historic streets of old Boston as he described the sense of frustration and bewilderment that had been creeping over him for much of the last year.

As long as I'd known him, George had been financially ambitious. He wasn't greedy or materialistic; he was a generous person who maintained a comfortable yet simple lifestyle. However, having grown up in a broken family that was always struggling economically, he was relentlessly committed to becoming rich. Or, more specifically, he was committed to creating what he described as "absolute financial security" for himself, his wife, and their kids. He was determined that his family would never need to worry about the kinds of things he'd struggled with as a child: having a stable home, enough to eat, and clean clothes. He wanted to be sure that his wife would not have to resume her career after their children were born, if she didn't want to; and that his kids could go to college even if they didn't get scholarships (which was how he'd paid for his education). While he was intensely focused on his own family's welfare, one of the things I admired about George was that this imperative for financial security did not end at home; he felt a strong responsibility for the well-being of the people he employed, too.

Early in our careers, we worked together at a hotel management company. After a few years, when he'd soaked up all the knowledge and experience he felt he needed, George left to launch a business providing a more efficient system for online hotel reservations. At the time, I admired his chutzpah at taking such a huge risk—betting his meager savings; maxing out his credit cards—on an unproven concept. But he knew what he was doing, and a year before we reconnected in Boston, his company had been acquired by a big hospitality industry conglomerate. With that deal, George went from simply earning a good income to having $10 million in the bank. He'd realized the goal of lifetime financial security for his family.

After selling the company, George had been contractually locked up—required to stay with the acquiring firm for one year. During that time he'd been doing almost exactly the same thing he had done before the sale. Few of the professional aspects of his life had changed: the company had weathered the recession well, revenues were on the uptick, and his new corporate bosses rarely interfered with his operations. When he'd called to set up our lunch in Boston, I'd assumed that he would be feeling on top of the world. Yet, as George explained as we walked, almost from day one of the new arrangement, he'd found less and less satisfaction in his work. In fact, his sense of dissatisfaction had grown to the point where he was really struggling now.

I was stunned, and my first reaction was to ask him how things were at home—was his marriage strong, were his kids doing okay? "Oh yeah, Amanda and the kids are great; they're my cornerstone," he said, then shook his head. "No, *I'm* the problem. Bringing my frustration with work home with me, I'm not much fun to be around."

I suggested to him that, in at least a couple of respects, his was a normal reaction. It's hard to find the same energy working for someone else after you've been the top dog. There's also an understandable letdown—a sense of lost momentum—when you've brought a major career goal to fruition, and done so much earlier than you'd dreamed possible.

Yes, George said, he understood that those things had dampened his enthusiasm, but he felt that he'd come to terms with them. He'd even accepted that it was time to walk away from the company he had built, which was a doubly difficult decision because the challenge of ensuring the livelihood of his "work family"—his longtime employees—had been a powerful and positive motivator for him.

All the questions I was raising were about the past, George explained, and the past wasn't the problem: the future was. He'd considered a series of new entrepreneurial ventures, but none felt right. He'd been in discussions about joining a consulting firm, only to back away at the last minute. Now he was even considering going to law school; he didn't particularly want to practice law, but at least it would give him a clear path and goal for a few years.

"Here's a guy who's fulfilled his career goals years ahead of what he'd originally anticipated," I explained to Howard, "and now he's dragging around in circles, unable to chart a new direction. He's a really driven person, full of energy—but he can't figure out where to direct that energy, going forward. Watching him today was like seeing an overheating boiler getting ready to explode."

Howard sat silently. I swallowed a couple bites of the sandwich, then continued. "He can't even enjoy the nonwork activities in his life. He's bored playing golf; he stopped going to the theater; and he's probably going to quit the community-organization boards he's on."

"Really?" said Howard, the first word he'd spoken since I started telling the story.

"Yeah. It was a very depressing conversation," I said.

Howard thought for a bit, then threw out a series of questions that surprised me because—at that moment—they seemed so beside the point. Question: Did I know if George played a lot of golf in college or early in his career? (Answer: It was something George picked up later. When I knew him in the early years, he loved bowling. The game bored me silly, but he got such a kick out of it that I let him drag me out to the lanes a couple times.)

Question: What were the community organizations George was involved with? (Answer: One was a local arts center, and the other was the American Lung Association.) Question: Is George an artist himself? Does someone in his family have lung disease? (Answer to both: No, I don't think so.)

After answering Howard's questions, I threw one back at him: "What the heck's all that got to do with his next career move?"

"Everything," he said, then stood up and disappeared into his den. He returned carrying a large plastic shopping bag filled with games and toys destined for his grandkids. He rummaged through it until he found what he wanted: a big jigsaw-puzzle box.

"My granddaughter loves these things," Howard said. "She's got this intuitive understanding of how to work them. Starts by forming the outside edges of the picture, then moves inward. She's creating a basic frame—a context—to use in making decisions about how to fit the rest of the pieces together."

"A strategic thinker at age ten," I said. "I guess she takes after her grandmother, huh?"

He smirked but otherwise ignored my jibe. "Clearly, this young success—George—has hit a major inflection point in his career and his life. And just as you can leverage a negative inflection point into a beneficial opportunity, a positive inflection point can become a real pain in the ass if you don't handle it well." He let that sink in for a moment before continuing.

"Remember when we talked about those astronauts who used the moon's gravity as an inflection point to get back home?"

"Sure," I mumbled as I worked on the second roast beef sandwich.

"Well, inflection points aren't very useful without a context, without a sense of how you want to use them. If Apollo 13's astronauts hadn't known exactly where they *were* relative to where they wanted to *end up,* their risky maneuver around the moon would have been a joyride to oblivion. Without knowing their desired end point, they wouldn't have been able to decide how fast they needed to go, how long to burn the engine, when to shut it down—any of that.

"Those astronauts actually had it easy, in a certain way," Howard continued. "They had one single objective on which everything depended. There was no ambiguity, no weighing of alternative places to go. They needed to get to one place—Earth—and quickly, before they got cooked. But here on terra firma, things are more complicated because we don't have that same kind of precise, singular goal for our life's work."

He shook the jigsaw box, and the puzzle pieces rattled around inside. "There are a whole lot of jigsaw pieces in anyone's life and career. But how do you know which piece to grab next if you don't know what the overall picture's supposed to look like—if you don't at least have a framework to consider?"

"So George has been handed a big new stack of jigsaw pieces, with no idea how to put them together," I said. Howard nodded, and I continued, thinking out loud, "He's a driven guy. Except without a direction, without even a compass to say which direction is which, he's driving himself crazy."

"Bingo!" he said, grabbing my now empty plate and bringing it over to the counter.

Well fed, and assuming our conversation about George was done, I began to pull my notebook and a few files from my briefcase. Yet when Howard came back to the table—with an enormous slice of peach pie and a glass of milk, and a look on his face that said, "Don't argue; just eat this"—it became clear that his mind was still on George's situation.

"What was that old saying? 'If you don't know where you're going, any road will take you there,'" he said. "It may be false nostalgia, but I think people used to give a lot more thought to the broader context of the big decisions they make about their lives. Not so much anymore, it seems."

I had to smile, because talking with Howard like this made

me feel like a student again, a student privileged to get one-on-one tutoring from one of Harvard's great minds.

"Maybe it's an unanticipated side effect of our hyperconnected, twenty-four/seven culture," I offered. "Life seems to be happening so quickly and so continuously that people are unaccustomed to taking time to think. And they're reluctant to 'waste time' thinking, instead of acting. This reminds me of something one of my business partners, Mike Wargotz, says, 'Hurry up and fail.'"

"You're probably on target," Howard said, "but it's a really counterproductive situation. Nine times out of ten, a person will *lose* time and *waste* energy if she just heads out to accomplish something without first considering why she's pursuing it and what success would look like." As I ate my pie, Howard continued.

"You know, Eric, I think there's another factor at work, too," he suggested. "In this hyperconnected society of ours, there's a huge emphasis on what I call 'celebrity success' culture: we increasingly equate being well known with success, and we turn successful people into celebrities. All this 'success' pervading our cultural atmosphere leaves people with two internalized assumptions.

"First, we believe we're all equally worthy of and prepared for success. You know, the alternative—having to admit that maybe we're not good enough to succeed at a particular thing we *want to succeed at*—is too painful for many people to even consider. Second, we just assume that everything *must* work out."

"You mean, we assume that it's life's responsibility to point the way for us?" I asked.

Howard nodded and paused as his mind reached out for just the right analogy. "It's as if many people think their lives come equipped with a personal GPS that shows the best career on-ramps and off-ramps—at the push of a button. Unfortunately, even the best GPS doesn't tell you *where* to go, only *how* to get to the specific place you've set as your destination.

"Ironically, it's often the folks who consider themselves smart or talented or hardworking who fall into that logical fallacy—because they figure their brains, talent, or diligence will automatically make clear how fast to go and what turns to take, even without their having first determined their goal."

We both considered that for a moment, then he motioned for us to head into the den. I didn't even bring my files with me: class was definitely still in session.

Howard sat back on the couch, put his feet up on the coffee table, and continued on an intellectual path clearly laid out in his head. "Eric, I can't tell you how many of my students try to construct the puzzle of their careers by identifying a few desirable pieces and building on those. Or, worse, they just go with the pieces they find in their hands," he said. "But a meaningful, satisfying life consists of the *entire* puzzle. It takes real thought to design and time to build. So when a person pursues one piece of their career and life puzzle predominately and without forethought—without regard for how it fits into a broader picture—trouble follows."

I knew that over the years, Howard had met many "successful" people who were miserably unhappy despite their very active lives, fancy titles, expensive cars, and vacation places in the mountains. I'd had innumerable similar experiences. These people excelled on the dimension of success measured by wealth, status, organizational authority, or some other narrow criteria. Yet they hadn't taken the time to understand how that dimension should fit into the more complex, long-term picture of their lives. They'd never considered how the primary goal they were pursuing should fit with other objectives—ones that might have been smaller-scale but were nevertheless important. Indeed, they hadn't recognized that ignoring the rest of the picture often comes at a significant emotional cost.

"To use a different analogy," Howard explained, "focusing almost exclusively on one goal is like exercising a single muscle:

your overall health doesn't improve; in fact, it's pretty unhealthy. And it sounds like that's exactly what your friend
George has done; all his planning and most of the energy he
expends have been focused on one piece of his life's puzzle."

Now, here was a point I didn't get. While George hadn't necessarily charted out a lifelong career vision, he had built what
seemed to me to be a pretty well-rounded life so far. Sure, he
worked hard. But he also spent lots of time with his family,
regularly engaged in a sport he enjoyed, participated in cultural
activities, and was involved in his community. I had to assume
that these things all brought him pleasure and enriched his life;
that they were all integral to how he defined himself. In fact, that
was one reason I was so unsettled by George's experience: he
wasn't just dissatisfied with his career situation, he was unhappy
with most aspects of his life—displeased with everything, it
seemed, except his family.

So I pushed back on Howard's point. "It seems to me that he
did have a multidimensional life," I said. "Career, family, social
activities, community work—and that this one positive change
has somehow unbalanced it."

Howard smiled impishly, as if he'd lured me into a trap on
the chessboard—a trap he now sprung. "Ah yes, all his social
activities, his community engagement, his golf. . . . On the
surface, sure, his life looks well-rounded—three-dimensional,
if you will. But I'd be willing to bet a platterful of roast beef
sandwiches that his life was, in fact, 'pseudo three-D.' "

I burst out laughing at yet another Howard-ism. "A 'pseudo-
three-D' life? What the heck's that mean?"

"It means that all of it was—whether he knew it or not—part
of his strategy for pursuing financial success, not distinct elements of a well-rounded life. An extension of one dimension
that appears to be multifaceted—three-dimensional—but really isn't. Pseudo three-D."

I began to follow. Howard was suggesting that George hadn't

taken up golf because he really liked it; nor gone to the sym-
phony because he loved classical music; nor accepted leadership
roles at the art center or with the Lung Association because he
was passionate about the organizations' missions. He engaged
in those activities because they were perfect ways to connect
with people—like corporate executives, bankers, investors, and
others—who could help his business grow.

Maybe it was a conscious strategy. More likely, given his present
degree of confusion and frustration, it was just an intuitive process
of leveraging connections. Without intending to do so—and
without making explicit choices about the trade-offs—he had
built an interconnected web of business relationships, community
engagement, and social activities that defined his life beyond the
family. But with one hugely positive turn of events, the whole
structure became almost pointless. Professionally and—to a certain extent—psychologically, George had found himself at a new
beginning. And he was clueless about how to start over, because
he didn't fully understand how he'd gotten there in the first place.

"Don't misunderstand, Eric; I actually admire George for
what he's done, for the sacrifices he's made for his real 'life goal.'"
I looked at him with a quizzical expression, and he explained,
"I'm suggesting that financial security wasn't George's ultimate
goal, but only a means to an end. I honestly think his real life
goal has been more fundamental: protecting and nurturing his
family—both his at-home family and the family he created in
his company. Getting rich and all the steps involved in it were
just elements of his all-consuming strategy for accomplishing
that goal."

I absorbed this analysis for a moment, then suggested, "So now
he needs to refocus. He should acknowledge 'protecting and
nurturing my family' as his primary goal, then take a fresh look
at what that means, given his new financial reality. Because financial support is only one facet of 'protecting and nurturing,'

and it's important that he consciously acknowledge the other facets—emotional, intellectual, spiritual, social . . ." Howard nodded vigorously, and I continued. "More than that, he should explicitly give himself permission to consider what other things are important to *him*—what will give him joy, give him a sense of personal engagement in things that are meaningful, give him a sense of satisfaction."

"Exactly," Howard said. "Now that he's got some time to spare, he should just stop for a bit. Tell him to stop driving hard and fast to find the next thing. Tell him to take time to think, broadly and deeply; to consider all the individual elements of who he is and what he wants in his life—large and small—and how they might relate to one another."

"Going back to your puzzle analogy," I offered, "he should create a solid frame around his life, a clear picture that will be the basis for responding effectively to this huge inflection point in his life."

"Yes, he should create a clear context for his decisions," he replied. "But I'm not talking about a rigid, permanent framework. It needs to be an evolving, flexible structure that enables him to have a holistic view of his future life and how day-to-day work and personal activities should fit into it."

"Why evolving and flexible?" I asked.

"Because our lives are flexible and evolving. The framework that you develop today will certainly inform your framework a year from now. But the very act of responding to an inflection point today will change the way you view your life tomorrow." He pointed at a beautiful chess set sitting on a shelf behind him. "It's much like a game of chess: once you've gotten a few moves into it, every subsequent move can change the entire complexion of the game. The most innocuous move can have huge long-term impact, and you want to be able to look at the way things are now, not just how they were before the last move.

Good chess players understand that—and so should each of us when we're thinking about our careers.

"The problem is that many people make the mistake of assuming their perspectives never shift as their careers and lives evolve—as they move closer to or slide further away from what they had previously determined were their long-term goals and hopes. They fall into the trap of not asking simple questions, like: 'Do I really want the same things today that I wanted last year?' 'Are the reasons I took this job five years ago still valid now?' 'Are the decision points I used to make my last choice the right ones to use in my next one?'"

"In other words," I said, "don't respond to the last inflection point. Focus on leveraging this *particular* inflection point in front of you at this *particular* point in time, based on today's perspective of what you want in your life, not yesterday's. Or, to quote a great sage: live life forward."

He chuckled at my use of his favorite phrase and said, "You got it."

"Okay, then George is in the perfect situation, because whatever framework he had before has been blown up—that much I'm sure he gets. But what does he do to construct this renewed picture? We assume that 'protect and nurture the family' is going to be a big piece of it, but where does he go from there? How should he start to frame the picture of what his future should be?"

At my question, Howard smiled brightly. "He should start at the end."

"Come again?"

"You heard me: start at the end. George should start by thinking about what he wants his life to have looked like when it's over. He's made a bunch of money. Great. But what's his legacy going to be? Looking long term, legacy is what we should all be thinking about. The earlier you think about it, the easier it will be to identify the path to get there—and the happier you'll be throughout your life.

"'Starting at the end' means investing time up front to develop an aspirational picture of your future as a guide for the decisions you make throughout your career and your life," he continued. "And sometimes the easiest way to define your legacy is simply to think about what you want people to say about you at your funeral." He stopped and looked at me, making sure I got it.

"I have to admit," I said after a moment of reflection, "of all the things I thought we'd talk about tonight, eulogies were not on the list. But that's what I love about you, Howard—you keep a guy on his toes."

"I could live with that on my tombstone," he joked, then grabbed his briefcase from beside the couch and turned his attention to preparing for the next day's meeting.

Remember the last time you faced an inflection point? A chance you had to confirm a path you were on, or to head off on a new one? Did you stick to your original course by default, in preference for the tried and true? Or did you pursue the option that everyone thought you "had to do"—the "once-in-a-lifetime opportunity" that you felt you couldn't pass up, even if your gut was telling you to let it go?

And how did you make your decision? If you're like most of us, you may have struggled with the pros and cons of specific options. You may have thought endlessly about the possibilities in front of you. Perhaps you focused so closely on every small element of each option that you found yourself in decision paralysis, unable to figure out what you "should" do.

Or, as Howard would suggest, did you take some time to stop, to bring all of your life's potential end points—all your myriad goals and hopes—together into a single picture? Did you then make a decision within the context of that whole-life picture?

It's easy to set a single goal and pursue it fervently. What I learned from Howard was the importance (and, yes, the challenge) of envisioning and pursuing not just that narrowly focused goal, but a broader personal legacy—a vision that holistically comprises the life you want to live.

Why is doing that so important? Because identifying your legacy is the essential precursor to creating the road map of how you want to live your life. It is the foundation for the decisions you make in your career. It is the key reference to use when responding to inflection points—both the humungous, life-changing kind that George faced, and the smaller-but-still-potent Friend and Foe inflection points that most of us face many times in our careers. As important, it is a perfect catalyst for creating your own inflection points.

How much easier is it to make all the step-by-step decisions you face—accept this job or that, live in the city or the suburbs, go to graduate school or take piano lessons—if you have a clear long-term destination in mind? The answer is obvious: enormously easier. But *easier* decisions are not the biggest—or even the most important—benefit. Legacy-driven decisions are also much more *effective*, much more likely to lead to a sense of satisfaction. In this respect, people can take a useful lesson from successful businesses.

Businesses succeed when they base tactical decisions on an overall corporate strategy, not on one small element of their operations. Those without a comprehensive strategy fail. They are often flashes in the pan—they start off strong, leveraging a brilliant product or a groundbreaking marketing approach; then they taper off, because they have no idea what to do after the "brilliant" and "groundbreaking" tactics run their course. On the other hand, the businesses that sustain their success over the long term have been able to develop a multifaceted picture of what they want to be. And they use that three-dimensional picture as a guide to move from where they are today to where they want to be in the future.

Just as Howard noted for George, an effective business strategy is not a rigid, unchanging picture. As successful companies learn more about themselves, their markets, and their products, they often shift their strategic goals. (In human terms, their legacy evolves.) But they do so with a clear set of reference points—embodied in their current vision—to use in determining exactly what new opportunities to pursue and what operational changes to make.

As individuals, many of us follow a career path built on tactical decisions made in isolation, without a broader context. We find ourselves lurching from one priority to the next. All of the facets of the life we want to have—salary, job title, house, social activities, intellectual pursuits, role in the community—are tactical. Figuring out how *all* those facets fit together is a strategy. Or, as Howard would say, it's business planning for your life's work.

"To undertake business planning for your own life," Howard explained to me, "you need to start at the strategic level. Develop an overall image of where you want to end up. And I don't mean the title you want at the height of your career or the position you hope to have eventually. Develop the strategic vision and then make decisions—respond to inflection points—in ways that make sense and that help you realize that image."

While businesses and individuals both need to invest time and energy in developing their strategic/legacy view, people face an interesting complication that organizations do not. For a business, financial "need" is clear and unambiguous: a company *needs* to make a profit and, over the long term, meeting that need is a key gauge of its success—a consistent measuring stick by which performance is, in large part, defined and judged. (Although, as Howard would be the first to point out, a company must have nonfinancial performance metrics as well, and, actually, profit can be viewed as simply a constraint on the company's fundamental mission. Apple and Facebook, for example, have changed key aspects of our culture, and Johnson & Johnson and Medtronic save people's lives—and the fact that they do those things enables them to be profitable.)

Human beings, on the other hand, have both needs and wants. For millions of people on this planet, fulfilling needs— something to eat, a place to sleep—takes virtually all of their energy and time; fulfilling wants is a wonderful extra, when it happens. On the other hand, the fact that you have the time to read this book—and I to write it—is indicative of the opportunity we've been afforded to pursue needs *and* wants, almost every day. We're lucky; but we're burdened, too, because having unfulfilled wants can feel quite painful. That's especially so in a society that tells us, "You can have it all. Indeed, you *should* have it all; and if you don't, maybe it's because you're just not smart enough, pretty enough, or diligent enough." This is what Howard was getting at when he said that the Apollo 13 astronauts had it easier in space: all their wants and needs were distilled down to the single goal of getting back to Earth alive. They had the luxury of simplicity, which most of us do not.

Despite the way it appeared on the surface, the inflection point that my friend George was struggling to respond to was not just financial. It represented a fundamental shift in the things he needed to focus on—a shift from needs to wants. It was a single chess move that changed the entire nature of the game. George's inflection point was one many of us would love to have. But it was a problem nevertheless because he had achieved career "success" but not satisfaction, and certainly not fulfillment. He hadn't recognized, let alone acknowledged, the importance of balancing needs and wants, and hadn't factored both into the life he'd created or the vision he had for himself. At least, he hadn't done so in a clear and emotionally honest way.

Howard would have told him that if you want to be satisfied and fulfilled, don't start by trying to figure out your next step.

Start by answering this question: "*Who* is it I want to be, and what is the legacy I want to leave?" George had indeed answered a piece of this question—he did achieve the financial security he so wanted for his family—but there were other parts of his life's picture that he had never taken the time to think about painting.

"Who you want to be is a reflection of your values," Howard says. "It's the manifestation of your most deeply held beliefs. And if we are to make full use of our opportunities in life, we must have a values-based vision of ourselves, of who we are and what we believe."

In all of our conversations about values, Howard never tried to define what those values should be for me—and I'm certainly not going to start down that long and winding path here. His lesson for me has always been more simple and direct: that my values should, indeed, be mine, not ideas I absorb unthinkingly from the culture around me; that my values must be the fundamental pillars around which I craft my legacy; and that they should be reflected in the tactical decisions I make about how best to pursue that legacy.

There are plenty of ways to get a sense of the options for who you want to be—plenty of ways to gather data points that you'll use in defining your desired legacy. However, when it comes to sorting it all out, there is really no substitute for "sittin' down and havin' a deep think," as Howard would say.

Whether you call it a "deep think" or an "honest interior dialogue," for many of us this kind of deep thought and self-analysis is new—maybe even uncomfortable. Considering who we want to be is not something we've tried to do in any focused or sustained manner. And having this dialogue is often antithetical to the pace of our lives and to the "right now" atmosphere that pervades our society. We want answers *now*. And success yesterday. But, really, most of us know—or can figure out—what we value, if only we would give ourselves the permission to explore it.

That sense of "self-permission" is important. The first step in defining your legacy is to realize that it is a conscious choice: you have the ability to shape who it is that you become over your lifetime, to shape the nature and path of your career in the context of your life. Once you accept the power to choose, there are myriad ways to engage in that all-important "deep think."

I particularly like the approach that Howard suggested for George: think about what you want people to say at your funeral. Consider how you'd want those you care about to describe you—on the most personal levels, separate from the structures and roles that define you to the rest of the world. Envision what you'd want your children to say when they describe you *to their children*. Or think about it this way: if a camera could take a "legacy" snapshot of you in the moment before you departed the earth, what do you want that picture to show?

The most fulfilled people I've met—both those with enormous wealth and those without—answer this question in personal terms that go beyond traditional career success. "I want my tombstone to read 'He was a friend to the world,'" the former chairman of the world's largest hotel company once told me. "I hope my legacy will be the individual girls whose lives I've changed by helping them learn to read," explained an extremely successful Turkish entrepreneur. And Bill Gates, speaking to Harvard graduates a few years ago, noted that he wants to be remembered not primarily for revolutionizing the personal computer industry, but for having played a small role in alleviating disease for the people of Africa. Each of them—and many others who have taken the time to draw a picture of their future lives and paths—have a broad, three-dimensional vision of themselves, of which professional and financial success is but a single element.

For them, legacy is not just a theoretical construct; it is a practical, highly effective tool that guides the major choices they make in their careers and their lives.

LORI SCHOR

You've probably never heard of Lori Schor, a smart, witty woman with a warm and infectious smile—and until recently, neither had I. She's not the CEO of a major corporation, and she's not likely to make a million-dollar philanthropic gift any time soon. She's just a well-educated professional woman, wife, mother, sister, and friend. But once we'd been introduced and started to talk, I realized how perfectly she embodied the concept of "starting at the end."

When I told her about Howard's belief that you must define *who* you want to be, long term, to make good short-term decisions—for example, by considering what you want said at your funeral—she nodded her head in recognition. "Howard must be a fan of T. S. Eliot," she said, and quoted from the poet's *Four Quartets*: "We shall not cease from exploration, and the end of all our exploring will be to arrive where we started. . . ."

We talked about the challenge of starting at the end as a way to guide one's response to inflection points. I asked her how she approached that challenge.

"Well, Howard's approach is good—but I'd go one step further," she said.

"One step beyond your funeral?" I laughed.

She nodded and paraphrased a piece of Jewish wisdom: "When I get to the gates of heaven, I won't be asked, 'Why weren't you more like Moses during your life?' or 'Why weren't you more like the best people around you?' I will be asked, 'Why were you not more like yourself?'"

As we talked more, I understood just how central this parable has been for her. It's such a tenet of her life that this is one of the blessings she offers her family each Friday night during her observation of the Jewish Sabbath: "Be who you are, and may you be blessed in all that you are." That blessing about sums up what she'd want people to say at her funeral: that she had fulfilled the promise of being herself.

"When I'm facing an inflection point in my life, I don't look primarily at external factors. I try to determine the best path to fulfilling who I am," she explained. "And your next question, of course, is, 'Okay, who are you, then?'"

I smiled as she answered her own question. "I am a multifaceted person, but my sense of self is based on a few pillars: I am a person of faith—both religiously and in my trust in people; I believe in the importance of education and continuous learning through life; I am grateful for all that I've been given and for the people in my life; and dedication to those I love is paramount."

She paused, then said, "I am also, by nature, a planner. I prefer action to inaction, but I'm not comfortable rushing into decisions and reactions. So I proactively seek out the information I need to make decisions. Then I move forward." She laughed to herself. "For example, I started reading *What to Expect When You're Expecting* a year before my husband and I even started trying to have a baby. Sure, some of my friends laughed at me. But I knew that while having a first child is obviously a major inflection point, the point when you decide, 'Yes, we're going to do this,' is a pretty big inflection point, too."

To an outside observer, Lori's professional life has been

successful, with an interesting variety of prestigious roles. She's been an urban planner, an attorney, a private-school administrator and educator, and director of a research fellowship program. But her career hasn't followed any traditional, linear path—seeking the ever-higher salary, bigger office, and fancier title—because it wasn't her goal to get to a particular place in a prescribed professional hierarchy. She's always tried to view her life as a whole, rather than as a set of linear points, and the major choices she made in her life were in response to the question "Who am I, and what is the best way to express that professionally, given the present circumstances in my life?"

That doesn't mean her career's inflection points were all friendly ones. In fact, the first major career inflection Lori faced—midway through college—was huge, complicated, and emotionally painful.

"From the time I was a child," Lori explained, "I *knew* that I was going to be an architect. And when I got into the architecture program of my choice in college, I assumed I was all set—that I'd just have to follow the standard path to success." That assumption might have been correct, except for one small but essential thing. "After my second year, I realized I had no talent for design," she said. She was able to grasp the concepts, theories, and techniques. She had all the basic skills. She was very creative. "I just wasn't skilled in the particular way an architect really needs to be," she said.

This realization forced her to look deep inside herself, reexamine all the aspects of who she was, and create a whole new path. It took more than a year of reevaluation, a year during which she left college, worked as a waitress, took classes on subjects that struck her as interesting, and considered her options. Recognizing and relying on her "inner planner," she expected to—and did—land on her feet again.

Having thought deeply about the things she was good at and the skills that brought her satisfaction—in other words, focusing on *who* she truly was, not simply on *what* she might be—she decided to become an urban planner. The latent emotional energy of her "architectural" inflection point was so powerful that within a few years, she'd finished college and then earned a master's degree in urban planning from the University of Pennsylvania.

"In retrospect, that long, difficult process reflects my approach to most major decisions in my life," Lori observed. "At each inflection point, I've gone back to the basics of who I am and used that information to guide my responses." Then she smiled brightly as the perfect analogy came to her mind, a basic principle she recalled from her urban-planning days. "When conducting a land survey, you identify a starting point, measure the distances and borders along the property, and return to that starting place. The final words on the description of the survey are 'Back to the point of beginning.' To me, that return to the start represents both a sense of completion and the realization of something brand new. And that's very satisfying."

CHAPTER FOUR

Juggling on the Balance Beam

It was the wrong time: my wife called to me in the middle of the night.
It took no time: the fear and desperation in her voice woke me immediately.
Time was short: so many things to do, so quickly.
Then, suddenly, time on our hands: hours into days into weeks.
Still, no time to relax: the calendar hung over us like a sword.
It was all a matter of time: on it, everything depended.
But finally, like sand in an hourglass: time came through.

IT'S HARD TO OVERESTIMATE the value of time. Time is one of the most important resources for any organization, from a Fortune 500 corporation to a nonprofit group to a local bakery. Time management is an essential skill for everyone from a CEO to a social worker to an IT manager to a cake decorator. In most jobs, you don't succeed if you don't manage your time effectively.

Managing time is an even greater imperative for us as individuals, because while a corporation is a perpetual entity, people are not. And a company can hire more people if the situation demands, but we can't hire someone to live our lives for us. Sure, there are some time-saving tasks that we can employ people to do for us, especially the things we don't like doing or that don't fit with our goals; for instance, instead of laundering and pressing our own clothes, we can pay for a dry cleaner.

But time-saving approaches only go so far. We really can't hire someone to do our careers for us or to earn the sense of professional satisfaction we seek. Nor does it make sense to hire someone to do activities that bring us joy.

As we pursue our life's work, one of the stiffest challenges we face is how to handle the constant demands on our time. We wonder how it's possible to address all the things we need and want in our lives: from family to work to community to friends to hobbies. And to do so in a way that enables us to look forward with some degree of pleasure to the day ahead, while making long-term progress toward our legacy vision.

For many people, career and family are the two most significant draws on time, and that's my situation as well. I've long understood the place that family plays in my own legacy vision and how my investment in family-focused time affects my career day to day. But a recent experience (one that occurred smack in the middle of writing this book) brought home in a *very* real way the challenge of pursuing all the elements of my legacy vision in the face of time's strict limitations.

It started at four o'clock on a cold Saturday morning in February. "Eric," my wife, Jennifer, called out. "You need to get up. Now!" The tone in her voice was one I'd never heard before, filled with notes of absolute, primal terror. "Call 911," she said, her voice shaking with fear. Jennifer was twenty-five weeks pregnant with our second son, and her water had broken— fifteen weeks early. Pulled out of a sound sleep, I didn't immediately understand all of what was happening, but I intuitively knew that our unborn child was in danger.

Up to that moment, things had been going well on the home and career fronts. Jennifer, formerly an elementary school teacher, was focusing her time on being a mom, and she loved it. Our three-year old son, Daniel, was blossoming and was a joy for his two sets of grandparents, who lived nearby. My work life was good, too: my company, Axcess, was thriving, giving me the chance to work with fascinating people and companies. In fact, just days earlier, I'd returned from Las Vegas, where I'd led marathon negotiations that brought about a partnership between two publicly traded companies—a partnership that was being hailed as "historic" for both of them.

Between family, the office, work on this book, and a handful of other personal and professional commitments and goals, I had a full plate. Regardless, I've always been good at juggling multiple challenges and making effective decisions about using my time. So, despite a really busy schedule, I felt in control.

Then, in an instant in the middle of a February night, the balance of my life shattered. My juggling act fell apart. All sense of control disappeared.

Thirty minutes after Jennifer first woke me—the longest half hour of my life—we wheeled her into the hospital ER. After hurried examinations, the doctors explained soberly that our unborn child weighed less than a pound and a half; that Jennifer could go into labor immediately; that for most women in her situation, the baby is born within seven days. If the baby decided to come then—three months early and unable to breathe on his own—we could do little to stop him. And, they concluded, however long it would take, Jennifer would not be leaving the hospital until the baby was delivered.

As we moved Jennifer from the ER to a hospital room, the nurse—sensing our fear and confusion—encouraged us to be forward-looking, to be thankful for each hour and each day that the baby hung in there. It was the most important piece of advice we received.

Without realizing it, our family began a two-month odyssey: eight weeks with Jennifer lying flat on her back, enduring medically supervised bed rest for twenty-three and a half hours a day, doing everything possible to stave off labor. We couldn't know at the outset how successful her efforts would be: defying all odds, our developing son would remain in the womb for sixty-one more days. The doctors told us it was a minor miracle.

The first couple of days after that four A.M. rush to the hospital were a blur, marked by a kind of terror I'd never known before. It was a terror that rendered meaningless many of the things that had consumed my focus just hours before: from my business to our house-hunting plans to work on this book. Now my attention was solely on my wife and on the well-being of our kids—the one still hanging tight in his mom's belly, and the one who awoke on Saturday morning to find his grandmother preparing breakfast instead of his mom or dad. It was only at six o'clock on Monday morning, the time that I would normally have been on the train to work, that reality dawned for me. For the foreseeable future—however long it would be—I was going to have to fundamentally rethink the way I prioritized my time, not to mention my emotional and intellectual energy.

The status quo was out the window. All my careful calibrations on balancing career, family, and my myriad personal and professional goals needed to be reconsidered—for a period that we hoped would stretch for months. My wants and needs took on a very narrow focus; my time and energy had to be weighted heavily toward Jennifer and Daniel. I wanted to spend every minute of every day with Jennifer, fearing what might happen when I was not there. (As if my presence could somehow forestall her labor.) And I needed to take over responsibility for Daniel's daily routine, to try to fill Jennifer's shoes as the primary toddler carpooler, birthday-party attender, and seesaw partner. I knew that those imperatives would leave little energy and focus for other facets of my life; that everything would need to take a backseat to our new family reality.

I suppose there were any number of ways I could have handled the situation, many of them perfectly reasonable from an objective perspective. I could, for example, have slept at home and spent all day with Jennifer. In theory, I could have gone into the office every other day. I guess I could have figured out a way to keep up some of my other activities, to retain some element of normalcy. For me, though, there was really just one option, only one right answer.

So, beginning that first night, I moved into Morristown Medical Center, the foldout recliner in Jennifer's room serving as my bed. Together we embarked on a 24/7 mission to keep Jennifer flat and fat—flat on her back and pregnant as long as possible. Day after day, we lived in that hospital room, grateful for the time that had passed and hoping to stretch the time before us.

Early on, as I struggled to adjust to this situation, work had no place in my schedule. I didn't check e-mail or connect with my company, leaving the business in the capable hands of my long-time business partner, Kirk. Gradually, as days went by and I accepted the new normal, I began to reengage with my professional life. I commandeered a back corner table in the hospital cafeteria for my new office space, equipped with a notebook, a laptop computer, and two cell phones. I arranged for members of my staff to travel from Manhattan to suburban Morristown for weekly meetings. Conversations with clients took place by phone or e-mail; I had virtually no meetings with people outside the company. What time I spent beyond the hospital confines was reserved almost exclusively for Daniel—shepherding him to and from nursery school, shuttling him between his grandparents' houses, taking him to the playground or to dinner at his favorite pizza place, and reading him bedtime stories.

This extended episode of imbalance and lack of control—so scary in one sense and, ultimately, wonderful in another—ended when our new son, Michael, was born at thirty-four weeks gestational age. Somehow, we'd all gotten through those sixty-one amazing days intact. Jennifer, Daniel, and Michael all healthy; grandparents resilient and happy; and my company continuing along well, if just a bit out of kilter for my absence.

It took a little while, but the balance of our lives returned. (Well, as much as any family's balance returns after adding a second child. I understand why people say that having two kids is three times the work!) And I returned to juggling a more predictable set of externally driven family and work challenges, and of internally driven personal and professional goals.

Effectively pursuing our life's work—having a satisfying life and a rewarding career—depends on successfully managing the allotment of time we've been given. It is, of course, a *finite* allotment: we're all going to die someday; and each day until then will last just twenty-four hours. So we face some big questions about how best to manage those hours and days:

> *How should we apportion our time among the various facets of who we are and who we want to be?*

> *Are we using our time in a way that leaves us feeling generally satisfied or dissatisfied?*

> *Are we managing time in a manner that enables us to fulfill our most important needs and wants?*

> *Are we unwittingly squandering this precious resource by being reactive and allowing events to manage us?*

If those questions aren't daunting enough, remember that time isn't the only resource that's finite. There are limits to our physical energies and stamina—whether we're working, mountain biking, helping the kids with math homework, fixing up the house, or just staying up late to watch *Monday Night Football* or *American Idol*. There are limits to our emotional energy and resiliency—whether we're handling an overbearing boss, caring for a sick parent, studying for a licensing exam, or trying to stick to a new diet. And there are, of course, limits to our financial resources.

I love the old proverb "To make God laugh, we make plans," which my friend Bonnie Reiss, the former secretary of education in California, shared with me years ago. It's a great reminder not to expect too much from our flawed human capacity for planning out our lives and managing our time. It suggests that, since life sometimes includes crazy and unpredictable events, it's quixotic to think we can continuously control and manage all our time or energy. And after our flat and fat experience, boy do I get that point.

However, if we let our day-to-day lives be guided *solely* by that perspective, we'd just accept events as they come; we'd make no effort to shape them to our benefit. And, to use the proverb's language, God is not *always* laughing at our efforts. So I remind myself that another term for a "crazy and unpredictable event" is *inflection point,* and that—as Howard has observed—we can conserve time and energy if we engage in some serious forethought about how to handle the inevitable inflection points in our lives.

In other words, having a "deep think" will enable us to make better decisions about how we're spending our time and our other precious personal resources. Even if life doesn't go according to our exact plan, the fact that we *created* the plan positions us to make the best possible use of the time and energy available for our careers. That's why Howard believes it's so important that we each create a legacy vision, a strategic picture of who we want to be and what we'd like our lives to look like when they're all done.

Still, Howard would remind any budding entrepreneur, "Strategy is just the start. Strategy tells you the destination, but tactics are where the rubber meets the road—in fact, it's where you choose which of the multiple roads to your strategic goal you're going to take."

The tactical level is where the tough choices get made—the decisions involving your time, energy, and money. The tactical level is, therefore, really challenging.

Remember the Apollo 13 astronauts? In one sense, they had it easy—one single, clear objective, no ambiguity, no weighing of alternative destinations and paths. Their tactical options were limited and their choices straightforward. In general, our day-to-day choices are infinitely less weighty than theirs were; yet our choices get vastly more complicated over the course of our earthbound careers. It can become quite difficult to choose among multiplying options for using our allotment of time and physical, emotional, and intellectual energy. Doing so in a way that leaves us with no regrets afterward is even tougher.

Many people describe this challenge as one of keeping their lives in "balance," and they seek a stable and comfortable "work/life balance." But if you use those terms as nouns in conversation with Howard, you're likely to get a deep scowl in response. "Most often, when I hear people talk about balance in their lives," he's told me, "they're conceiving of it in static terms—as if they could arrange the facets of their lives just so, and then stand there with twenty pounds of priorities perfectly balanced in each hand and their feet firmly planted in one place. I suppose that works well if you're an unmoving statue, but most people I know are in motion. They're trying to move forward, and as they do, the relative weight of their various goals and priorities keeps changing. Not to mention the fact that the tides of life keep moving around them, sweeping the sand out from under their feet.

"We need to think of 'balance' as a dynamic *verb*, not as a stationary noun," Howard believes.

"So," I asked one day after observing his frustration at yet another expression of stationary balance, "if balancing in place is too static a metaphor, what's a better one? What image more accurately captures the challenge of pursuing your life's work in a satisfying way?"

He thought for a moment, then broke into a broad smile and said, "It's like juggling an egg, a tennis ball, and a knife, while walking on a balance beam—at the Olympics."

"That's a weirdly precise answer," I responded. "Why exactly that image?"

"Because," he said, "making good day-to-day tactical choices requires thoughtful juggling, a keen sense of balance despite distraction, and the courage to continue putting one foot in front of the other—and it is, literally and figuratively, the challenge of a lifetime."

Well, that's not a simple metaphor, is it? But I can't think of one that better describes the complexities of our lives. Or one that better conveys the different—and subtly shifting—weights, shapes, and impacts of the things we deal with as we try to move our careers forward.

We all juggle on the balance beam every day. For instance, there's the young father, trying to advance in a field where success demands lots of after-work time socializing with colleagues or clients; he's seeking the right balance as he juggles the need to build social capital for his career with the desire to head right home for family time. There's the up-and-coming corporate manager who's trying to stay on the beam while juggling her long work hours, a part-time MBA program, and a desire to spend more time getting to know her fiancé's friends and family. There's the guy who's offered a high-profile project that will take him out of town for the next two weeks, but who knows that it would mean missing two consecutive sessions with the "Little Brother" he's mentoring—which would throw that little guy off balance. Then there's his colleague, who's also offered a place on the project team but realizes it would require her to drop out of the local theater production in which she has, finally, earned a lead role. And don't forget their third colleague—the one who's overweight and has a family history of diabetes, and knows that all the running around during the two-week project will lead him to completely blow the diet and exercise routine he's just getting used to.

Keeping our lives going, pursuing all the things we want to do—all that we want to be—is often stressful. It can be emotionally and physically draining. That's especially true in our current cultural moment, where there's an explicit assumption that you'll respond to a friend's text or a client's e-mail *now,* and an implicit expectation that you'll be the best you can be all the time: the best mother, wife, sister, daughter, certified professional accountant, yoga student, and church bake-sale organizer—every single day. It reminds me of the line Lily Tomlin made famous: "The trouble with the rat race is that even if you win, you're still a rat." Our challenge is to figure out how to manage the many facets of our life's work—and to move toward our legacy vision—without getting drawn into the rat race.

Whether we're facing a family crisis or just trying to live a full life, each of us needs to develop an ability to juggle and balance effectively. It's essential to having a satisfying career. So after my wife and new son came home and once I got back into the swing of work (and book writing), this imperative became the focus of several conversations with Howard.

Harkening back to his juggling-on-the-balance-beam metaphor, during one of our walk-and-talks I asked, "What does successful juggling and balancing feel like? As we move along the balance beam of our careers, how do we know when we're doing it right?"

"In simplest terms, Eric, you know you're balancing effectively when you're maintaining comfortable reserves of physical, emotional, intellectual, and financial resources—when you've got sufficient quantities left in each tank. And, by extension, you're doing it wrong when you ain't got nuttin' left in one of your tanks and you're running on fumes in another.

"That's not to say that every tank has to be equally full all the time. In fact, there will be plenty of situations where, for a limited period, you run low on one of them. For example, my physical energy was really low for a while after my heart attack. But I was balancing well because my emotional and intellectual tanks were pretty full; they carried me until I was able to get a refill of physical stamina."

"And juggling?" I asked.

"In broad terms, successful juggling means pursuing the facets of our life's work—what I call our various selves and dimensions—in a way that allows us to move toward our legacy vision. To mix my metaphors, when we're juggling well, we are succeeding in putting the puzzle pieces together in a way that fits our picture of who we want to be. And that give us a sense of general satisfaction."

Here he paused, then went back to make sure I understood the significance of those last few words. "General satisfaction— meaning most of the time you are satisfied, but not always or not completely. It's an important point, because there are always going to be ebbs and flows; to expect complete, unbroken happiness and satisfaction is setting yourself up for disappointment. So, for myself, I don't expect to be happy one hundred percent of the time, but I need to be happy for some part of almost every day. I don't have to win every professional contest, but my satisfaction depends on winning the ones that are really meaningful. And I need to feel that I'm moving in the right general direction, toward my legacy vision."

Later in the day, after I'd gone on to other meetings, Howard sent me an e-mail. It said:

Continuing our conversation. . . . Edgar Degas, the nineteenth-century painter, once said, "There is a kind of success that is indistinguishable from panic." We often use the frantic pace of a "successful" life as an excuse for not taking the time to think deeply about what's getting crowded out. We're running so hard, so fast—and that feels good for a time, but at some point you stop running and you wonder, "What the heck am I doing here?" So here's another way to know if you're succeeding at juggling and balancing: you're actually making time to sit down and think about why you're using your time and energy the way you are—and where you want it to get you.

I absorbed Howard's ideas on juggling and balancing for a few days. Then, over lunch later in the week, I asked him to delve a little deeper in his explanation. "When we were discussing juggling and balancing last time, you talked about our life's work in terms of selves and dimensions. What did you mean?"

"Okay," he said, grabbing a handful of yellow sweetener packets and laying seven of them in a row on the table. "In the context of our broader lives, there are a variety of selves that we juggle—each represented by one of these packets. I think that most of us juggle some combination of these seven, although it can vary from person to person." Those seven selves were:

1. Family self (whether parent, child, sibling, in-law, etc.)

2. Social/Community self (friendships and communal engagement)

3. Spiritual self (in terms of religion or philosophy or emotional outlook)

4. Physical self (your physical health and well-being)

5. Material self (the immediate environment in which you live and the things you have around you)

6. Avocational self (hobbies and nonprofessional activities)

7. Career self (from both short- and long-term perspectives)

(You'll note there's no "financial" self, because money is one of the resources directed toward our various selves.)

"For each of these selves there are three main questions to answer," he continued.

"Who do I want to be?

"How much do I want to experience in this self?

"And how important is this self relative to each of the others?

"Those answers will guide the choices you make about exactly what to juggle."

"The decision you come to, then, is how much of your supply of personal resources you put into juggling each self, right?" I asked. "And that leads back to the process of balancing— judiciously allocating your time, energy, and money according to your assessment of the relative importance of each of your selves?"

Howard nodded. "It's a continuing cycle—a dynamic process of movement and subtle correction. Sometimes it's intuitive, like the unconscious muscle movements in our legs and torso that keep us balanced as we walk down the street. Other times, such as when you're facing a new situation or when the consequences of losing your balance are significant, it needs to be more conscious. For example, when you're hiking on a rocky hillside, you take a second to look ahead and say to yourself, 'Okay, that next rock is sloping downward, so I'll need to lean forward and then immediately shift my balance laterally toward the flat rock on the right.'"

"All right," I continued, "those seven little packets are the selves—but what are the dimensions?"

Howard now picked up a bunch of blue sweetener packets and arrayed them in columns below the yellow ones representing the selves. Some of the columns had just one blue packet, others had several. "Each of these selves can have multiple dimensions," he explained. "For instance, I could put a handful down under my Family self—representing my dimensions of 'father,' 'husband,' 'grandfather,' 'brother-in-law,' and so on. Similarly, under Social/Community I'd put a few representing the dimensions of 'close friend,' 'colleague,' 'organization board member,' and probably several others."

"In the end, any person with a reasonably full life is going to have a lot of blue packets," I observed. "That's a whole lot of juggling and balancing. The permutations are endless."

"Well, that's what makes life both fun and challenging," he replied, with an ironic laugh.

We continued our conversation, talking about the individual yellow and blue packets arrayed before us as if they actually embodied our various selves and dimensions. I won't bore you with the details of the discussion about our Physical selves (where, Howard noted, we both needed to invest more time on the exercise dimension) or our Avocational selves (which for Howard is multidimensional, and for me is—to put it mildly—not).

But his thoughts on the dimensions of the Career self were particularly interesting. "Sure, the day-to-day job is a major piece of almost everybody's juggling-and-balancing challenge. That's a no-brainer. However, people tend to overlook the career dimensions that represent the different professional skills and capacities we hope to utilize and, more broadly, the variety of professions in which we are interested."

In the shorter term, these dimensions become part of the juggling-and-balancing challenge when we decide to put concerted effort into honing a particular skill or expanding areas of expertise. For example, when taking the next step in your career requires testing for a special software certification, or earning the certified public accountant designation, or just attending public speaking classes to improve your communication skills. These dimensions also come into play when expanding your repertoire requires an investment of intellectual and psychological energy in a relatively weak area—such as when you need to concentrate on being more organized, or overcoming the introvert in you, or managing your work schedule more efficiently.

In discussing these dimensions of the Career self, Howard emphasized that it's about more than just how much time we spend on the job, day to day. "It's about identifying the various facets of *who* you want to be in the context of your current job and career path and allocating your personal resources to those facets."

The Career self has an important long-term dimension, too: the various, distinct kinds of professional activities that you hope to engage in during your life. "Time was," Howard observed, "just about everyone entered a profession and stayed there for life. Many people still do, happily and productively. But as our economy and society have evolved, folks are pursuing a variety of professions over the course of their lives—some by necessity as entire industries have shrunk or gone out of existence, and some by choice. And, increasingly, people will choose to pursue multiple professional dimensions. The key to doing that successfully, with the fewest hurdles and detours and the most consistent satisfaction, is to anticipate what you'll need to do to make the transitions between them. If planned carefully, small, incremental investments of time and energy can pay off big down the line. But you've got to have thought about those facets of who you are, professionally, and fed that thinking into your short-term choices."

Over the course of his four-decade career, Howard's professional roles have included business school professor, university administrator, corporate executive, money manager and investor, philanthropist, and author—six somewhat linked but distinctly different roles. Some of those roles he's pursued simultaneously; others sequentially. His choices evolved from a deep understanding of the various dimensions of who he wanted to be, professionally and personally; a recognition of the skills and capacities he wanted to utilize and develop; and careful decisions about how and when to invest his time and energy in pursuing new paths.

"You've got to view the various near- and long-term Career dimensions as part and parcel of your legacy vision," Howard explained. "This may sound like a 'Duh! Of course' kind of point. But it's the rare person who truly recognizes at the outset of her career all the facets of her professional interests. For most of us, it's like opening the layers of an onion as we gain experience of the work world and a greater understanding of ourselves. So we need to be open to this discovery process and to incorporate our evolving self-knowledge into our legacy vision and our juggling-and-balancing decisions."

As our lunch wound down, a waiter brought over two lattes, and since the table was nearly covered with sweetener packets, he politely began to restack them in their little holders, making room for the cups. "Let's not move those," Howard said to him, resetting the packets into their previous rows and columns. "We'll just squeeze the cups over on the side here." After the waiter left, I looked at Howard quizzically.

"One more important point," he responded. "A point perfectly illustrated by our friend the waiter." He took a long sip of his drink, then said, "You can't make really effective juggling-and-balancing decisions if you don't recognize that each of these selves and dimensions are distinct things. Sometimes they're related; still, each is different.

"But it's easy to fall into the trap of lumping everything together. And when you do, the decisions about how to allocate time and energy become both overwhelming and ineffectual."

"It's kind of the reverse of the old saying 'can't see the forest for the trees,'" I suggested. "In this case, you can't find the path between the individual trees, because all you see is the one big, dark, impenetrable forest."

"Nicely put," he said. "On a day-to-day basis, we humans have a tendency to let all of our challenges mush together, becoming a single problem that's greater than the sum of its parts. So when we are feeling out of balance or about to drop one of the things we're juggling, it's very important to tease apart the different strands of the challenge so that the whole thing isn't overwhelming.

"When I've taken the time to do that, I've often found that a small shift in how I use my personal resources has a big impact on my overall sense of satisfaction."

All of us are jugglers and balancers on the balance beam of life, trying to handle a variety of priorities, wants, and needs. Some of these are like tennis balls; they're relatively easy to handle and there are few negative implications if we drop one. The challenge with them is simply how many can we juggle at any one time. Others are eggs, easy to handle but fragile; so we probably need to juggle fewer of them. And at one point or another, we all find that a sharp knife, a bowling ball, or an unwieldy crystal vase gets tossed into the act—and that's when things get really interesting, challenging, and even scary.

Understanding the broad elements of who you are—your multifarious "selves" and "dimensions"—is fundamental to making clear and effective juggling-and-balancing decisions. It's not a once-in-a-lifetime process; you can't say, "I've thought it through and I'm done and now I'll just go hit that balance beam." The process of managing your time, energy, intellect, and emotional vitality is a dynamic one. You can't set your allocation on autopilot and expect it to keep working for you. And you can't set unrealistic expectations.

Juggling and balancing effectively requires that we make clear, legacy-driven choices about what we're trying to keep in the air and how we sequence our movements down the beam. Because the ultimate grade in life is not based on how far and fast we've walked the beam or how many things we've juggled—it's based on how much we've enjoyed the exercise.

SOLEDAD O'BRIEN

I am exhausted.

Well, okay, not literally exhausted—I am vicariously and sympathetically exhausted.

The cause? A conversation I just had with Soledad O'Brien, the hugely respected, award-winning news anchor and special correspondent . . . and documentary filmmaker . . . and author . . . and wife and mother of four young kids . . . and philanthropist. Any one of those could be a person's full-time job, yet she has managed to keep all of them going. How? I don't know. I used to pride myself on handling a busy schedule, but her schedule can be so punishing—including strings of nonstop, twenty-hour days—that I'm tired just thinking about what "busy" means in Soledad terms.

Given the chance for a freewheeling conversation, there are lots of topics I'd have liked to ask her about—from her reflections on growing up as an Aussie-Afro-Cuban girl in a lily-white Long Island suburb; to her experiences reporting on Hurricane Katrina, the Southeast Asia tsunami, and war in the Middle East; to the foundation that she and her husband, Brad, created to help promising young women in challenging situations. But wanting to be respectful of her time, I limited my questions to one primary (and obvious) topic: How does she stay sane while juggling so many different facets of an amazingly complex life? How do she and Brad—himself a busy and accomplished investment banker—balance the demands on them as professionals, parents, and engaged citizens?

"I think that, first, balance is connected to how we view the world. People, generally, are less likely to be wasting time and energy if they have an appreciation of the opportunities and privileges they're given. It's often much easier to feel satisfied by what you've got in your life when you see it in context. My parents instilled that idea in our family. For example, when we went on a vacation and stayed in a nice hotel, my dad would make a point of driving us through the neighborhoods where all the workers lived, so we saw who made it possible for us to be comfortable and how they lived. And if we went into New York City for a day of shopping, he'd take us first to the Bowery so we understood that many people didn't get to wear nice clothes.

"Brad and I try to do the same thing, to make sure the kids have a balanced sense of expectation and reality. When I went to Haiti to report on life there since the earthquake, I brought my kids with me so that they could get a sense of the day-to-day experience of children just like them who lived in this very tough situation. It's experiences like that that help us understand that a car breaking down isn't a crisis, losing a material thing is not a crisis—a tsunami is a crisis.

"I also believe that maintaining balance is not just a matter of how much time you spend on something. It matters *how* you spend it, how well you use it. My mother, who worked full time as a teacher and raised six kids, spent a lot more time at home than I do. But I'm able to spend more time actually doing things directly with my kids than my parents did. Sometimes it's everybody playing games or just wrestling around on the floor together. Other times it's more focused: one child loves to visit with little kids at a hospital nearby, so we do that; one loves to play baseball, so we do that; one just wants to sit on your lap and be read to, so we do that. We also plan focused getaways—Brad will take the two girls somewhere for a weekend, and I'll take the two boys. Making and keeping those plans is one of the 'rules' we have in the family that help us keep focused on the right things, even when schedules are really crazy."

I asked Soledad what other rules they've adopted for juggling the myriad facets of their lives. She thought for a moment, then laughed and said, "First rule: the parents must keep it together for the kids, and we can't both 'crash and burn' emotionally at the same time. That means, no matter what we're dealing with in our careers, the kids don't feel the impact—we might talk to them about tough stuff we're wrestling with, but we don't let them feel the fallout. It also means that if Brad and I both start feeling big challenges coming on we pull back and figure out which one is going to be the positive, supportive, optimistic partner.

"The next rule is accepting that everything is fixable and discussable—that there are no unsolvable problems, no disagreement or issue that can't be talked out. That's especially true if you take the long view of a situation, if you look not just at today and tomorrow, but you also ask, 'What's this going to mean a year or ten years from now?'

"Another really important rule is: everyone votes and there are no martyrs. We're each entitled to a say in big decisions; and we're each entitled to happiness—entitled to say, 'This is really important to me' and have everyone else accept that. Often, that means Brad or I are giving up something we want. But it also means that—sometimes, for limited periods of time—family doesn't come first. And everybody understands that if there's a big breaking news event, I drop pretty much everything to cover it— because doing my job is *really* important to me.

"The final rule is: keep your commitments. If you agree to do something—big or small, involving a few minutes or whole days—make sure you follow through. If people know they can count on you, their lives are more stable—and your life is more firmly balanced, too."

With that she paused, then said, "You asked me why I maintain the kind of overwhelming schedule that I do. If there's any single answer, it's because I've made commitments—to people, to organizations, to my family, to myself. It's very important to me to keep those commitments. I may not be able to keep up this pace forever, but I'll keep making those commitments for as long as I can keep fulfilling them."

CHAPTER FIVE

Is the Juice Worth the Squeeze?

*Is it worth squeezing a gallon of fresh grapefruit juice if you really want
a glass of orange juice?*

IN OUR HIGH-ACHIEVER CULTURE, there's an increasingly
strong tendency to think that we should accept no limits on
what we can do. As a result, even if we consciously recognize
the daily cap that life places on our time, we frequently believe—at least subconsciously—that we should accept no limitation on what we can accomplish within each day, month, and
year we're allotted. Technology has ramped up our ability to
achieve more, we tell ourselves; multitasking is the promised
path to fulfilling all our goals.

But this is not a wholly new phenomenon of the Internet age.
Our culture didn't suddenly shift with the founding of Google
or the introduction of the iPhone. The feeling that we're somehow "less" if we aren't doing "more" has been growing for decades, and has simply been amplified by technology.

This never-doing-enough culture is something that Howard
has thought deeply about—especially as it comes into play for his
ambitious students as they move through their careers. It was
one focus of his book *Just Enough*, a wide-ranging, research-
based look at how high achievers set their career, financial, and
personal ambitions. In *Just Enough,* Howard and his co-author,

Laura Nash, considered the risks and pitfalls of trying to accomplish everything on one's agenda, fully and perfectly, all the time. And they posited that the never-doing-enough mentality derives, in part, from what they called "celebrity culture."

In celebrity culture, success is glamorized for its own sake, and new levels of achievement immediately become the norm to be superseded, rather than accomplishments to be appreciated. Celebrity culture represents the ancient stories of Sisyphus (who was condemned to eternally push a boulder up a hill) and Tantalus (whose prize was always just out of reach), combined into a myth for our own times: we are constantly striving for more, pushing uphill with unending effort because the object we desire is forever just beyond our reach. Merely doing well, moving forward in our lives, being happy most days—doesn't seem enough when we get caught up in celebrity culture. As a result, *Just Enough* suggests, we feel we have to be almighty at everything in order to consider ourselves anything at all.

"On top of that," Howard has observed, "we make ourselves miserable by engaging in endless comparisons, because there's always someone ahead of us on any single element we choose to measure—someone prettier, richer, more athletic, funnier; someone who's a better parent, a more devoted spouse, or a more well-rounded person. When we judge ourselves by the metrics of celebrity culture, we've lost the game before it's even begun."

I'm certainly not immune to the impact of celebrity culture—nor to the creeping of the never-good-enough, never-doing-enough perspective into my subconscious mind. I even fell prey to it, now and then, during my family's two-month "flat and fat" hospital experience. Although I never questioned my initial decisions about how I would allocate my time and energy—Jennifer and Daniel and unborn Michael came first; everyone and everything else was secondary, at best—periodically I still found myself feeling frustrated and anxious about the things I wasn't getting done. I wondered if I might be able to accomplish more if I'd only put out a little more effort or devised a slightly more effective approach. This book, and my sense of commitment to Howard, was one of my points of anxiety. While there certainly were a lot of quiet evening hours at the hospital when I could have focused on writing, I found that I had little energy for it. I was husbanding that intellectual and emotional energy—figuratively and literally.

Some of that maybe-I-should-be-accomplishing-more frustration and anxiety came out during a phone call with Howard halfway through my wife's hospital stay. In that conversation, reflexively and without thinking much about it, I apologized to him for not making as much progress on this book as I'd planned. "I know that I'm not supposed to be working on it right now, and I know that I'm not supposed to be feeling bad about it," I said, "but the fact is that some part of me still does feel bad. I really don't want to disappoint you on this."

"I know," he said gently and with complete understanding. "You're the kind of guy who can do a number of things really well; and it's very easy for you to slip, almost unconsciously, into the assumption that you should be able to do *everything* well, even now. So let me make it simple," he continued with a deliberate pace and deep feeling in his voice. "Stop wasting your anxiety on me . . . and stop trying to get an A on everything."

"What do you mean?" I asked.

"Eric, I know you understand this deep down, but I'm going to say it again because it's easy to forget in the day-to-day hurly-burly of life," he began. Then he reminded me of something we'd discussed more than once in our walk-and-talk conversations. "It's possible to get straight A's when you're a student. The school grading system is an artificial construct in which it's possible to excel at everything—it's designed to enable intelligent people to achieve consistently high grades with a reasonable investment of time and energy. But life is not a classroom. We can't get an A on every facet of life every single day. Our lives are too complex; there are too many variables to control. It's almost one of the physical laws of the universe, like you can't be in two places at the same time."

He continued, with a laugh, "And for highly motivated people, there are few more frustrating situations than realizing that the goals you've set will require a shift in the basic laws of time and space."

Howard's words did indeed bring to mind the many times I wished I could clone myself, or slip 120 minutes in between 4:59 and 5:00 P.M., or develop the capacity for simultaneous telepathic communication with family, co-workers, and friends. And I recalled the plaintive words of my friend Warren Adams, an entrepreneur who is one of the fathers of social networking. Despite being an amazingly accomplished and wealthy man, Warren once told me, "Eric, I wake up each morning wondering who I'm going to disappoint today, because there are more demands on my time than I could possibly handle. And in that respect, I don't think I'm much different from a twenty-six-year-old guy just out of grad school or a forty-three-year-old working mom."

On the phone, Howard continued his thought. "We've got to accept that we can't maximize ourselves on all dimensions at the same time. We cannot pursue all of our goals simultaneously, nor satisfy all of our desires right away. The more deeply we accept that fact, the less time and emotional energy we waste trying to work against it. Ultimately, recognizing this inherent human limitation is essential to achieving a sense of satisfaction, day to day, in our careers and lives."

He continued on in a kind, paternal voice. "I'd give you an A-plus as a husband and father, especially for your long, sustained effort. You'd get a C-plus on your job, keeping your projects moving but not aiming for big wins. Even without looking at you, I'm guessing that you'd get a D at taking care of yourself—you sound tired, and I'll bet you haven't been to the gym for a while. And as a son, a friend, and an author, you get an 'incomplete.' There's little time or energy left over for those things, but you'll have plenty of opportunity to make up those grades when your life settles down."

I was quiet for a moment, letting his words sink in, then I asked, "So what grades do you aim for in your life?"

"Hmm, interesting question," he mused. "I suppose that, generally, I don't aim for an A-plus on any individual dimension. There are few times when A-plus effort is absolutely necessary, and getting that close to perfection requires a huge and unsustainable effort. You're experiencing the costs of an A-plus effort right now." I grunted in agreement, thinking of how my A-plus grades as a husband and father were coming at a cost to some other dimension.

"But to answer your question more broadly," he said, "I want to get the best average grade I can. With the understanding that I don't want to get an F on anything—because if I'm willing to accept an F, I shouldn't be trying to do it in the first place."

He paused, then offered, "All in all, I'm looking for an A-minus or B-plus average—over the long term and across the different dimensions of my life. It's a conscious decision, because well-rounded, balanced people have myriad interests and pursuits; and there's an inverse relationship between the intensity of effort in any one area and the number of areas in which we can invest energy."

"So you've given yourself permission to get a good-but-not-stellar average in order to pursue a wider range of goals," I observed.

"Yes, and with all the external pressures today, I think it's important that we give ourselves explicit permission to get that A-minus or B-plus average," Howard said. "I know a lot of people who aren't willing to aspire to anything less than an A across the board. And as a former mathematician, I can tell you that in the end it just doesn't add up. Sooner or later, these people fall out of balance. Some of the things they're juggling start slipping through their fingers."

"That's not necessarily a problem if they've made a conscious decision about what they'll let slip," I pointed out.

"But that's just it—they haven't!" he said. "In refusing to accept a lesser grade on any element of their lives, they've made everything equal. They've chosen *not to choose*—"

"And so, life chooses for them," I finished his point for him. "Something gets dropped, and it's only when that something turns out to have been a delicate item—like a relationship that falls apart or a longtime dream that goes unrealized—that the implications become clear."

"You got it," he said. "The grades that we strive for in the different dimensions of our lives are a way of making choices. And choices—explicit and clearly thought out—are essential to successful juggling and balancing. People who try to get an A on everything usually haven't taken the time to understand the cost of *not choosing,* and therefore . . ." His voice trailed off and then he started laughing.

"What's funny?" I asked.

"More ironic than funny," he answered. "Here I am, giving a superfluous lecture about choices to a guy who very clearly knows the necessity of making them. And I'm doing it at a time when the last thing he needs is a lecture."

"Well, it didn't feel like a lecture. And I don't think it was superfluous," I said. "Making choices and learning not to be uncomfortable with them—those are two different things."

"That's a wise observation," he replied, "and one worth talking about once your life gets back to normal. For now, though, get off the phone, go for a walk, and let the winter air clear your head."

Howard retired from his regular teaching responsibilities at Harvard Business School in July 2011. He explained, "Even though

I've still got plenty in the tank, age seventy is the right time for me to make way and let someone else have the opportunity. I've always thought that one of the important lessons in life is to recognize when it's your time to 'leave the stage.' Mine is now."

The school marked his retirement in a number of ways, including creating the Howard H. Stevenson Professorship of Business Administration—a huge, singular honor at Harvard. The new professorship was announced at a celebratory dinner at which many of Howard's friends and colleagues shared their thoughts on what he'd meant to them and to the university. One of those folks, former HBS dean Jay Light, remarked on the amazing and enduring phenomenon of Howard's incredible energy over the years—energy expended on activities ranging from teaching, research, and writing to launching and leading businesses and advancing the work of nonprofit organizations like NPR and major environmental groups. "Howard has been a nonstop ball of energy and an inspiration to us all," Jay said.

That description of Howard's seemingly indefatigable spirit and vitality was right on target. But Howard is not superman; he can't change the laws of space and time. Even he has had to make choices about how and where he expended his time and his physical, emotional, and intellectual energies. And one of the things I most admire about him is his approach to some of the tough juggling-and-balancing choices in his life—small and large ones alike.

For example, several years ago, when I was first anticipating fatherhood and its time pressures, he told me about an early career choice he made. "There was a period, when my children were young and I was first building Baupost [the very successful money management firm he co-founded and nurtured], that I was getting a B minus or a C plus in the overall father dimension. I was at the office long hours or traveling a lot, and there were aspects of the kids' daily lives that I wasn't deeply engaged in. While it wasn't ideal, the situation represented clear decisions my wife and I had made about how to create the best long-term outcome for our family. But I'd also made the specific choice that whenever I was at home with the kids I wasn't going to divide my focus; they were the priority then, and I was going to be as responsive and engaged as possible. To that end, I set a rule for myself: regardless of what I was doing—reading a book or listening to music or cleaning out the garage—if one of the kids asked me to fix a toy or help with homework or talk through a problem, I'd stop and do it right then, no question. I'd determined that the emotional value of responding immediately to their concern would be substantial and far higher than the corresponding value of whatever else I might have been doing."

Making a quantitative assessment of emotional return may seem like a dry, unemotional way of approaching interactions with your children. Yet Howard was (and is) anything but unemotional. He was simply applying one of his best skills—clearheaded analysis—to one of his most important challenges: how to give his kids what they needed most from him in the short term, while maximizing both his sense of professional satisfaction and his ability to ensure their long-term financial security. It's a challenge almost every working parent faces, and Howard's quantitative assessment was just another way of sitting down and asking himself, "What kind of father do I want to be and how do I accomplish that vision?" However, by giving his "rule" some advance thought, he didn't find himself just reacting in the moment on a case-by-case basis, and he was able to create a consistent expectation in his kids' minds. He applied this kind of close analysis to many aspects of his career and family life, quite successfully. The proof, mathematical or otherwise, is in the results. Having become friends with several of Howard's children, I can attest that they are deeply attached to him. The kids' (and twelve grandkids') love for him seems boundless, as does the genuine pleasure they take in being with him.

Several years after that first example, when he was in his late forties and his career seemed to be hitting on all cylinders, Howard was faced with a larger and more complicated set of choices regarding his family and his career—choices borne of very painful circumstances. One day, Howard's wife simply walked away from their marriage, leaving home and family behind. Howard and his three sons were floored by the sense of abandonment they felt, but he was determined to move them past the shock to regain their equilibrium as quickly as possible. Six months later—something of a record in the legal annals—a divorce was granted, and Howard effectively became a single parent.

"To that point, I'd been investing most of my time and my emotional and intellectual energy in three places: my family, Harvard, and my 'second job' at Baupost," he had explained to me, decades later, over a couple of stiff drinks. "With the divorce, I needed to rechannel to my family a big chunk of time and energy that had been flowing into my career. Something had to go." So he chose to give up his leadership role at Baupost and stay at HBS. Few people would see a faculty position at Harvard as a consolation prize—and Howard certainly didn't view it that way—but the choice to leave Baupost did have major downsides. He gave up a job he loved and a future income in the tens of millions of dollars. And he had to reconcile himself to walking away from a business entity he had nurtured—which was ironic, given that he was doing it in order to nurture the three human entities he'd created.

"It was a situation where I needed to earn a consistently good grade as a father, for an extended period," he explained. "I couldn't risk some aspect of my family responsibilities slipping through my fingers. Sure, my ego and my wallet both took big hits from my leaving the Baupost leadership. Yet they were insignificant compared to the emotional value I got from the kids. The additional money certainly would have been nice to have; we weren't rich. But once we'd crossed the financial threshold between covering 'needs' and satisfying 'wants,' the value of having more time and energy for my kids far outweighed any incremental monetary value."

Did you notice that Howard used the word *value* in describing both the minor and major choices he made in allocating his time and energy? It was a deliberately chosen word, because he's long recognized that there is a cost associated with each of the choices we make about our life's work. And the only way to truly assess cost is to understand the *relative personal value* of one choice versus another.

Songwriter Lucy Kaplansky captures this idea in her song "End of the Day," when she asks, "How much did it cost you? How much did you pay? And are you sorry at the end of the day?"

To me, this deceptively simple lyric carries a weighty truth: what we're consciously paying in the short term can underestimate the actual long-term cost of a poorly considered choice; and we need to look back from the "end of the day" to most effectively assess what that cost will have been. In this respect, Kaplansky's words echo Howard's wisdom that "starting at the end" is the best way to gauge the value of the options we choose among for allocating our time and energy.

Howard's definition of active balance in life—never letting any of your key resources dwindle down to an empty tank—highlights the direct relationship between the cost of choices (which reduce those resources) and your ability to maintain balance-in-motion while juggling the multiple facets of life. That's why, Howard has often reminded me, "You've got to ask yourself if the juice is worth the squeeze. Are you getting satisfaction equivalent to the time and energy you're investing in your choices?"

This little bit of Howard-speak—"Is the juice worth the squeeze?"—actually conveys two related but distinct imperatives. First, understand the direct product of the time and energy you're putting into something, and why you're seeking it.

Second, evaluate if that product is really the most satisfying way to invest your effort, given your broader goals. So your response to the first might be, "I'm getting a gallon of grapefruit juice from my effort and I'm squeezing the grapefruit because I'm thirsty for fresh juice." But your response to the second might be, "I really have a taste for orange juice, and I'd be very happy with just a glass." In which case, Howard would say, before anything else, make sure you're in the right orchard!

There are many ways to translate the juice/squeeze metaphor into practice. One of the most important is considering the costs and the resulting value of striving for an ambitious professional goal. That might mean asking, for example, "What are the costs of becoming a partner in the firm before I'm thirty-five? How do the costs shift if some of the variables change, such as pushing back my target age to forty-five? What are the benefits I'm seeking—what's the immediate and longer-term satisfaction value I expect to receive from achieving this goal at thirty-five? At forty-five?"

The same kinds of probing questions can be asked about the costs of pursuing personal goals. What is someone giving up if, for example, they commit to a rigorous course of preparation to become a deacon in their church? Or to years-long training for the national amateur ballroom dancing competition? Are the costs—in terms of career, family, finances, et cetera—equal to or less than the personal satisfaction gained, now and in the future?

"Don't be afraid to ask the questions and to acknowledge the true answers," Howard always says. "Sit down and say, 'Self, it's just you and me, so let's be straight with each other.' I can almost guarantee that the benefit will far outweigh the cost in the emotional energy you're investing."

"Now, today's question is, 'How do you think about costs in a way that enables you to make clear choices about allocating

your time and energy—and be comfortable with them?'"
Howard was standing at the front of a seminar room, speaking
as if he were launching into a formal lecture to a room full of
students. Except the real class had ended an hour ago; the last
of his students had just trickled out after an extended session of
informal banter, and the only other person left in the room was
me. As it happened, the class had been part of a multifaceted
course Howard had developed, Building a Business in the Context of Life—surely one of the most unusual and creative business school courses anywhere. With the blustery winter weather
precluding a walk around campus, the seminar room was a comfortable place to talk, and the just-concluded class was an apt
lead-in to our continuing conversation about making effective,
satisfying juggling-and-balancing choices.

"You know, Eric, some choices are easy, even if the costs and
consequences are not. Some choices are hard, because all the
options carry similar values, good or bad. And some choices,"
Howard said with a slight Yoda-like smirk playing on his face,
"we simply make hard for ourselves because we haven't done
our homework."

"Homework, huh?"

"You bet," he replied. "Making juggling-and-balancing
choices is a lot like solving equations on an algebra test. Both
often require you to assign a value to loosely defined variables,
and both are a hell of a lot easier if you've done your homework," said Howard the former mathematician.

"Okay, hit me with those 'homework assignments,' Professor
Stevenson."

Howard grabbed a blue marker and started drawing on the
whiteboard. "The overarching, continuing assignment—you
won't be surprised to hear—is assessing how a particular choice
connects generally to your legacy vision and to the 'selves' and
'dimensions' that you value most highly."

"Because why put time into squeezing out a gallon of fresh

grapefruit juice if what you really want is a glass of orange juice," I interjected.

"By god, you *have* been listening all these years!" He laughed, then pointed to an old-fashioned scale he'd drawn on the board. "Put a different way, an ounce of gold and an ounce of lead both weigh the same. But they have vastly different intrinsic values. Similarly, an hour spent reading to your daughter has an intrinsic value different than that of an hour spent playing basketball with friends; and both have intrinsic values different than that of an hour spent studying for a licensing exam or volunteering at a homeless shelter or painting the garage."

"But, unlike the commodities market setting the value of gold versus lead versus uranium," I offered, "the intrinsic value of an hour of your time is set solely by you," I offered.

"Another gold star for the man in the third row," he quipped. "The intrinsic value of any significant choice you make about allocating your time and energy should be based on how it moves you closer to your legacy vision. But, as we've said, the toughest calls are usually between choices that appear, on the surface, to be equally valuable in advancing different aspects of who you want to be. That's where the more focused homework assignments come in—helping to clarify the costs involved in a choice, and the potential short-term and long-term value to be derived from it."

Howard turned back to the board and began to write out a series of choice-specific homework assignments. Sitting quietly, watching him work, I found it fascinating to follow his thought process as he defined the assignments in his mind, refined the wording on the board, and periodically reorganized and consolidated the list. After about ten minutes, he closed the marker and sat down, the better for us both to behold his work: a series of five assignments, presented as concise imperatives. Then he walked me through them.

The first assignment was "Consider the Need/Want Spectrum." We're constantly juggling the "needs" in our lives with the "wants"—working to fulfill the needs and have a reasonable amount of time and energy for the wants. Howard explained, "Generally, fulfilling needs has a higher intrinsic value than fulfilling wants. And it's often clear whether a choice involves a want or a need. To me, taking time off periodically to recharge your batteries is a need, but having a four-week-long vacation in Tahiti is a want. Working long hours to be able to put a roof over your head reflects an undeniable need, but working double shifts in order to have the biggest house on the block reflects a want."

"So the goal of this assignment is to clarify whether you're considering a choice among needs, among wants, or between a need and a want," I summarized.

"Yes, but," he said, leaning in to emphasize his point, "understand that most of the choices we're talking about really fall on a spectrum. On one end is basic food, shelter, and health; on the other is diamond necklaces, round-the-world cruises, and mansions. The kinds of choices that are most difficult to make are the ones that fall in the middle, that are neither black nor white. That includes the wants that are so strong it's difficult to separate them out from needs. For example, a friend of mine gets really sad if she can't take time each day to play her piano; it is so much a part of who she wants to be that it's become, in practical terms, a need. There's also the guy who feels he has to run seven miles a day, virtually every day; it's hard for him to separate out the health-oriented need—which could probably be satisfied with a three-mile run five times a week—from the want to feel he's indestructible.

"So the goal is not just to determine what's a need and what's a want, but to understand—in relative terms—where your options and choices sit on the broad need/want spectrum," he concluded.

The second assignment was "Recognize Both Investment

and Opportunity Costs." Howard explained, "Almost every choice of consequence—whether agreeing to a strategic business alliance or becoming den mother for the local Girl Scout troop—involves two kinds of costs. There's the investment cost, the things you do—the time and energy you expend—in order to pursue the choice. And there's the opportunity cost, the things you won't be able to do—the options you're forgoing because you've invested resources elsewhere. I think that people tend to focus mostly, and most consciously, on investment costs, on what's being expended. But if we pay close attention to our decision-making processes on the most important choices, especially those where we feel unable to decide, we'll often see we're hung up on a subconscious worry about the opportunity cost," he suggested. "Sometimes, just seeing that distinction frees us up to make the choice. Other times, with just a little more thoughtful analysis, we realize that options we think we're closing off aren't really open in the first place!"

The third assignment was "Get Specific About Upsides and Downsides." Don't fool yourself about the nature of the choice and what will logically follow, Howard urged. "Be sure you weigh everything. Be as specific as possible about the investment and opportunity costs involved in a particular choice, and be clear and honest about the benefits you're expecting. For example, don't just say you're going to invest time and energy in exploring new job opportunities; rather, say that over the next two months you're going to spend an hour each weekday evening researching the kinds of jobs available and doing networking; and that you'll take a break from your recreational softball league for that period in order to free up the time. Then be clear about the anticipated benefit: is it a fifteen percent higher salary, or a job using a specific skill, or a more relaxed work culture? Also clarify the likely effect of getting those benefits: if getting that salary increase requires you to work an additional ten hours a week, what will you lose in giving up that time?"

The fourth assignment was "Consider Proportionality and Commensurability." While investment cost and opportunity cost are linked, they don't necessarily have to be proportional. "In other words, investment cost doesn't always equal the opportunity lost," he explained. "Small investments can have outsized benefit down the line; and large investments of time and energy can prove valueless if they don't truly serve who you want to be." Similarly, he pointed out, costs—and benefits, too—are not always commensurate; that is, they can't be weighed on the same scale and can't be exchanged on a clear one-to-one basis. "If you can't establish a relative value between two things, there's no logical way to trade one for the other. So, for example, while the phrase 'time means money' is accurate in some respects, there are only certain ways that money can purchase time; and it's rare that money can be traded for intellectual energy or emotional engagement." Some people also confuse themselves by thinking that necessities can be valued commensurately—can be traded off one to one. But, by definition, you can't exchange one necessity for another. "Trade-offs only work when you can do without the thing being traded away. One of the reasons people start feeling anxious and dissatisfied with their careers and lives is that, without having thought deeply about it, they've made a trade-off of necessities," he noted.

The final assignment was "Sequence Your Goals." Sometimes, Howard observed, we feel extraordinary pressure from the number and diversity of our options and goals. Under that pressure, we tend to conflate all the things we *could* and *want* to do—creating one big Gordian knot of stuff we think we *must* do, right now. To counter that self-imposed pressure, we need to take a broader and longer-term perspective. "My mother wasn't formally educated beyond high school, but she was smart and sharp—of real pioneer stock," Howard told me with a wistful smile. "And one of the most insightful things she ever said to me was, 'Howard, remember that you may be able to have anything you want in life—just not at once.'" Truer words were never spoken. The wise Mrs. Stevenson's point was that by carefully sequencing your goals—thinking about which dimensions are best emphasized now and which later—you will have a greater sense of satisfaction, day to day. "The challenge in our instant-gratification society is to keep your eye on the middle and long distance," Howard observed. "When you're evaluating choices for how to invest your time and energy, aim not for instant gratification but for 'instant progress' toward your legacy vision. Manage the competing elements of your career and life by thoughtfully sequencing your most important goals, and then making choices based on moving that process along. Sequencing your progress gives you the flexibility to heavily weigh one dimension for now, knowing that you'll shift the weight to another important dimension later. And that enables you to have a sense of balance as you pursue the various selves and dimensions that almost assuredly can't be realized at once—but that may be attainable over a lifetime. You just have to remember not to ignore anything really important as you shift priorities."

"That reminds me of the old joke 'How do you eat an elephant?'" I quipped.

Beating me to the punch line, he responded, "One bite at a time." Then he said, "Which reminds *me*," and quickly gathered his papers.

"Off to lunch?" I asked, knowing that having lunch with a friend or colleague was an almost sacred ritual for Howard.

"You bet I am," he replied, then chuckled and said, "And therein lies my final piece of wisdom on this subject. I make a point of having lunch with people whose company I enjoy, as frequently as possible, because that one-hour time investment gives me a sense of renewal—a boost of emotional and intellectual energy as much as nutritional energy—that carries me forward no matter how long the day becomes. So if after all the homework, a person is still uncertain about a tough choice on allocating time, I'd say simply: make the choice that gives you the most energy."

CARTER CAST

One day last summer, Howard e-mailed me the text of a speech given by a former high-flying corporate executive to a big group of Fortune 500 and nonprofit leaders. "You should read this," Howard said. "It's really compelling." The speech, entitled "The Drama of Comparative Living," was both intelligent and heartfelt. As I read it, one phrase in particular jumped out at me:

> *And that is my epiphany . . . I can choose not to see things in their relation to others, but only in their relation to myself—in relation to my own spiritual and intellectual development.*

Wow, I thought, this guy and Howard are really on the same wavelength. So I e-mailed him, explained the book project with Howard, and asked if he'd make some time to talk with me. Astoundingly—because he didn't know me from Adam—the author replied almost immediately. "I'm happy to talk with you," Carter Cast wrote, "because, believe it or not, I just finished reading Howard's book *Just Enough*." We spoke a few days later, and I learned the amazing backstory to the speech.

By most standard measures, Carter Cast has had a very successful life and career—driven by intense focus, discipline, and determination. Those qualities helped him as a competitive swimmer (beginning at age four): through a mixture of talent and hard work, Carter earned his way to two Olympic trials in the 400-meter individual medley—one of the more grueling races to swim, because it requires excellence at four different strokes. Those qualities were also an asset to him as a student earning a bachelor's degree from Stanford and an MBA from Northwestern's Kellogg Graduate School of Management.

After school, Carter's focus, diligence, and smarts quickly drove him ahead in the business world. First there were key roles at Pepsi, where he helped market Pizza Hut, Taco Bell, and Frito-Lay. Then he went to Electronic Arts, where as marketing VP he launched the Sims games. Next he became senior VP for the online retail jewelry start-up Blue Nile. And his career was still gaining speed (and intensity): soon he became CEO of Walmart.com—which, under his leadership, became one of the biggest e-commerce sites in the world—and CEO of online retailer Hayneedle.

He was a star—no, a megastar—of the burgeoning e-commerce industry.

And then he said: "Stop. Time-out. Something's not right."

"Since the time I started swimming as a child, I had been driven, focused, determined to reach the top," Carter told me. "But there's only so long you can go on constantly pushing. As a result, my health suffered. My family suffered. And I felt hollow." So he stepped back from an amazingly successful career. Instead, he took time to heal—and to look deep inside to understand what had been driving him. The speech that I'd read was one of his first efforts to share publicly some of the things he'd learned about himself and his experience.

"For much of my adult life," he explained, "a subtle form of fear has been my constant companion. Fear that I am not enough, that I don't measure up to some ever-moving standard of worthiness. It's been an anxiety over the gap between what is and what I think I should be: I should be more educated, like many of my friends; I should have made more money, like some of my former colleagues.

"Philosopher Bertrand Russell called the results of this kind of feeling 'worry fatigue,' and described the situation as a kind of envy that 'consists in seeing things never in themselves, but only in their relations,'" Carter explained. "While this feeling has been around as long as man, it's increased in our present age because technology and media have given us a far greater ability to compare ourselves to others. It often pushes those comparisons in our faces. Think about it: only a few hundred years ago, one blacksmith compared his product and status to those of the other blacksmith in his village; now, we blacksmiths compare our work to that of all the blacksmiths in all the villages across the world."

This comparative perspective matters when we're competing in a zero-sum situation, where for every winner there must be a loser, Carter observed. "However, for most of us, daily life is far from a zero-sum situation. Our society need not be driven by a zero-sum mentality. That's why, I believe, we should each think about not participating in what I've called the 'drama of comparative living.'"

What does this mean for him in practical terms? "It's meant trying to use my focus and discipline to stop comparing myself to others—to their achievements, their wins, their acquisitions. I'm working hard to see myself only in relation to my own spiritual, intellectual, and professional development. At night, I try to reflect on the fact that my progress as a human being is measured only by where I was at a prior state of development. I remind myself that I don't have to keep trying to keep up with the beat of an imaginary metronome, following someone else's decision on the pace of my life."

And what are the implications of this perspective for Carter's career? When I spoke with him, he was serving as a clinical professor at Northwestern, doing some consulting, and reading deeply and widely on philosophy, sociology, and business. "Right now I'm really enjoying the chance to think and write and share my ideas with people," he said. "Will I jump back into the corporate world? I honestly don't know. Down the road, I may get excited by a business opportunity. But what I know is that if I pursue that opportunity, I'm going to have a vastly different perspective and a whole different approach. And the only person I'm going to be competing against will be myself."

CHAPTER SIX

Cheating at Solitaire

If you're tying your sense of professional satisfaction to specific career goals, you want to know you've got what it takes to achieve them.

ONE OF THE THINGS I've cherished about my relationship with Howard is that he and I have been able to sustain it over time, distance, and the changing circumstances of our lives and careers. Our friendship initially developed through talking and working directly together, first as teacher and student, then as colleagues. Over the last few years since I left Harvard to become president of Axcess Worldwide, our interactions have more frequently been by phone and e-mail. Still, when we get together we're able to pick right up, as if it's been a matter of days rather than weeks between our visits. And, luckily, my business travel often brings me to the Boston area.

That was the case one summer day when I'd flown up to do a series of presentations on a client's international development project. Howard and I had arranged to meet that evening at Upstairs on the Square, a favorite restaurant not far from his office. "I'm having a drink there after work with a former student looking for my advice," he'd explained. "But we should be done by six-thirty; then you and I can grab dinner."

As it turned out, my meeting ran long and I arrived at the restaurant a little late. I saw Howard sitting at a table and started over to him, assuming he'd been waiting for me. Halfway there, I realized that he was still engaged in his previous conversation. Normally, I'd have walked over and introduced myself to the former student; a friend of Howard's often became a friend of mine. But a focused, intent look on Howard's face made me hold back. Instead, I took a seat at the bar and waited for them to finish what I could tell—even from a distance— was a cordial but difficult conversation.

In a few moments, they both stood, and Howard walked his companion over to the restaurant exit not far from where I sat. As they passed, I heard him say to Howard, "Yes, I am feeling disappointed. But I didn't come to have you tell me what I wanted to hear, I came to get your honest assessment." He paused to gather his thoughts. "Most people believe they're being nice by dancing around an issue—by not giving objective, constructive criticism. They're caring, but they're not straightforward, and they're not helpful. You, however, are all three. Thank you." He gave Howard a warm, two-handed handshake, turned, and headed out the door.

I walked over to Howard, and he put his arm around my shoulder. "If you don't mind, Eric, I could use a change of venue and some fresh air before dinner." I nodded, he went back to settle the bill at his table, then we walked out into the cooling summer evening. We turned in to Harvard Square, walking past shops and street performers, sharing the brick-lined sidewalks with folks of all ages: high school students touring the university campus, college students just back from summer break, young professionals heading home from work, parents with strollers, and multigenerational families rounding out their vacations.

We spent some time catching up on recent events—new clients at Axcess, the latest challenges at National Public Radio (where Howard was board chair), my son Daniel's budding bilingual skills in English and Spanish, the exploits of Howard's oldest grandkids. Eventually, a little curious, I asked him about his earlier conversation at Upstairs on the Square. "It looked pretty serious," I said.

Howard took a deep breath. "Yes, it was. A difficult conversation. Although he handled it well, all in all," he said. We walked on a bit, then he explained the situation. "So this guy, James, was a student of mine about ten years ago. Very smart, analytical, logical, a little on the introverted side. He's a nice guy, honest, very ambitious—but not in a cutthroat way. Since he left HBS, he's been working at a real-estate investment trust, on the team that negotiates large acquisitions and sales. He's feeling stuck. The company's happy with his work—keeps giving him raises— but he's getting bored with the same-old same-old. And his bosses won't give him the professional development opportunities he's looking for. When he asks why he's not getting the plum assignments—the chance to break out of his narrowly defined role—he's getting the run around rather than clear answers. This has been going on for a a couple of years, and he was hoping I could help him figure out how to move forward."

"And what did you tell him that was so difficult for him to hear?" I asked.

"I had to tell him that he's cheating at solitaire," Howard replied with a tinge of frustration in his voice.

That was a phrase I hadn't heard before. "What does that mean, 'cheating at solitaire'?" I asked.

"Did you ever play the card game solitaire?" he asked.

"Sure, when I was a kid."

"What happened when you were on the verge of winning and realized you'd never get the one card needed to finish the game?"

"Sometime I'd just give it up and start again." I smiled sheepishly and added, "And sometimes I'd bend the rules a little to get to the card I needed."

"As did we all," he said. "It's just a game, and you're playing against yourself, so it doesn't really matter if you pretend to have the cards necessary to win." He stopped walking, leaned over, and poked his finger at my chest. "But now it's not a game. We're adults, playing in the real world. And when I say someone is cheating at solitaire, I mean they're cheating themselves. Pretending they have the right cards to get where they want to—when they don't."

"And the 'right cards' are?"

"The skills and talents they'll need to achieve the specific professional objectives they've set for themselves," he explained. "And, by extension, to achieve their broader personal goals in life."

"And what cards are missing for James? What does he *not* have in his hand that's keeping him from winning?" I asked.

Howard motioned for us to cross the street, and we walked into the historic Cambridge Common. Once the assembly ground for a key Revolutionary War battle, on that day the common was the setting for skirmishes between after-work softball teams. We gravitated to a bench near a ball field, sat down, and watched a game while we talked.

Howard explained that James's missing card was an intuitive grasp of complex interpersonal relations in high-pressure business situations. James didn't understand the subtle dynamics at work in an ongoing negotiation process. He didn't recognize the signals being sent by the people on the other side of the table; so, too often, he made ineffective tactical suggestions to his colleagues. Worse, he often missed the signals being sent by his own team; as a result, he sometimes undermined the on-the-fly course corrections his senior colleagues made during negotiating sessions. Despite these shortcomings, no one doubted James's good intentions nor questioned his intelligence and diligence—he often worked longer hours than even the team leaders, and frequently dazzled people with the depth and pinpoint accuracy of his technical assessments.

"So, bottom line," Howard summarized, "he's good at key parts of the job; and he plays an important, clearly defined role in the company. Except his ambitions are for more—he wants to head a project team, lead the negotiations at the table, be a rainmaker for the firm. It's been extraordinarily frustrating for him, watching other people get the assignments he wants and achieve the goals he thinks he's earned for himself. But the fact is, he will never hit those goals," Howard concluded, glumly.

"That's a really tough spot he's found himself in," I said. "It's amazing that no one's explained the situation to him before."

"Maybe they have, and he wasn't ready to hear it," Howard responded. "Or maybe none of his superiors and colleagues cared enough to try to figure out where the mismatch was. A lot of work cultures are that way, unfortunately."

I thought about James's situation for a moment. "Kind of reminds me of the old joke about the two hikers and the bear that starts chasing them," I said. "One guy stops to change from hiking boots into running shoes; the other guy says, 'Are you crazy? You can't outrun that bear.' And the first guy says, 'I don't need to outrun the bear—I just need to outrun you.'"

"Yeah, if you put that joke into a career context—especially in a tough economy—not being honest with yourself starts to have real consequences," Howard replied, with an ironic chuckle. "That bear could represent anything from losing a big promotion to being the one who gets laid off during an economic downturn. In the long run, that bear represented the gnawing frustration of not ever being able to hit your goals."

"So how does somebody figure out for themselves if they are cheating at solitaire?" I asked. "I mean, if you're going to tie your sense of professional satisfaction to specific short- or long-term goals—if you're weaving these goals into your legacy vision and allocating time to them—you want to know you've got what it takes to achieve them."

"Right you are," Howard said, then sat back in deep thought.

After a bit, he continued, "I suppose the best way to figure out if you're cheating at solitaire is to answer—as honestly as possible—two simple questions.

"One: do I have the *core capacities*—knowledge, skills, and personal characteristics—to do a job really well?

"Two: if my sense of career satisfaction is based on achieving a narrowly defined goal—like gaining entry to a very selective profession, getting a specific job, or working at a particular organization—does the depth of my core capacities compare advantageously to the capacities of people with the same goal?

"Frankly," he concluded, "in a tough job market, the second question is as important as the first."

"But core capacities aren't the *sole* factor in whether we achieve our short- and long-term career goals," I pushed back. "Hard work, luck, timing, juggling-and-balancing choices, and sequencing decisions all play a part."

"Of course, any of those things can provide a short-term advantage," he said. "However, in my experience, over the long term they pale in comparison to the question of whether you've got the skills and talents to advance on a particular career path." He paused, then added, "And it's a big problem when people invest heavily in career goals built around core capacities they *have,* without deeply considering—or worse, deliberately ignoring—the ones they are *missing.* "

I chewed on that for a bit, then asked, "How are you defining core capacities? 'Cause I can throw a ball and run down a baseline, but I'm never going to earn a living playing professional baseball."

"No, you're not—I doubt you can hit a big league curveball," he chuckled. "That's a core capacity that you're missing. But let's not use athletics as an example; it's misleading, because capacity in most professions is not so obviously delineated as it is with batting averages and on-base percentages." He looked around at the other people watching the softball game, as if considering each person's profession in turn.

"Without getting bogged down in nuance, you could say there are three broad categories of core capacities," he explained. "There are physical skills, such as a singer's vocal range, a surgeon's steady hand, or a white-water rafting guide's stamina. There are intellectual abilities, such as an interior designer's eye for color, a public relations executive's memory for faces and names, or a tax attorney's facility with organizing complex information. And there are personality characteristics, such as ease in meeting new people, flexibility in dealing with novel experiences, diligence in solving complex challenges, personal integrity, and empathy for other people's situations." He stopped for a second, then added, "For what it's worth, in our knowledge- and relationship-driven economy, I find that it's the latter type of core capacities—personality characteristics and 'emotional intelligence'—where people most tend to cheat at solitaire."

"It's interesting," I mused. "At one time I gave serious thought to becoming an attorney; but even though I liked the idea of being trained in the law and thought I might be analytical enough to be a successful attorney, I had to admit to myself that I didn't think I had a strong enough memory for such a knowledge-based profession. Similarly, when I considered medical school for a brief period, I realized that since I don't function well without a full night's sleep almost every night, I'd never make it through the grind of clinical rotations and residency—so becoming a doctor was off the table. Both realizations were humbling."

"In those situations, your lack of one or another requisite capacity was clear, and even though you didn't like it, you could easily see that those careers weren't right for you," Howard replied, then smiled mischievously. "But if I recall correctly, there was at least one career path you started down because

your lack of capacity was not so clear, until you'd became en-
lightened by experience."

Howard was alluding to what my wife calls "the KaBloom
ka-boom." Early in my career I bought several KaBloom flower-
shop franchises. Although I didn't care much about the floral
business (investing mistake number one), I'd learned a lot about
franchising from having worked in corporate management for
a large franchising conglomerate. Given the opportunity to invest in what was touted as the "Starbucks of the floral industry,"
I took it. The venture seemed a great match for my strengths in
entrepreneurial business, marketing, and management. Turned
out I was wrong, because—in addition to the fact that the underlying KaBloom strategy was flawed—I'd overestimated my
capacity to take on the "all-in" financial risk I had romanti-
cized throughout college. And when the venture started to go
south, I realized that the "bet the farm, double-down, mortgage your house if necessary" entrepreneurial approach that's
the lore of many a business book was not for me. I had the
stomach for thoughtful, calculated risk, but not the unmiti-
gated, bottomless risk I took with this investment.

"I guess you can call it enlightenment," I said. "It was a really
difficult experience. Frankly, I had never failed before—in career terms, anyway—and at the outset it never crossed my mind
that I might fail with the KaBloom stores. But the experience
taught me that I needed to drill deeper on the skills and characteristics needed to excel in future career choices. Looking
back, the flaw in my plan seems pretty obvious, and I wish I'd
understood the risk-tolerance mismatch earlier. I could have
avoided the emotional pain, not to mention the financial loss
involved in unwinding the investment."

"Maybe . . . but we can't live our lives looking back," he replied. "You've heard me say it a thousand times: there is a high
emotional cost in living backward; we're happiest when we live

life forward, guided by experience and unimpeded by regret. So don't look at it as losing money on a deal. View it as the cost for acquiring an important piece of information: the fact that you're not suited for specific jobs or broad career goals requiring high tolerance for financial risk. I'd say that's a pretty useful bit of data for a businessperson to have."

Howard's point, obviously, applied beyond my own little KaBloom ka-boom. "When you're in a position to know, up front, that you don't have a capacity necessary for achieving a particular career goal, don't ignore that information," he said. "But when it's unclear if the capacity is there—or when it's just not possible to know the full range of capacities needed—then run the experiment. And try to construct it so that it's the lowest cost experiment you can manage."

"How do you constrain the costs of this experiment?" I asked.

"In a number of ways," he replied. "First, going into it, set finite limits on the resources you're willing to expend—whether it's time, energy, or, as in your KaBloom experience, money. Second, be explicit about the outcome or benefits you're expecting, and make sure you're comfortable with the resulting cost/benefit ratio. Third, be clear about the capacities you're testing; and confirm that there are no simpler or less costly ways to test them, individually. Finally, as best you can, make sure you're running a realistic and complete experiment: don't play doubles tennis to test your capacities as a singles player; don't test just your clinical nursing skills if your goal is launching a home-nursing agency."

"And once you've got the experiment running?" I asked.

"Track the data," he said. "See how it feels, actively gauge the emerging results, and compare your expectations to the reality. Pay close attention to the core capacities and specialized skills exhibited by the people who are most successful, and consider how you feel about your capacities in those areas. And at all

times"—he gently slapped the bench to emphasize his point—
"be intellectually and emotionally honest with yourself about
the experience."

Pointing back in the general direction of Upstairs on the
Square, Howard said, "In many respects, James's experience
was not very different from your franchise experiment. You
both made some correct assessments about the capacities required and at least one big misassessment—in your case, your
risk tolerance level, and in his case, his capacity for subtle interpersonal relations. Where you two diverged was in the lessons
you drew from your respective experiences. James wasn't analyzing the full range of data from his experiment. He wasn't
paying close attention to all of the capacities displayed by people whose roles he aspired to. Beyond that, he ignored the not-
so-subtle clues about the factors that were hampering his
progress toward his goals. And—most important—he was emotionally dishonest with himself, ignoring his own discomfort at
the reactions he was getting from both colleagues and people
across the table."

Perhaps, I thought, if James's company had an effective performance evaluation system or review process, it would have
helped him get an objective sense of what was going on. But
clearly they didn't; nor did the deal makers in the room—his
nominal colleagues—feel invested in addressing his lack of a
core capacity for success. It was only when Howard helped
connect the dots by offering straightforward observations on
James's strengths and weaknesses that it clicked for him.

"You know," I suggested, "in one respect I feel bad for him.
More than ten years into this career path, James has hit a big,
troubling inflection point and needs to rethink a whole series of
assumptions about his life's work. On the other hand, this
could be a situation where a Foe inflection point is merely a
Friend in disguise. The knowledge and experience he's gained
on the deal-making teams will be really advantageous if he

pursues a more analytically oriented career path. He could use those to leverage the core capacities he does have."

"I agree," Howard replied. "But it's not going to be easy for him. He'd really dug in, psychologically, to a certain set of career goals. And he's felt somewhat battered, emotionally, by the increasingly negative response he's been getting from his colleagues and bosses. It's going to take some real work to get himself up and running again on a new path, and I don't know if—" He stopped midsentence, gave me a quizzical look, then said, "Want to do an old friend a favor?"

It took just a second for me to understand what he was asking. "What's his phone number?" I replied.

"Thanks," he said as he pulled James's business card from his pocket. "After all, brainstorming and pep talks are two of your core capacities." As I plugged the contact info into my phone, Howard stood up, stretched, and said, "Now I've got my appetite back. Let's go to this new place near my house. They've got a small, eclectic menu—but everything they do, they do well, and it all works together."

"I'm curious about something, Howard," I said as we waited for a table at the restaurant. "How did *you* approach the whole challenge of figuring out your core capacities, identifying where you might have competitive advantages, and matching them to career goals?"

"Wow, that requires some dredging of the memory banks," he responded, with a hint of nostalgia in his voice. He thought about the question until we'd been seated for dinner, then he offered his answer. "Coming out of college at Stanford, I had a number of viable career options. My choice involved a three-point analysis: identifying the tasks I most enjoyed doing, pinpointing the things I excelled at, and considering where I might have a competitive advantage relative to others with similar interests and skills. For a while, I considered system engineering, and I used a couple of summer jobs at IBM as my experiment—and learned that I lacked a real passion for the field.

"I'd majored in mathematics, and that was an area where I focused my analysis. I enjoyed math and was quite good at it. But as I approached graduation and compared myself to some of my classmates, I realized I was never going to be as good at it as they were. They really loved it, worked harder at it, and had more natural success with it. On top of that, there was a limited range of jobs we'd be competing for in the field, and the competition would be fierce. Today, computers have opened up huge opportunities for using mathematics to address a range of important questions, but the opportunities were much narrower in 1963. So given all those factors, I took a career focused on mathematics off the table.

"Another serious option for me was a military career," Howard continued. "I came from a family with a strong military heritage. My father was a commander in the Navy, and my older brother was one of the youngest captains in the Marine Corps. I probably could have become a good strategist or logistics guy. But, being both a bit of an introvert and an intellectual free spirit, I knew I didn't have a military leadership kind of personality. While there was no real barrier to a military profession, I didn't have a passion for it, nor did I think I had any personal competitive advantage to employ there."

"So you decided on business and business education?" I asked.

"Well, my choice wasn't quite as cut-and-dried as that," he replied. "I decided to go to business school because it was a subject that interested me. I didn't know if business was a *deep* interest, and I didn't know if I had what it took to succeed, but I was comfortable running the experiment. Especially because I knew that studying at Harvard Business School wouldn't *preclude* me from pursuing any of my nonbusiness career interests, and would likely expose me to options I hadn't even considered before.

"It was only once I got to HBS that my ideal career path became clear. In fact, it was a specific series of conversations with Professor Myles Mace, a master of corporate management, that turned out to be the first major inflection point in my professional life. Myles helped me understand that business and business education were areas where I could be passionate and effective—and have a competitive advantage relative to others."

"Was there some grand Harvardian epiphany?" I joked.

"No." He laughed. "No angel choruses singing, no fireworks going off over the Charles River . . . but yes, I do still remember the moment when it clicked for me. Myles had been telling me about his own professional path, and he said, 'You know, Howard, the fact is that I've essentially based my entire career on asking three simple questions: Where did you get that number? What does it mean? Why are you trying to bullshit me?'

"Talk about a 'hedgehog' or a 'one-trick pony'—basing his career on a narrow area of expertise! But he understood how universally important those kinds of simple, fundamental questions are for organizations large and small, profit-making and nonprofit. Some people may have thought these were silly questions or ignored them; but as soon as I heard them, it all made sense for me. I understood how the simple act of asking good questions can ascertain an organization's strengths and weaknesses.

"In further conversations, Myles helped me recognize that I was really good at figuring out the key strategic questions to ask in business situations—that I intuitively knew the important points to delve into and push on. I came to understand that the capacity to ask the right questions was a competitive advantage for me, and that capacity has been the cornerstone for my life's work.

"Could I have been a respectable systems engineer or the

mathematician most of my college friends expected me to become? Sure. Or an able military officer, which was what some
of my family expected? Probably. But would I have excelled at
either of those? Become as successful in those fields as I've become in business and business education? I don't think so, because neither my passions nor my competitive advantages would
have been fully engaged. And none of these professions would
have enabled me to accomplish my legacy vision."

Through that evening's dinner and subsequent conversations,
Howard and I continued to explore his notion of cheating at
solitaire, and why people fall into it. He explained that most
people don't intentionally cheat at solitaire. Rather, they succumb to a series of fallacies, which leads them to misjudge their
core capacities.

For example, there's the Hard Work Fallacy: the belief that
determined effort will always overcome an enduring shortcoming. In other words, thinking that achieving an ambitious career
goal is simply a matter of saying, "This is what I want to do and
where I want to be and I'm just going to work as hard as necessary to get there!" Many people view boundless self-improvement
as an inalienable right, indivisible from the American Dream—
even as a natural extension of the pioneer spirit that drove
American economic development in the eighteenth and nineteenth centuries. Howard has great sympathy for that shoulder-
to-the-wagon-wheel spirit, because his ancestors were among
the pioneers who settled the western United States. But he also
knows—from decades of firsthand engagement in analyzing
organizations and from direct observation of many people's career tracks—that hard work is not a universal solution to weakness in core capacities. In his experience, when hard work has
enabled someone to succeed despite a shortcoming in a core

capacity, it's because the intense effort has fundamentally expanded or deepened their skill set and erased the shortcoming. And it's been effective only where a very clearly defined capacity was subject to improvement and the gap to be overcome was not huge. Don't misunderstand: Howard wasn't suggesting that one should never try; but he *was* saying that it's important to approach the challenge with eyes wide open.

Then there's the Smarts Fallacy: assuming that being really smart in general guarantees you'll have no problem picking up a specific skill set. Howard, who's seen a lot of really smart people in his time, has found that many of them think they are equally smart and talented at *whatever* they do—and that many who don't start out thinking it are pressured into *acting* that way by our very competitive culture. They think that success in school makes them good enough to achieve *any* goal they set for themselves. "You'd be surprised by how many really smart people make career decisions saying to themselves, 'I'm smart and good at X and Z, so I'm sure that I can be great at Y, too,'" Howard once told me. "But it's like saying 'I am an excellent three-hundred-pound wrestler, so I'll also be a great pole vaulter.'" His point wasn't that you can't be a three-hundred-pound wrestler/pole vaulter. With amazing determination—and a super-strong, high-tech pole—you might clear the bar and feel satisfied in that accomplishment. But if you set yourself a goal of competing in the Olympics as a three-hundred-pound pole vaulter, you're setting yourself up for failure and disappointment.

The Smarts Fallacy has a cousin: the Magnification Fallacy, which occurs when we assume that a particular capacity we have is somehow more special than that of our peers, even when we have no objective data to back us up. We're also "magnifying" when we just assume that the capacities we possess are the most important ones for the job. Howard describes magnifiers as "folks who shoot arrows at a blank target, then draw a bull's-eye around the spots they hit."

There's also the Joy/Passion Fallacy: assuming that we're good at the things we *want* to be good at because they give us joy or engage our passions. Of course, enjoying what you do is essential, and if you don't like a fundamental aspect of the job, you likely won't excel at it. Moreover, passion for a career path or goal can itself be a competitive advantage. But joy and passion alone are insufficient to overcome shortcomings in skill or relevant knowledge or talent. That's why Howard needed to tell James, "You can't let *wanting* to be good at something keep you from objectively assessing if you *are* good at it."

Finally, there's the "Wishing Will Make It So" Fallacy, which comes into play when someone seriously underestimates the challenges involved in pursuing a particular career path or ambitious goal. It's sort of a mirror image of the Hard Work Fallacy, because the folks who succumb to the Wishing Fallacy think that simply closing their eyes and believing real hard in their success will make it so—easy, no muss and no fuss. Howard would be the first to confirm the importance of self-confidence, optimism, and aspiration—of reaching beyond your comfort zone. These qualities are essential for achieving career satisfaction. "But there's a big difference between having well-founded confidence that you'll achieve your goals and assuming that the whole thing will be a piece of cake," he notes. "It's the difference between thinking and yearning, planning and hoping, knowing and desiring. It's the difference between grappling with the hurdles in your path and waiting for them to move themselves out of your way."

I think that Lori Schor, whom you met earlier, is a great example of how *not* to succumb to the various fallacies that lead to cheating at solitaire. She loved doing architectural designs. She had her heart and mind set on becoming an architect. She certainly had the intelligence to earn an architecture degree. And no one in her program worked harder to master the field. Yet when she objectively compared her core capacities with those of her fellow students and honestly analyzed her instructors' feedback on her projects, she recognized that she didn't have the "design gene." She had a good eye for design—she could tell when someone was doing great work—but that eye told her that her own designs wouldn't measure up to the standards and competition of the marketplace. While it was a painful experience, Lori's intellectual and emotional honesty enabled her to recognize the situation relatively early; in this respect, she was lucky. Too many people don't see their limitations in core capacities until they hit a major bump well down their career path. Then, suddenly, their professional expectations, sense of self-worth, and deep passions all run into a brick wall of reality . . . and that hurts.

In considering all these fallacies, here's Howard's bottom line: "Career success and satisfaction isn't a matter of luck. The people who achieve their professional goals—whether it's to become CEO or to be recognized as the best graphic artist in the company—do it because they have made a strong match between what they're *really* good at, what they like doing, and what the profession demands."

That's why, if you tell Howard you're pursuing an ambitious career goal because you've got a passion for it and will be satisfied by the *pursuit* of the goal, regardless of outcome, he'll say "Go for it!" But if you tell him that *achieving* that goal is essential to your career satisfaction, he'll advise you to have a deep, honest think about the cards in your hand. In the long run, you'll be happier for doing so.

JEFF LEOPOLD

In conversation over coffee on a rainy Thursday morning, it's clear that Jeff Leopold loves his job and works hard at it. Jeff is a Lexington, Massachusetts–based consultant who conducts searches for top executives and board members at high-tech companies. "The way I know I enjoy my work is that I wake up without an alarm at about six o'clock every morning, eager and ready to dive in—even if it means meetings or phone conversations over the weekend," he explained. "My work sometimes bleeds into family or personal time, but I'm okay with it because I have a blast doing what I do." He leaves unsaid the corollary fact: his firm is growing and he's busier than ever—even in the midst of tough economic times—because he both likes his job and does it very, very well.

Ironically, part of the reason that Jeff is so successful and effective as an executive headhunter today is that he learned some important lessons from a very unsatisfying experience early in his career. Back in 1991, with his newly minted MBA from the University of Michigan, Jeff became one of a carefully chosen few to be recruited to a young company called Microsoft. "On paper, I had all the skills I'd need to succeed there," he recalled. "I was analytical, organized, and well versed in my field. And the very fact that Microsoft even offered me the job—it was a hugely competitive process—reinforced my own high expectations of what I'd accomplish there."

But what he didn't understand—what he couldn't have understood at the time—was that despite all his strengths, he was destined not to succeed at Microsoft. His strengths turned out not to be the big competitive advantages he assumed they would be. In fact, they undercut his ability to succeed in a corporate environment the likes of which he'd never experienced before. "At the end of the day," he explained, "I found myself at a competitive *disadvantage* because I didn't know how to make myself successful in that unique corporate culture." That's why, just two years after joining the company, Jeff left Microsoft. Talking to him now, nearly twenty years later, I could see that the experience still caused clear discomfort. (And a certain wistfulness: if he'd stayed longer and vested his stock options, he would have seen a nice financial windfall.)

"The Microsoft culture was a crucible that quickly exposed the relative weaknesses that lurked between a person's strengths—and kept those weaknesses in the spotlight," Jeff noted. "My weakness, at that time, was an inability to connect with the company's anything-it-takes, ignore-received-wisdom culture.

"You see, going into the job, I didn't understand that most of the people there were missionaries, out to change the world through software. I was viewing my job through the staid, analytical, and organized frame that had made me successful in previous jobs and in grad school. But the people who succeeded at Microsoft were passionate about their mission, and their passion drove them to do things differently than I would naturally do them. They asked questions differently, viewed problem solving differently, understood customers' needs in a different, more subtle way. And that 'difference' was what enabled some people to succeed wildly and others to feel out of synch."

Expending all kinds of energy to succeed but still struggling with the Microsoft way of doing things, Jeff was increasingly unhappy. It didn't help that during one horribly memorable product-strategy session, a concept he offered was absolutely skewered by Bill Gates. "He began with, 'Jeff, that's the stupidest idea I've heard all week,' and it went downhill from there," Jeff recalled. "I know it wasn't intentional on his part and that there was nothing personal in Bill's very hard-nosed criticism of my work products. He simply had a quasi-religious zeal about testing any idea, and he spoke in very direct terms when pointing out its flaws. I certainly wasn't alone in earning his criticism—it happened all the time—but I wasn't prepared for it."

Eventually, a colleague pulled Jeff aside and said, "I know you're not happy here and you're trying to figure it all out. The thing is, you're a really sharp guy, but you need to consider the possibility that you're not smart in the way you need to be smart here."

"I was stunned. Speechless," Jeff recalled, "because I first took the guy's message to be 'Yeah, maybe you've got an MBA from Michigan but you're not all that smart—certainly not as smart as the successful people here.' After some thought, though, I understood what he really meant: you can't use your smarts *effectively* here, because the Microsoft culture demands that you think in ways you aren't used to thinking—and it doesn't wait for people to catch up.

"He was right, of course," Jeff said. "I had come to Microsoft with a too-narrow perspective on how to get the job done. I'd hamstrung myself by imposing intellectual limitations on ways to solve problems. And, to top it off, I didn't have the same gut-level passion as colleagues who believed that they were 'democratizing the business world' through their software.

"It was all gut-wrenching to admit it to myself," he

remembered. "It felt like a failure, and I'd never experienced professional failure before."

But in Jeff's short-term failure were the seeds for long-term success and satisfaction. A painful, negative inflection point became the catalyst for a new and productive path. The experience gave him valuable lessons that shaped his professional life thereafter and became the foundation for future achievements. In this regard, he exemplified Howard's belief that the most effective people will leverage data from even the most negative situations, using it to build their capacities. Jeff represents a very rare breed: people who, through deep intellectual and emotional honesty, are able to turn an area of relative weakness into an extraordinary strength.

"Big lesson number one from my Microsoft experience," he explained, "is that being analytical and methodical in problem solving is necessary, but it's not enough. Finding great solutions demands creativity and flexibility—requires that we come at problems from new, unexpected directions and without rigid preconceptions.

"Big lesson number two: how you think about yourself in your professional context has the potential to shackle or unshackle your skills and creativity. A narrow perspective limits your capacities. Giving yourself freedom to think broadly and freely creates more opportunities to solve problems.

"And big lesson number three: don't mess with culture! I learned firsthand how significant a factor organizational culture is, and I began studying how individuals' degree of 'fit' with the corporate culture around them affects their performance."

His diligent study paid off, and Jeff believes that his success in executive search—and the reason he's working

extra hard these days—grows directly from his keen sen-
sitivity to interactions between existing organizational
culture and potential new leaders. And, of course, from
his creative, no-blinders approach to finding just the right
person for a top job.

CHAPTER SEVEN

Everyone's Outside

Confidence is not the same as arrogance; expressing the fact that you're good at something is not the same as self-promotion.

Howard and i ate an excellent dinner the night he met with James, after our long walk around Harvard Square and our discussion on cheating at solitaire. For me, the meal was spiced by the bits of insight and wisdom Howard shared with me as he reflected further on the huge inflection point that his former student had experienced. Finally, though, it was time to leave. We settled the bill; I excused myself to make a pit stop, then met Howard outside the restaurant. As I walked up to him, I laughed and said, "Washing my hands in the men's room reminded me of this story I've got to tell you."

"By all means," he said with more than a drop of sarcasm in his voice, "because you know how I love bathroom humor at the end of a good meal."

"Don't worry, it's more bathroom irony than bathroom humor," I said. "Besides, it's a perfect counterpoint to our conversation about cheating at solitaire."

Howard shook his head in mock disgust, and as we walked to his car I launched into my tale. "Last week, I was having a drink with this guy, Bert, who's the manager of an event-planning company we've started using. We were just kibbitzing about families, hobbies, backgrounds—that kind of stuff. When I asked him about the key inflection points and choices that got him to where he is now, he told me about two or three of his more significant, career-shaping decisions. One in particular struck me as surprising, funny, and interesting."

"This being the one about the bathroom?" Howard asked.

"Right," I said, then paused as Howard unlocked his car and we climbed in. He'd insisted on driving me back to my hotel, and I continued my story as we headed back across Cambridge and through the busy streets of downtown Boston.

"For five years early in his career," I explained, "Bert was in guest services for a big Chicago hospital, and he basically enjoyed the work. He's an 'idea' guy and was always offering up ideas for reducing costs or improving services for patients and families. Sometimes his boss adopted the ideas; usually she didn't. She rarely explained why she turned down his ideas—but, being young, enthusiastic, and idealistic, Bert assumed there were good reasons.

"One evening, Bert's at a farewell party for two of his colleagues; one was taking another job and the other was going to grad school. Midway through the party, Bert takes a bathroom break, and as he's washing his hands, his boss's boss—the department vice president—walks up to the next sink. Bert's worked directly with the VP on small projects here and there, and of course he says hello. The VP nods and starts washing his hands but doesn't say anything for a minute. Then he grabs a paper towel and, without actually looking at Bert, says, 'Son, I'm gonna give you a piece of advice, something that I'll deny I ever said. Figure out how to make the next farewell party be for you.' Bert's confused and he starts to ask a question, but the VP shakes his head and says, 'Just listen.' So Bert shuts up; the VP takes a deep breath and continues. 'You're a smart, talented young guy. But we don't know how to use somebody with your abilities. . . . Some of that's my fault, I guess. Some of it's your boss's fault—she's not the most self-confident person in the world. And some of it is just how the organization works. It's sad, but it's reality.' Then the VP drops the towel in the trash, says, 'Enjoy the rest of the party,' and walks out."

Howard shook his head in amazement and said, "I'd call that a sinkside epiphany."

"That's pretty much how Bert saw it," I replied. "It was a wake-up call, and it took a few days to digest what he'd heard. It simply had never occurred to him that an organization wouldn't be able to recognize and use good people; that his boss might be trashing his ideas just because she felt challenged by Bert's creativity; and that, for whatever reason, the higher-ups weren't willing to change the situation."

"How did Bert use this revelation?" Howard asked.

"Once he got over the shock, he took the VP's advice. He started thinking about what he wanted and where he wanted to be in the next step of his career. Once he got himself in gear, things moved pretty quickly, and his farewell party took place about four months later. But what's also interesting is the longer-term lesson he took from the experience. He decided never to let himself fall into that situation again—never to let an organization set limits on how fully he used his skills. Since that time, he's been much more proactive in assessing whether a job is tapping his capabilities. During annual reviews, for example, he always makes a point to discuss how his skills could be more effectively used or built on in the coming year, and where he feels they're not being fully used.

"And, Howard, you'll love this," I continued. "Whenever he's considering a job offer, he tells a prospective boss about his 'bathroom epiphany' and asks how they'd deal with a similar situation. It's spurred some fruitful conversations. Although in one case, he got such a strange and revealing response that he turned down the job cold."

"Good for him," Howard said, tapping the steering wheel in applause.

We drove on in silence for a minute, then as we pulled up near my hotel I said, "Bert's really figured out how to leverage that early-career inflection point. . . . But you see the question his story raises, given James's experience with cheating at solitaire?"

Howard smiled and nodded in understanding. "What's your schedule look like for tomorrow?" he asked. I had free time the next morning, so we made plans to play tourist and see some of the historic sites near my hotel. "With all the day-to-day pressures," Howard observed, "it's been too easy to forget all the great stuff around us."

The next day, our walk started at the memorial to Colonel Robert Gould Shaw and the pathbreaking regiment of African-American soldiers who fought in the Civil War—and whose story was told in the movie *Glory*. We worked our way over to the Old North Church, where, deep in the night of April 18, 1775, two signal lights in the steeple spurred Paul Revere on to his famous ride. (An inflection point if there ever was one!) During our little historical tour, we talked about how interpretations of events like the Revolution and the Civil War shaped our sense of the contemporary world—and vice versa. Then, since the Old North Church sits in the North End—Boston's "Little Italy" neighborhood—we ducked into a café.

Once we were settled in with our cold drinks, Howard shifted the conversation back to the previous evening's subject. "Now, to the question you were suggesting last night," he began. "Cheating at solitaire is when you overestimate what you're good at," he said. "The other side of the coin can be just as bad: not seeing your strengths for what they are and not using them to their full potential. This is a common problem, because most of us are conditioned to humility—to not tooting our own horn. That's why it's useful to remind ourselves, now and again, that confidence is not the same as arrogance; expressing the fact that you're good at something is not the same as self-promotion."

Howard took a long sip from his drink, then continued, "We're also conditioned to put great stock in what our surrounding community says about us, notably our work community. For many people that plays out as letting their employer define who they are and what they're good at. Their default setting is believing that the organization 'knows' what it needs and how best to knit together people's skills into an effective whole. Some well-run organizations *do* understand these things, and they get it right frequently. However, a hell of a lot more places *don't*—they just can't figure out how to make effective use of employees' skills and talents.

"Sometimes it's a function of a highly structured and inflexible organizational culture. Other times it's because an organization is focused on results rather than performance—which is a problem when there's often no correlation between how effectively someone works and the outcome of those efforts. This happens a lot, because many organizations overlook simple luck as a key component of results, whereas performance comes from the combination of effort and skill. The fund-raising profession is a good example: a good organization will focus on the fact that you made one hundred visits to donors this year; a less effective organization will focus on the dollars you brought in—regardless of how much was the result of luck and quirky timing, not good work."

He paused to consider, then continued, "The other big problem is that too few managers—even the well-intentioned ones—really know how to develop staff. It requires a different type of skill than is required to keep things on track, day to day; and it demands a higher level of effort. So the average manager is stymied when someone on his staff wants to leverage skills that fall outside of a traditional job description. Then, of course, you've got a manager like Bert's immediate boss, who—insecure and afraid to let someone else shine—deliberately constrains her staff."

"That reminds me of your old saying," I said. "'A-level managers hire A-level staff, and B-level level managers hire C-level staff.' In this case, you could add one more step: 'C-level managers force their teams to be C-level.'"

"All too true." Howard sighed.

"I gotta tell you, lately I've run into a lot of people who are in the kind of situation Bert was," I said. "Some of them are even experiencing what you could call an existential crisis because of the disconnect between what they're capable of doing and what the organization expects and will enable them to do."

"That's pretty strong. Why do you say 'existential crisis'?" Howard asked.

I thought for a moment before responding. "Because it undermines their morale *and* makes them question themselves morally," I said, taking a breath before I elaborated on a subject that really bothered me. "With the economy the way it's been, they're afraid to make a change. They stay in jobs where they're working harder but falling behind in learning and professional growth. Intellectually, they feel 'dumbed down' and hemmed in by the limited expectations of the organization around them. A friend who's in exactly this situation says it's like training for a marathon always surrounded by teammates running slower than they're able. She can't break out of that pack—physically and psychologically—and she's worried that if she's stuck there long enough her core abilities will deteriorate. It's a morale killer and really depressing for her.

"These situations also become moral issues for high-capacity people like her," I continued. "Even though they're meeting their employers' expectations—their bosses have made clear they're not interested in getting more from their employees— they've got qualms about not putting out their best. If they're getting paid for a job, they feel it's wrong not to give one hundred percent effort. Sometimes it's fun for a bit—they think 'Hey, I don't have to work so hard this week!.' But over time it grates on them, ethically, not to strive for excellence, not to offer help when it's needed, not to suggest an alternate approach when something's not working. So they keep giving their all, for months or even years. They push on despite the constant frustration of hearing 'That's a good idea, but we're just not interested in pursuing it' or 'That's a really good piece of work, but we're not going to use it,' or 'Thanks for offering to help, but we'll muddle along without your assistance' until, eventually, they're faced with the choice between changing their ethical perspective—giving less than full effort—or going crazy with frustration and even resentment.

"And with the economy having been so tough for so long, it feels like a no-win situation for many of these folks. They can't stay in a soul-sucking work environment—if they stick there too long they'll find themselves caught in a steadily deepening rut. But there are significant risks in venturing out—especially if they feel they've lost their edge."

Howard nodded, put his hand on my arm, and said, "Believe me, I can completely empathize with the people you're describing. They feel they've got no options—they're told just to dig in and be happy to have a good job. They feel caught in a maze. That was just how many of my HBS colleagues felt thirty years ago." A wry smiled crossed him face. "But folks often underestimate the degree of freedom they actually have to navigate a path between hard realities. There are ways out of even the most demonic labyrinth—although they require proactivity, not passive anticipation of the next opportunity.

"Remember, successful companies are the ones that figure how to 'lean into' changing economic situations. They take the time to reaffirm their vision and goals, then they invest in themselves; they identify their strengths and build on them—preparing to capitalize on the opportunities they intuitively know will come. Individuals can do this, too. In fact, I believe that we have a responsibility—to ourselves and to the people who depend on us—to do exactly the same thing."

Howard signaled to the waitress for two more cold drinks. "We all have the potential to find a satisfying role with an employer who acknowledges and makes the best use of the skills we bring to the table. When we don't actively seek out that situation, we're not cheating at solitaire, we're just cheating ourselves. And ultimately, that's the worst situation to be in."

Only the most supremely confident or arrogant people have never questioned their capacities or wrestled with finding the best environment for fully realizing those capacities. Mindy Grossman, the president of HSN, Inc. (formerly known as Home Shopping Network) and a very experienced executive, once told me, "One of my biggest motivators is not wanting to disappoint the people who are depending on me." Wendy Kopp, the founder and CEO of Teach For America (TFA), still grapples with a persistent worry that she'll prove unequal to the task of leading the growing national organization she started as an inexperienced college senior—even if TFA's stunning success seems to prove her worries misplaced.

It's especially easy to underestimate or mischaracterize your skills and potential when you're just starting out on a career path, considering a new job, or taking on a fresh challenge. It even happens to established Harvard Business School professors. When Howard retired from the active faculty and HBS created the Howard H. Stevenson Professorship of Business Administration in his honor, the position went to a guy named Tom Eisenmann. While Tom was already a respected member of the Harvard faculty, he was still awed by the idea of what he described as "stepping into the master's shoes."

"Having had Howard as a teacher and mentor since grad school, this was both an incredible honor and a little scary," Tom told me after his appointment was announced. "After all, he shaped my life's work in fundamental ways—even helping me when I stumbled early in my teaching career. And when I learned I was moving into what had been his office for decades, I felt a weird mix of pride and embarrassment: it seemed presumptuous for this cub to sit in the old lion's den." To calm his spirit and harness good karma, Tom asked Howard to leave something of his in the office. Howard left him a statue of Ganesha, the Hindu god of wisdom, commerce, and humility—the Lord of Beginnings and the Remover of Obstacles. "It was a perfect token of encouragement for someone beginning a new phase of his career," Tom reflected. "And perfect, too, for someone like me who teaches people to be effective entrepreneurs—masters of new beginnings and removing obstacles."

There certainly have been plenty of times when I've questioned if I had what it took to pursue the path I'd chosen, both early in my career and at inflection points throughout it. Over time, I've learned to anticipate the insecurities and fears that come with new or uncertain situations—and to make a plan for managing them.

However, I hadn't yet figured this out when, as a freshly minted Cornell graduate, I started working for the entrepreneurial founder of the Joie de Vivre hotel chain, Chip Conley. Whip smart, with an amazingly creative, think-outside-the-box mind, Chip had a high tolerance for his employees' off-the-wall ideas. So, as an overly confident twenty-two-year old, I was constantly throwing out suggestions and schemes for new products and services or "better" strategies. After four years of college at one of the world's best hotel schools, I clearly should have had answers on every issue, right? Now, many years later, I wince at how I must have looked to those more experienced and wiser than I was.

When my answers proved impractical or naïve, as many inevitably were, Chip would patiently explain the fundamental flaw in my plan or the piece of the problem that I'd overlooked. After a while—after dozens of my ideas had been shown to be interesting but not feasible—I started questioning myself. Was I really any good at this? Was I fooling myself in thinking I could hit the ambitious career goals I'd laid out for myself? Would I have been better off taking a more traditional banking, consulting, or corporate position?

One day when I must have been looking particularly glum, Chip asked me what was up. I told him my concern: that maybe I wasn't as good at my job as he needed me to be; that I didn't feel as effective as my colleagues seemed to be.

"Don't be stupid; you're doing fine," Chip reassured me. "I brought you in because you come up with interesting ideas. I didn't hire you to have all the answers."

I told him I appreciated what he was saying; but it seemed that most of the folks I worked with were much better at getting answers than I was.

"They may be," Chip said, in a rare display of disgust. "But that's because many of them are tackling only the easy questions or offering safe answers to the tougher questions. They aren't taking risks or pushing the envelope. You don't see the churning that goes on inside their heads as they try to manage how they're viewed.

"You are pushing the envelope every minute of every day—and, frankly, sometimes it's a bit much," Chip continued, confirming my suspicion that I was indeed at times driving him crazy, "but I'd much rather have you doing that than being hesitant because you're afraid of what others will think of you.

"Remember," Chip continued, "everybody's outside looks better than your own inside."

"Um . . . what?" I asked, trying to figure out how we got to discussing anatomy.

He had a good laugh at my confusion, then said, "It's human nature to focus on the strengths and talents people display on the outside, and to assume they don't have any unseen weaknesses. We also tend to discount our own strengths and magnify the depth of weaknesses we see in ourselves. But if you could put yourself inside other people's heads, you'd probably see they've got their own worries and failures of confidence." (I've found that Chip's observation applies to organizations, too: whatever the size, mission, operational structure, or culture, an organization invariably looks better to outsiders than to insiders. Virtually every company, college, nonprofit agency, business franchise, or consulting firm I've seen up close appears more efficient and effective to the rest of the world than to those experiencing its inner workings—the people who see the organization in its underwear, so to speak.)

I understood Chip's point about seeing things with others' eyes and through the filter of their own insecurities. And I appreciated his confidence in me. But I still wasn't completely clear on exactly what he saw me bringing to the table at Joie de Vivre. So I swallowed my pride and asked him point-blank, "Why did you hire me, if not to come up with the right answers?"

"I hired you to ask the questions that will eventually lead us to the right answers," he said. "You tend to see a few steps further down the road than other people—like a hockey player who can anticipate where the puck will be two passes ahead. Right now, your anticipation's a bit off; but once you get a little more experience, you're going to start beating others to the puck."

Now, many years later, as Howard and I sat in the café, I recalled that conversation. "Previously, I'd never crystalized my skills in the way that Chip explained them," I told Howard. "His thoughts were really important in helping me identify my competitive advantages, the areas where I excelled professionally. But

I wouldn't have gotten that information if I'd just listened to my inner doubts when I was just starting my career."

Howard nodded and repeated to himself, " 'Everybody's outside looks better than your own inside.' I think Chip's somewhat oddball phrase captures something important. It's very easy for our basic insecurities to interfere with our ability to make a rational assessment of our capacities. Plenty of folks get their heads stuck in an old or narrow version of who they are and what they're good at. So it's important to periodically push the 'refresh' button on your self-assessment—and then be proactive in pursuing work roles that match that new version. Because it's the rare, lucky person whose boss comes in one day and says, 'You're cut out for more; you may feel secure in your current situation, but you've got the skills to be successful in a more challenging role.' "

"Sounds like Bert was one of those lucky few," I noted. "But for the rest of us—the ones who have to drive their own career development—how do we most effectively leverage our skills and potential?"

Howard sipped his drink and thought a bit before responding. "There are several keys to doing that successfully.

"First, don't get hung up on weaknesses. Focus on your strengths and how to build on them." I looked at him skeptically and he continued, "I know, that's pretty counterintuitive to the way most people think. From kindergarten, we're trained to identify weaknesses and work hard to improve them. We devote huge amounts of time and energy to improving areas of weakness. Except, humans have a thousand weaknesses and just a relative handful of strengths. And since weaknesses usually overlap with things we don't enjoy, improvement requires a big investment of intellectual and emotional energy. On both counts, focusing on weaknesses is a losing proposition," he said.

"But there are baseline capacities for every job, and sometimes you've got to improve an area of weakness to hit that baseline," I pushed back.

"Granted. But beyond that, don't dwell on what you can't do well. Become excellent at what you're already good at, and then build from those areas of strength. And remember that you don't have to be *perfect* at something in order to rank it as one of your strengths."

"You know, when I first started working in Manhattan," I said, "I wondered why the tallest buildings are clustered in midtown, with relatively smaller buildings at the upper and lower ends of the island. I finally figured out that it's because midtown is where bedrock comes up toward the surface and provides the strongest base on which to build. It's a great metaphor for your point: build the foundation of your career on the most solid ground available."

"Yup," Howard replied. "And study after study of successful leaders bears out that idea—they succeed by focusing on what they do well and continuing to do it. They make up for their weaknesses by surrounding themselves with people who are strong in these areas. That's why I say identify the things you excel at, then find a role and an organization that enable you to do more of it."

The second key element to pursuing one's career potential, Howard suggested, is to envision the ideal context for doing what you're good at. Think back on where you've been and what you've done to this point, and ask a series of questions about the setting and circumstances:

In what situations and on what tasks have I felt really good about my abilities and accomplishments—whether on the job, at home, in volunteer positions, or in social settings?

What are the places and situations where people have sought my help or been eager to have me on their team?

*What patterns or commonalities do I find in those instances; and
based on that information, what appear to be the conditions in
which I am best able to utilize my strengths?*

*What kinds of roles involve those conditions; and where are these
roles found, whether at my current employer or elsewhere?*

"You should develop answers to each of these questions for
yourself," Howard said, "and then pose a version of these questions to people who know you well—your spouse, your good
friends, trusted current and former colleagues. Explain that
you're seeking guidance on your strengths and how best to use
them, but be appreciative of anything they have to offer, positive or negative. Take it all in as useful data."

As you work through these questions, he noted, be sure to
recognize that your strengths might be effectively applied in
situations that aren't immediately obvious. "Keep an open mind
about the places, paths, or specific roles that might allow you to
best utilize your strengths and pursue your legacy vision. Look
outside the predefined career tracks that someone with your
skill set would traditionally pursue.

"Remember," he stressed, "you don't have to be an 'entrepreneur' to be entrepreneurial in building your career."

That quip reminded me of a woman I'd met a few years ago,
Barbara, who took just this entrepreneurial approach. I told
Howard Barbara's story, explaining that her most apparent
strengths were her energetic personality, her intelligence, and
her self-starter mentality—and her black belts in the Korean
martial arts of Tae Kwon Do and Hapkido. She enjoyed working with people, but her experiences as a human resources and
training specialist in several organizations had soured her on
that career track, and on traditional nine-to-five office environments in general. So Barbara put her skills together in a wholly
different way: she created a workplace-based women's self-

defense training course and convinced a series of businesses, health-care providers, and other groups to sponsor them for their employees and clients. Over time, her project expanded to include general physical fitness classes, as well as programs on workplace bullying. "She knew she wouldn't get rich from this career path; and there were challenges she hadn't anticipated, like financial management and billing," I told Howard. "But she was happy with her life, day to day. She felt good about the way she'd leveraged and built on her key strengths. And she liked how this new approach to her career moved her toward her long-term vision."

"Who would even know that such a business is possible?" Howard joked. "But it's great that Barbara pushed beyond traditional career tracks to capitalize on her passions and skills."

By then the clock was winding toward noon; I had a client meeting to get to and Howard was having lunch with his son Andy. We downed the last of our drinks, then started back to my hotel, where he'd left his car. As we walked, Howard offered a final thought.

"You know, Eric, we've been focusing on situations where it's clear that a person's not going to be able to leverage their skills in their current situation. But, obviously, there are plenty of situations where that's not the case—where there are realistic chances for learning and professional growth, if some short-term hurdles can be overcome. In that case, you want to make sure you've fully played out the opportunities where you are.

"So, for example, it feels really bad getting passed over for a promotion or not being chosen for a juicy project, especially the first time you experience it. But that doesn't necessarily mean you've hit an immovable roadblock. If it's me, I'm going to start by engaging with the decision makers—in a nondefensive way—to understand their reasons. I'm asking what concrete steps I can take to be better positioned for the next opportunity. And I'm talking with them about opportunities for incremental growth—for expanding my current job to include new tasks and challenges that will enable me to develop new skills and demonstrate the capabilities my bosses are looking for."

"And if you don't get a productive response?" I asked.

"Well, then, as you hear me say all the time, use all the data they give you. Negative or unconstructive responses can be as useful as positive ones—more useful, in fact—if you're honest with yourself in hearing the message," Howard replied, punctuating the last phrase with a light slap on my shoulder.

When we got to his car, I gave Howard a hug. He wished me a safe trip back to New York, sent his love to Jennifer and the kids, and climbed into his car. As I watched him drive away, I thought again how lucky I was to know this savvy and sincere man. Despite an amazing list of accomplishments over a long, distinguished career—his very successful outside—he empathizes with others' insides. He understands the inner trepidations of the twenty-something in her first job and the frustrations of a forty-something who's looking for a renewed sense of challenge in his career in ways few others seem to. It is one of the many things that make Howard so wise.

And one of the observations he'd offer to each of them is this: most of the people who are both accomplished and happy in their life's work are not driven by overbearing confidence or an incontrovertible sense of their superior skills; they're guided simply by a determination to continue moving toward a vision that is its own definition of excellence and success.

BOB PITTMAN

I'm sitting here, having just come away from a deep and wide-ranging conversation with Bob Pittman, and my mind's eye is trying to reconcile two incongruous images.

The first is the picture that the world has of Bob today: a true pioneer in the cable and digital entertainment industry; one of the most accomplished and honored marketing minds of his generation; a philanthropic leader and winner of the Robert F. Kennedy Foundation's Ripple of Hope Award for his contributions to the advancement of education and the fight against poverty.

That picture has been formed through several decades of extraordinary accomplishment. Bob is the guy who launched MTV and VH1; who turned a network for preschool kids into today's Nickelodeon and Nick-at-Night; and who made MTV Networks into cable TV's first profitable network. Later, as president of America Online, he helped drive AOL's phenomenal growth—and the related expansion of online communication and commerce as key elements of American society—and was a major player in the blockbuster merger of AOL and Time Warner. Most recently, after taking a few years out of the limelight to work in venture capital and help launch a series of start-ups, Bob took on another big, high-profile challenge: leading Clear Channel Communications, one of the world's biggest diversified media companies—which owns the largest group of radio stations (850 and counting) and perhaps the largest number of outdoor advertising properties in the world, and runs the iHeartRadio digital music service. Throughout those years, Bob also made a mark in the philanthropic and nonprofit world—helping to create LiveAid at MTV; developing Internet-based education programs at AOL; chairing the boards of the Robin Hood Foundation, which fights poverty in New York City, and the New York Public Theater; and serving on the board of the Alliance for Lupus Research.

Juxtapose that present, "top-of-the-world" image of

Bob Pittman with this one: a young man born in Jackson, Mississippi, and raised in the racially segregated American south of the 1950s and '60s; son of a white Methodist minister who incurred the wrath of the Ku Klux Klan for advocating racial integration of the Methodist church structure; a kid from a poor family who worked through high school and college.

At a first, superficial glance, it's hard to see that early version of Bob Pittman in the man he has since become. Even his voice—uninflected by accent, flowing with the deep, clear tones of the radio disk jockey that he was early in his career—belies his beginnings. But as you dig a little deeper in conversation with him, you see the intellectual, moral, and emotional connections between the boy then and the man now. And then you come to a connection that is one of the most significant.

That then-and-now connection is the continuing psychological impact of an early experience that sits deeply inside of him, that has affected the way he views himself and the way he came to interact with the world around him. It was the experience of a six-year-old boy who was thrown from a horse and, as a result, lost an eye.

"As I reflect back on my life, losing my eye may have had the greatest impact of any experience I had," Bob had recalled. "In those times, in that place, kids could be merciless in their treatment of someone with a physical disability. Dealing with that kind of abuse, day after day, I felt like an outsider. More than that, I had to get used to people viewing me not as who I was, but only as 'the kid without an eye.'"

I had asked him how his reactions to that experience manifested themselves as he moved through his career.

"Well, first, it was incentive for me to escape Mississippi: I took radio jobs—first announcing, then programming—in Milwaukee, Detroit, Pittsburgh, and Chicago, and finally landed in New York City when I took on programming for WNBC," he replied. "Actually, I was the first in my family to leave the South— maybe the first since my people arrived in Mississippi in the early 1800s.

"It also made me even more attuned to the civil rights battles of the 1960s—because I experienced a taste of the same rejection by society around me—and has driven a lot of my community work since.

"From a career perspective, it's probably contributed to my strong drive and my wanting to go from challenge to challenge. It's also made me look at things in a different way than I might normally have—given me a natural inclination to see situations from a different perspective than a lot of people around me. That's been a big factor in my ability to do what I've done.

"Also, I am really committed to helping people be better, to helping them achieve everything they've got the talent for. If I have a particular strength as a leader, it's building a team, getting everyone seeing the important role they play in what we're doing, and getting them excited about our mission, together."

I had asked Bob if he looks back with any sense of anger or frustration toward those childhood experiences.

"Those tough memories are still with me, without a doubt. But I'm an optimist by nature," he'd explained, "and I believe that life is one hundred percent about the journey—it's a collection of experiences, and even the negative ones give you something. And all of those experiences have brought me here.

"Everything in life is a stepping-stone to something new," he concluded, "and the key to contentment, I believe, is to view it all with amazement and curiosity."

CHAPTER EIGHT

The Mosaic in the Mirror

You can't just reach up and take a suit off the rack marked "successful" or "fulfilled" or "rich." It ain't gonna work.

HOWARD WAS BORN at a time of change and conflict in the world, a period when the United States was emerging from many years of hard economic times and facing a military conflict unlike any it had experienced before. Although the same might be said for a child born in this past decade, Howard was born in June 1941. The Great Depression of the thirties had finally ended, but a world war raged. Six months later, Pearl Harbor was attacked—a shock to the American psyche such as was not experienced again for sixty years, until September 11, 2001.

In those challenging times in the small town of Holladay, Utah, it was natural for a boy to look to the older, more experienced people around him for guidance on navigating a confusing, swiftly changing world. Howard found some of that guidance in the Boy Scouts; he joined at age twelve and proceeded with amazing speed to earn the merit badges needed to become an Eagle Scout by age thirteen. He took useful lessons from the Scouting code, beginning with "Be prepared," the Scouting motto that is also the perfect mantra for an entrepreneur. He also gained a deep appreciation for the opportunities born of collaboration and a sense of obligation to serve the community.

Religion was a big part of life in Utah, and for a while Howard sought guidance from the faith in which he was raised, the Church of Jesus Christ of Latter-day Saints. He was and still is a spiritual person; but as his natural analytical perspective emerged in his early teens, he found himself less comfortable with the leaps of faith embodied in the Mormon theology. Although many in his family and community were disappointed by his lack of religious vigor and he often felt like an outsider, Howard found a moral compass in some of the core values of the faith, notably the importance of family and of continuous learning.

Debates on religion aside, Howard found boundless support and guidance from his family. When Howard was born, his father, Ralph, was in the Navy—was, in fact, serving at Pearl Harbor when the Japanese bombs fell. The Stevenson family was living not far from the naval base, and six-month-old Howard would have heard those bombs exploding. Ralph served with great distinction in World War II, commanding communication units during some of the most difficult military battles in the Pacific. After the war, he launched a career based on his communications expertise and technical skills—first opening a radio supply store, then installing custom sound systems, and finally serving as a manufacturer's representative for a huge swath of territory in the western United States.

Ralph was a warm and engaging man and a supportive father; he welcomed Howard's questions about his life and his work. There were many lessons that Howard took from his father's career. Some were conveyed in words: why he sold this product, not that one; why he did business with this person, not the other. The most important lessons were about the values that guided his father—values conveyed not merely in words but through Ralph's actions, day in and day out. The two of his dad's values that I've heard Howard speak of most frequently are "Offer help to anyone who asks for it" and "Deliver more value than you're paid for."

"Given those principles," Howard once joked, "it's no surprise that my dad never became a wealthy man. On the other hand, his conscience never kept him up at night and he was welcomed wherever he went." From my perspective, Howard has been able to adopt his father's values, then build on them. He's always ready to lend a hand to colleagues, students, and friends alike. As a businessman, he found ways to both deliver unexpected value to his clients and make a profit. As a result, like his father, he's welcomed wherever he goes; in fact, he's sought after to go more places and see more people than he could possibly visit in a lifetime.

Dorothy Stevenson, Howard's mother, was a strong presence in his life. Though she had just a high school diploma, she possessed great intellect and a strong curiosity—traits that she clearly passed on to and nurtured in Howard. A deeply spiritual woman, she also had a bit of the maverick streak about her—for example, becoming the first female licensed ham radio operator in Utah—and this streak is another characteristic that Howard clearly displays.

Howard's aunt, uncle, and two of his grandparents lived nearby; deeply engaged in his life, they all left marks on the person he was to become. He clearly picked up the financial acumen displayed by his aunt, a professional accountant. His uncle was a creative-minded businessman who chose not to see limits that others felt bound by and who believed there are no bad ideas, just untested ones. And his grandfather, an outdoorsman who climbed mountains till he was eighty-five, instilled in Howard a sense of adventure and an appreciation for the environment.

Looking back at Howard's family and early years gives a sense of where he came from. To a certain extent, you can "reverse engineer" the Howard of today. But you can't draw a straight line from the traits, perspectives, and experiences he took from his upbringing in 1940s and '50s Utah to the man he's become and to the place he's carved in the world today. More than almost any other highly accomplished person I know, Howard is a "self-made man." Certainly self-made in financial terms, because his parents never made a lot of money, which Howard has done. Self-made in a career sense, because the word *entrepreneurship* didn't even exist when Howard went to high school, and he'd never met someone with an MBA before he went to college in 1959.

His is a self-made legacy as well. While he revered his family, respected the community surrounding him, and learned much from his teachers, Howard never modeled himself after any one person. He never hitched himself to anyone's star; never followed another's road map. Instead, to guide himself, he constructed an integrated "mosaic"—a selection of experiences, lessons, observations, principles, and ideas that he consciously wove into the broader picture of who he is, what he does and why, and where he's going.

Howard's notion of this mosaic is one of the things that most fascinates me about him. I really appreciate the idea that you can draw from the experiences and knowledge of people around you, without feeling that you need to be just like them. That you can put together a multifaceted picture of who you want to be without feeling isolated because that picture is different from the image created by the assumptions and expectations of people around you.

I grew up in a middle-class family in rural New Jersey. We were just an hour's drive from New York City, but my little hometown seemed light-years away socially, culturally, and economically. College was far from a given for many of the kids in my high school. My mom was a middle school teacher for thirty years, and her paycheck helped smooth out the financial ups and downs from my father's uneven career and various small-business ventures. They both worked hard, and though we didn't have many frills in our lives, my older sister and I never worried about food, clothing, or shelter. We weren't poor and we weren't rich. We were like a lot of families coping with the economic roller coaster of the 1980s and early '90s—or with the tough times during these last few years.

Growing up, I felt a certain sense of "apartness." At home, my parents often joked that I'd been switched at birth with somebody else's kid. They were relatively straight-laced, low-key, middle-of-the-road kind of folks. I was always trying something new, looking for the next adventure, pushing the very traditional envelope surrounding me. That narrow, mellow envelope extended to the community we lived in, where I was about the only Jewish kid in my high school class. Luckily for me, my best friend, Vikram, whose tradition-minded parents had immigrated from India, was similarly trying to deal with feelings of "apartness" and to push past the various intellectual and social confines around him.

Vikram and I shared a certain sense of isolation in a career sense, too. We wanted to engage the world and climb some professional mountains, but few of our peers shared our interest in ambitious, out-of-the-box goals. We had no pack of friends encouraging and challenging one another with crazy ideas and career dreams. We also didn't have a lot of obvious role models—no one to offer us guidance on the best paths to take as we set out into the foothills of our careers. This was less of a problem for Vikram than it was for me; he was always an amazingly focused, confident, and self-directed guy. Early on, he set his sights on a specific career path—the clearly marked road to becoming an investor—and then just went at it with unrelenting energy. (He's now a very successful investor, lecturer at Yale, and author.)

My career options were less clearly defined, and there were

few obvious paths blazed ahead of me. (Put yourself in my place as a high school freshman in 1988. What's the obvious career path for someone whose ambition is to try new things, build relationships, and build businesses?) So I was feeling a little lost—like wandering at dusk without a compass in the hilly forests of northwestern New Jersey.

As it turned out, however, my first guides were just waiting for me to stumble across them, at the place where the forest meets the waters of Lake Hopatcong, New Jersey's largest lake. More precisely, they were busy cooking dinners, pouring drinks, and schmoozing customers at the Jefferson House, a summer restaurant right on the lakeshore.

Billy and Allan Orth were the two brothers who owned and ran the Jefferson House. The guys—then in their late thirties and early forties, respectively—had run the restaurant for twenty years, ever since their middle-aged father died soon after buying the place. Over that time, they'd built a profitable and multifaceted business: the restaurant in the summer and a catering operation in the off-season.

I first met them the summer after I finished ninth grade. My family had eaten at the Jefferson House several times, and I loved its calm views of the rippling lake and surrounding forests. I liked watching the boats pull up to docks right below the waterside tables. And I was intrigued by the owners, who reminded me—I swear—of nothing so much as big, cuddly, friendly Sesame Street Muppets. When it came time to get a summer job, I could think of no better place to work. Despite having very little experience, I was able to impress the guys with my enthusiasm and talk my way into a job grilling burgers and fajita fixings and deep-frying tons of french fries.

When I started working for them, Allan and Billy were already wealthy from the restaurant and their catering business. They could have retired at any time. But money was beside the point. They enjoyed the work they did every day, seemingly drawing life energy from the heat of the grill and the laughter of their customers.

Allan had trained as a computer scientist before jumping into the food business. In his free time he'd build computers and tinker with every possible tool and system in the Jefferson House. His physical appearance—he was a big, well-fed guy with rumpled hair and a scraggly beard, who wore old shorts and polo shirts—masked a sharp intellect and a surprising agility in navigating a busy, cramped kitchen. He ran the back of the house like clockwork. I always found it humorous that a guy who spent much of his career happily flipping burgers quite literally could have worked at NASA.

Billy worked the front of the restaurant, schmoozing with longtime customers and managing the staff who served food, tended bar, and bused tables. He was an expert at keeping everybody happy. His huge personality, warmth, and wit did the trick, even when the staff were feeling harried, guests were weary from an extra-long wait for the better tables, or, infrequently, someone had had too many beers. As a young guy, I also appreciated that Billy could use a different kind of leverage when necessary—as when he gently "helped" one very obnoxious and physically abusive guy take a dip in the lake, to the general applause of the customers and staff. (Allan, always ready with practical solutions to problems, stood a few feet away, prepared to wield the iron skillet he'd brought from the kitchen when the commotion started.) Billy was the first real "relationship guy" I had ever met. He decided I was the right person to help his brother at the grill, enabling Allan to focus on the rest of the kitchen and get a break now and then.

For three summers, I spent almost every day in the restaurant's hot, loud, crowded kitchen—and I loved it. I loved working with Allan, a funny, caring, and thoroughly crazy guy. I loved spending my breaks hanging out at a dockside table, shooting the bull with Billy and an endless stream of friendly, talkative customers. And just before closing, when the kitchen shut down, I made a point of drifting back to the table and hanging out with the brothers as they wound down from their long day. They talked about lots of stuff, including plenty of bull. But there were also periodic mini tutorials for me on running a business, managing staff, and handling the day-to-day challenges of being a responsible adult (which neither Allan nor Billy admitted to being).

There are any number of reasons I look back so fondly on those summers. It was a gorgeous location, and I could relax just standing on the dock and watching the wind rippling across the lake. The most important reasons, however, are Allan and Billy themselves and the way they guided me to the path I'm following today. Though I didn't recognize it then, they were the first entrepreneurs I'd ever met, and they planted a seed that's grown steadily since. They demonstrated for me, by their example, the power of building relationships with the people working around you; they worked together as a team, and they treated everyone around them—employees and customers—as members of a big extended family. They were endlessly supportive of my career ambitions, and they wrote the recommendation letters I attached to my Cornell application. To this day, they are among my biggest boosters, greeting me—and now my sons—with open arms and warm words whenever I see them.

Billy and Allan played a huge role in my life. They helped me build a bridge between the boy I was then and the man I have become; between the community in which I grew up and the much wider professional and personal community I have become part of over the past twenty-five years. Although I have not sought to do everything as they would have done it, I view them as my first role models. They are men to be emulated for the caring way they treat the people around them and for making business decisions guided by their personal values. I believe they were also my first mentors—advancing my education and career through their support and counsel, and by sharing their experiences as creative "business builders." In those ways they helped shape my life's work.

There are many times I've seen Howard frustrated at people for doing or saying dumb things, repeatedly. (He rarely reacts negatively the first time, preferring to give someone the benefit of the doubt. It's the second time that you see the telltale downcast eyes and subtle shake of the head.) And, on a number of occasions, I've seen him express real anger when someone seemed to be willfully misunderstanding or misrepresenting a situation.

Yet one instance in particular stands out in my mind—because *I* was the person frustrating the hell out of him.

It happened one day while we were sitting at Logan Airport waiting for a flight. We were engaged in one of our many discussions about developing a legacy vision for our life's work. He asked me a question I found hard to answer—about how I might reconcile two conflicting goals—and I gave him a flippant answer: "Well, actually, Howard, I figured I'd write a case study on your life and then just follow it." He waved away my response and asked the question again. "No, really," I responded. "What better plan could I have than following in your footsteps?" I meant it lightly and flatteringly. But in retrospect, I have to admit that I may have also been looking for an easy way around the important choice implied in his question, a choice I had been trying to pretend didn't exist.

Howard focused right in on the part of me that was willing to cop out, to take the easy route by just adopting the "Howard Stevenson model." The look on his face—warm and inquisitive the previous moment—turned intense and focused. "Making me a role model is one thing," he said with an edge in his voice, "but I'll be damned if I watch you become a Howard Stevenson clone."

He could have slapped me across the face and it wouldn't have had as much impact. I just sat there for a moment, stunned and feeling sheepish.

I think he'd surprised himself by the strength of his response, and he carefully pondered his next words. "Look, Eric," he started again in a much milder tone, "I am deeply touched that you think so well of me and how I've lived my life; that you see me as a role model of sorts."

"Not 'of sorts,'" I said.

"Okay," he said, gently waving away my reply. "Perhaps I reacted so strongly because it's very, very tempting for someone in my position to cultivate a cadre of professional clones—former students who validate my thoughts and experiences by replicating them in their own lives. It happens all the time in higher education; doesn't matter if it's in business or English or physics. You also see these clones at the upper echelons of organizations—big and small, profit and nonprofit—where the leaders have encouraged a cult of personality. But I've worked hard not to do that, and I've called it out when I've seen it around me.

"Also, I reacted strongly because I've seen how easily people adopt a one-size-fits-all approach to their careers—even when those clothes clearly don't fit." He stopped, put a welcome smile on his face, and continued with mischief in his voice. "And when you get a bunch of people doing both, you're surrounded by a group of clones in clown suits. Sure, it works for a little while and everyone seems to be having fun. In the long run, though, most of these folks are dissatisfied with their careers. They end up looking in the mirror, trying to figure out who's in there, professionally."

Howard was interrupted by the boarding announcement for our plane. We picked up our bags and he continued as we moved to the gate. "Many folks—and not only young people—

fall into the trap of believing they can simply adopt a role model's legacy and path. It's a trap because as compelling as another's vision might be, you can't make it wholly, truly yours. A legacy is tailored to fit just one person. What brings satisfaction to a role model does so because of myriad factors and experiences unique to that person. The old saying is true: you can't step in the same river twice. In the same way, you can't follow a role model's exact steps, expecting the same outcome. That person hasn't experienced what you've experienced, doesn't have the same memories, doesn't love the same people . . . just isn't you."

He smiled at the attendant who took his ticket, then finished his thought. "You can't just reach up and take a suit off the rack marked 'successful' or 'fulfilled' or 'rich.' It ain't gonna work. So you need to be mindful of who you model yourself after. And why. And what parts of that model you're keying in on. And how you'll use that image when you're setting goals and making choices."

Filing down the gangway to the plane, I thought about Howard's points. Clearly, it's easier to take an off-the-shelf model for key life choices; and latching onto the things that other people value is simpler than working to identify your own values and goals. So it may seem a better approach—faster and more efficient.

But in the long run, it isn't real—or more efficient or sustainable.

And even if you truly down deep want to be a carbon copy . . . sorry, there's no way to do it. I would love to be just like the person Howard is today—except I don't want a divorce or a bad heart or an academic career (and, frankly, I could do without the classical music). I'd love to have Chip Conley's career—except I can't live in San Francisco, because my wife and kids won't leave the grandparents and cousins in New Jersey; and, as I mull it over, I think I may actually have a cooler job right now than he does.

The beauty of the human condition, Howard was reminding me, is that everyone is different and always will be, no matter how much we try to fit—or society tries to fit us—into a cookie cutter. (One of his favorite quotes is Charles Schulz's playful admonition, "Be yourself. Everyone else is taken!")

A better approach, he was suggesting, is to use a role model's perspectives as a catalyst for your own honest interior dialogue. Observe and consider the elements of the legacy that others have defined for themselves. But then, instead of just adopting that model, use the information to prompt your own deep thinking about what's truly meaningful and satisfying.

As I thought further about our conversation, it was clear from both the intensity and the substance of Howard's reaction that he'd given great thought to the subject of role models. I wanted to hear more. So after we'd settled into our seats on the plane, I asked him, "If you were choosing a role model today, how would you go about it? What would you be looking to a role model for?"

He considered the question. "I guess I have a few suggestions. First, I would remind myself what a role model is and isn't." He paused, smiled impishly, and said, "A role model is an adult imaginary friend." This comment was classic Howard: innocent and sweet, simple and insightful, playful and effective. "Role models are stories—a mixture of the story that someone tells about his or her life and the story that we choose to see and hear. Role models are, mostly, static images in our mind, snapshots that aren't easily updated. Role models are a mechanism for predicting one's future; but—for the reasons we just talked about—they aren't precise predictors.

"And, from my experience, it's a mistake to focus on a single individual as *the* role model. A role model should be a composite of many separate images. The best role model is actually a mosaic created from the characteristics of multiple people who collectively form an integrated image of the kind of person you want to be. And each individual element should connect to one or more of your specific selves and dimensions, in the short or long term."

"I'm trying to envision how the average gray-haired-eminence role model would respond to being described as somebody's 'adult imaginary friend,'" I said. "But your notion of the 'mosaic role model' resonates. I get it."

"Good, because my second suggestions grows from that idea," Howard replied. "I'd think about the perspective from which I'm viewing a potential role model. There are, generally speaking, three broad perspectives: legacy, career, and organization or professional. These provide different views—although there's inevitably some overlap—and it's important to recognize which 'window' you're looking through."

When contemplating a potential role model through the legacy window, he explained, you're looking at someone whose qualities reflect your fundamental sense of who you are and who you want to be. You look to them to help you define and refine your own legacy by examining the one they've established for themselves. You're not just adopting their legacy vision wholesale; you're observing the constituent elements of that vision—such as the ethical stands they take, the way they invest their personal energy, the place that family and close friends have in their lives, whether they display empathy and personal connection, and how they demonstrate diligence and commitment. Essentially, you're asking what impact they hope to have on the world and what light that shines on your legacy goals.

In considering a role model through the career window, Howard offered, you're looking at a person whose choice of jobs and career path offers hints for how your career might proceed. "This is a narrower perspective than the legacy view. It's the window to use when you're trying to assess things like your competitive advantages, the places where you could develop collateral strengths for long-term growth, and ways to sidestep problems or bridge areas of weakness," he suggested.

The organizational or professional window is the narrowest of the three, Howard noted. "It is a very targeted view, focused on the strategy and tactics of achieving your goals within a specific organization or profession. You watch an organizational/professional role model for clues on how to demonstrate your current capacities, identify growth opportunities at your present employer, move up the organizational hierarchy, or carve out a specific niche within your profession."

"I'd imagine there's a lot more 'predictive value' in an organizational/professional role model," I offered. "The field of vision is smaller, the number of variables is greatly reduced, and you could make better predictions based on the snapshot. Still, they'd be relatively narrow, short-term predictions, and it'd be a bad idea to just string together a series of short-term predictions—to construct your mosaic role model from a handful of organizational perspectives."

"You make a good point," Howard replied. "It's important to integrate all three perspectives. And I'm not suggesting that a person just go out and identify one each from columns A, B, and C. You want to thoughtfully connect the many facets of who you are."

"So how many individual people are represented in your mosaic role model?" I asked him.

He sat back to think about it. "Oh well—lots, I guess. A dozen, two dozen, maybe more? I haven't ever tried to count. Certainly my parents; my wife, Fredi; a handful of HBS and business colleagues . . . and I've viewed plenty of people as role models at discrete steps in my career. It's kind of a pyramid: fewer legacy role models, more career role models, many more organizational role models.

"But the number really isn't the point," he said, thumping

my knee with his hand. "The point is, do I have a complete, multidimensional picture of who I am, where I'm going, and how I'll get there? And if I don't, whom can I look at to help clarify what's missing? The fact is, even if I could give you a number today, it would likely change. I've had plenty of past role models—but as I've moved on to new challenges, those models have receded and I've looked to others to help illuminate the next part of the road ahead. Right now, my lens is 'Who's happily retired and what can I learn from them?' "

The flight attendant rolled his cart past and we accepted a couple of diet sodas. Howard took his time pouring and drinking; but when he was done, he dove right back into our conversation.

"This next suggestion is really important," he said. "To use a metaphor from my long-ago days as a Boy Scout: pick a role model who's earned the same merit badges that you're working toward."

"Whoa—you lost me there. Merit badges?" I asked.

"In Scouting, there are scores of subjects where you can do focused work and study; when you demonstrate clear skills or knowledge in an area, you get a merit badge. There are more than a hundred badges, but you can't possibly go after all of them. Even Eagle Scouts, the highest rank in Scouting, only earn twenty-one badges. It's the same in life—except that life's merit badges are defined by your vision, your values, and the 'selves' you've prioritized.

"If you want to earn a specific badge—whether it's being a good parent, being famous, being well-educated, serving your community, or getting rich—you should seek a role model who's earned that badge themselves. But don't stop there," he emphasized, "because earning a badge in one area necessarily means not earning it in other areas. So you should recognize how earning one particular merit badge has affected that person's ability to pursue other badges that are important to you, too. Understand, for example, if your model for the quickly-climbing-the-organizational-ladder badge completely ignored the badges for physical fitness and good health that are also important to you."

"On the surface, what you're saying seems so obvious," I observed, "but in practice I guess it's not intuitive for someone to stop and assess what makes a particular role model so appealing."

"The problem is that when we see someone who is seemingly successful, it's natural to strive to replicate her success—without understanding the implications of that success for the other aspects of her life. When you start a new job, for example, it makes a certain amount of sense to key in on the organization's 'stars' and try to emulate them. It's a good way to get your bearings in a new environment and to understand what the organization values. But if you focus on only one element of who they are, you can end up emulating someone whose overall vision is quite different from yours.

"So, looking across the board, a woman who wants a family and a home life isn't aiming for the same merit badges as an executive who is intending to make a zillion dollars before she's forty. A guy who places a high value on workplace friendships and on being liked by colleagues is going for a different set of badges than the results-oriented manager who prizes productivity and efficiency. Even two people on seemingly parallel paths aren't necessarily trying to earn the same badges: a hard-working young plastic surgeon who wants to focus on post-cancer reconstructive surgery and a senior colleague specializing in beauty-enhancement procedures are likely aiming for a different collection of badges. Neither collection is inherently better or worse—they just have very different implications for how someone leads their life and where they invest their personal resources.

"That's why, ultimately, a mismatch with a role model will lead to frustration in one of two forms: you feel inadequate because you're not living up to the model image; or you live up to the image and come home each night laden with a sense of personal or professional dissatisfaction."

Howard paused to hand his empty soda can to the flight attendant; then, with a much more serious tone in his voice, he said, "People are so different that it takes a lot of work to identify another person who really, truly is a model. Even when, superficially, we think it's a clear match." It was evident that he was thinking back on a difficult experience of his own. "During my first stint teaching at Harvard, I discovered that many of the senior faculty members didn't value the same things professionally that I did. At first I thought, 'How can that be? Aren't we all here for the same general reasons?' But it became clear that the answer was no."

"Where was the disconnect?" I asked.

"There were two main problems for me. First, my colleagues were very focused on educating business managers, and few saw value in the field that really interested me—entrepreneurship. Many tried to dissuade me from pursuing it; in fact, when I wrote a teaching case study focused on a visionary entrepreneur, they said I'd set case writing back twenty years." He chuckled ruefully. "Second, many of them weren't open to new ideas—which to me is what education should be all about—and had very different perspectives on what it meant to be a good teacher. Frankly, a lot of them were bored by doing the same thing, year after year.

"At some point, I got it: the people I hoped to emulate didn't want the same things I did. They defined success differently, and on top of that they weren't very happy. That's why I resigned from Harvard and was sure I would never return. It was hard to find the 'me' in that environment. I was convinced that the whole 'HBS professor role model' was inherently wrong for me, because the individuals I was observing weren't models I wanted."

When Howard first told me about this period in his life, when he was a young professor looking to establish himself, I was stunned by both his decision to quit Harvard and the courage it took to do it. University professors around the world dream of teaching at Harvard. For him to just walk away from HBS at the age of thirty-six—to decline an offer of full tenure and lifetime employment, which is what he did—was unheard of. But eventually, I realized that it was the only thing he could have done; that for him it was a relatively straightforward decision. The people around him weren't interested in the same merit badges. As a result, they didn't fit his vision of who he wanted to be. He had developed—far earlier in life than most of us—a picture of what he wanted his legacy to be; and at that point, he just couldn't envision HBS helping him achieve it. As it turned out, Howard's departure was a harbinger of change at the school. Within a few years, a new dean brought a fresh perspective on the role of the faculty, and HBS evolved in significant ways. Howard—a natural teacher—was lured back and asked to create the school's entrepreneurship program. In time, he found a new crop of colleagues and came to see several of them as role models, each in his or her focused aspect.

"And that leads me to my final thought on this topic—for today, anyway," he said. "It is a highly ironic point, given that I've spent this entire flight pontificating about my life and the way I've chosen and used role models. Ready? Here it is," he said with mock gravity and self-importance. "Listen respectfully to your role models, but don't believe everything you hear."

I laughed out loud, startling the woman across the aisle. "Yes, O Great One," I replied to Howard. "Tell me more and I will surely doubt all that you say." It was his turn to incur the woman's ire with his laughter.

"Most people, when looking back, overemphasize the intentionality of their lives and careers," he began. "Someone sits at their feet, stares up adoringly, and says, 'Tell us how you did it all.' And the role model says, 'Well, I started at A and knew I wanted to get to Z, and each step in between was clear, synchronized, and fluid.'

"They're sincere in recalling it that way—usually, anyway— but subconsciously they've polished off the rough edges, glossed over the places where they stumbled, and played up the level of confidence and certainty they felt at each step. The real story might be that, yes, they started at A and ended at Z—but perhaps it took a long time to realize that Z was where they were headed, and maybe they didn't actually go in alpha order, or even had to take a few backward steps along the way. . . . You get the idea."

"I do, and it goes back to your first point," I said. "Role models are stories that we tell ourselves to help us understand who we are, where we're going, and how best to get there. Ultimately, we've got to decide how to connect those stories to the real world we encounter every day."

"Just so." He nodded. "By all means, seek out people whom you want to be like, whose paths seem well worth following. But take the time to understand their goals—now and at the inflection points that brought them to be the person so interesting to you. Don't presume that the success you see in them is unalloyed. And by all means, don't buy anyone's cookie cutter."

NANCY G. BRINKER

Eric Brinker and I have been friends for more than fifteen years—since his first job out of college, working for me in a big corporate conglomerate. Throughout that time, one of the things I've marveled at is his composure: although he's the son of a hugely successful businessman father and a famous mother, Eric is one of the most grounded and balanced guys I know. He's hardworking, innovative, and loyal to family and friends. Meeting him, your reaction is simply, "That's a nice guy."

Despite my long friendship with Eric, it was only quite recently that I had a chance to talk face-to-face with his mom, Ambassador Nancy Brinker. Frankly, going into that first conversation, I wasn't completely sure what kind of person to expect. On the one hand, I assumed that the apple doesn't fall far from the tree. On the other, I knew that Nancy was a determined, high-profile woman whose name and accomplishments were recognized and lauded around the world. President Barack Obama, for example, described her as "a catalyst to ease suffering in the world" as he awarded her the Presidential Medal of Freedom a few years ago; and *Time* magazine named her among the one hundred most influential people in the world. As I'd learned from experiences throughout my career, great accomplishment and humility don't always go together.

The reality, however, is that I found Nancy Brinker to be a generous, modest, and reserved person. Before I could even thank her for making time to see me, she started our conversation by saying how happy *she* was to meet *me,* an old friend of her son's. Then, as we settled down to talk about Howard and this book, she said, sincerely, "I'm not quite sure why you want to have me in your book. I'm not smart like a Harvard professor. Do you know that I had the lowest SAT scores in the entire state of Illinois? And I had to work very hard to earn good grades in high school. In fact, my ninety-two-year-old mother still jokes that all these big universities giving me honorary degrees now would never have accepted me for college," she said, laughing. "But I'm happy to help if I can."

Her protests aside, Nancy is *very* smart and she quickly understood why I wanted to talk with her: because, even without meaning to, she has become a role model for many, many people.

"I do think that role models are very important in a person's life—they certainly have been for me," Nancy recalled. "I've been able to look up to a long line of exemplary women in my family, women who were really engaged in helping their communities." Her grandmother, an immigrant from Germany, helped start the first Red Cross chapter in Peoria, Illinois. Her mother helped found the area's first Girl Scout camp and was passionately committed to the idea that those who do well have an obligation to do good. "When I was a kid, she would frequently go through our clothes closets, and anything we hadn't worn in the last month she donated to a local charity—whether we wanted to give it away or not. If we weren't going to use it, she believed, it should go to someone who would."

That sense of commitment to community was carried on by Nancy's older sister, Susan. "She was the world's best volunteer, and cared deeply about other people," Nancy remembered.

Susan's battle with breast cancer—and, ultimately, her death from the disease at age thirty-six, in 1980—created a huge inflection point for her younger sister. The inflection point took the form of Nancy's promise to Susan to find a way to beat breast cancer and spare other women the physically and emotionally painful experience Susan had gone through. To fulfill the promise, Nancy created Susan G. Komen for the Cure, one of the leading organizations fighting breast cancer around the world; and that inflection point has defined, clearly and powerfully, the path Nancy has taken over the last three decades. (That path—the story of the promise and of the building of Susan G. Komen for the Cure—is detailed in Nancy's 2010 book, *Promise Me*.)

Nancy has invested enormous passion, energy, intelligence, and determination in making Komen a powerful engine for advancing science, medicine, and public health. Since its founding, the organization has funded an estimated $2 billion in breast cancer research, education, screening, and treatment programs. It's helping women (and men) in fifty countries. And its signature event, the Susan G. Komen Race for the Cure, draws supporters from across the globe—growing from 800 participants in 1983 to more than 1.5 million today.

"I feel a little uncomfortable when people talk about how I'm so broadly known and admired—how they see me as a role model. It's definitely not something I've aimed for," she explained. "Believe me, celebrity has never been a goal, and I share many of Howard's concerns about celebrity culture. However, I am a very pragmatic person. Being well known and respected is a powerful tool, and I willingly use that tool to achieve my ultimate goal: overcoming breast cancer as a threat to the lives of millions of women around the world."

Still, she recognizes that not everyone who admires her will be motivated by the same goal; and not everyone who shares her goal will admire her. She knows that each person will take on the challenge that most stirs her or his passions. So I asked her to generalize a bit, to talk about the qualities or ideas that she most hoped people would see her modeling. A woman of Nancy's breadth and experience—from daughter, sister, wife, and mother to businesswoman, diplomat, author, foundation executive, and evangelist for biomedical research—has many lessons to share. Three of her thoughts particularly struck me, perhaps because they resonated with ideas Howard and I had discussed.

"Mary Lasker—the great New York philanthropist—was an important role model for me in building Komen," Nancy recalled. "I got to know her late in her life, when she was this wise and experienced older woman. I marveled at how she was able to build a coalition of supporters. She helped me recognize that real change requires creating a critical mass of people moving in the same direction. I came to understand that if you want to tackle big problems, you've got to be willing to set ambitious goals, establish real and innovative collaborations, and make mutual commitments and be accountable for fulfilling those commitments. When you have those things, you can create what I call a culture of 'extreme entrepreneurism'—where people trust each other and have the confidence to take risks and make mistakes on the way to making important advancements."

When it comes to those driving those advancements, "I am a great believer in the power of evolutionary growth and sustainable change—in the benefit of sticking with things, even when they're tough, if you know they are right," Nancy explained. "Things that happen overnight usually lack depth and staying power. Big wins are not the only measure of success. In many situations—biomedical research being a perfect example—the biggest win can come from putting the smallest piece of the puzzle into place. I like to tell people that at Komen we create activists one person, one community, one state, one nation at a time."

And, like Howard, Nancy believes that you must have a clear and growing vision of who you want to be. "To me, that vision is never finished; you're never complete," she said. "You must evolve every day. Ideally, you never wholly become the person you want to be, because the world is changing ahead of you each day. So you learn to constantly embrace the new and evolve your own vision to include that new world."

CHAPTER NINE

Find Your Catalysts

*As long as I've got something to offer, I feel a sense of obligation to offer it.
And as long as I can take in new experiences and face new challenges, I'll
be able to benefit from someone who's further down a similar path.*

Do you know what a catalyst is?" Howard asked me a few
weeks after he'd recovered from his heart attack and returned to work full-time. That morning, we'd been talking
extensively about the big ideas he felt should be in this book. In
the middle of that conversation, he caught me by surprise with
this question out of left field.

I hesitated in answering, struggling to recall the definition
I'd learned in a long-ago science class (and vividly remember-
ing that my lowest grade in college was in a science class called
Physics for Poets). "Um . . . a catalyst helps make things happen,
right?" I replied.

"Technically, a catalyst kicks off or enhances a chemical reaction and, because it is unchanged, has a continuing effect. Catalysts are important in everything from digesting food to complex
chemical manufacturing processes," he continued. "In a sense,
we want this book to be a catalyst—driving a reader's thoughts,
questions, and actions on his or her life's work. But there's an
inherent problem." He paused, and I waited for him to continue, not sure if we were talking about science or careers.

"The problem with this book being a kind of career catalyst is that . . . it's a book," he said.

I must have had a blank look on my face because he laughed and asked rhetorically, "What the heck do I mean by that?" I nodded, and he elaborated. "The catalytic effect of this kind of book will come from our giving folks a new way to think about their life's work, and offering them actionable ideas for moving toward career satisfaction. Right?"

"That's my exact goal," I replied. "To suggest effective ways to combine thought and action. I'd like readers to feel that this book is like a wise, caring friend who sits down, says 'Let's figure this out together,' and offers little nudges to start the process and keep it moving—just like a catalyst."

"That sounds fantastic," Howard said, giving the table a slap. "But as close as we might come to that idea, the fact is that a book is not a human being; it's an inanimate object. We may offer a good framework for how folks can figure out the right questions to ask, the best way to get the answers, and how to act on them. Still, it's a one-way flow of information; there's no opportunity for readers to directly interact with you or me about how our ideas apply to them. Nor are we necessarily the right people to consult on their specific, unique situations, because we don't know them.

"So we've got to make clear how important it is to sit down and have real, substantive back-and-forth with flesh-and-blood people—to seek concrete and specific guidance on the questions and challenges someone's grappling with."

I got his point immediately, because flesh-and-blood catalysts have been extremely important in helping me move toward the kind of life I want: a life with meaning and achievement, and with no regrets. "The challenge, of course, is that these helpful people—these catalysts—usually don't just drop into your lap when you need them," I noted. "In fact, you may not realize you need them until after an inflection point has come and gone.

You've got to consciously and proactively create a team around you; a group of people who are invested in your success."

"That's exactly the message we should convey," he said. "And I know exactly where we should start."

In addition to having a doctorate from Harvard, Howard is a pretty cultured guy. He collects art from around the globe and loves classical music. He reads endlessly, especially history, political affairs, and science. In fact, his favorite book may be Richard Dawkins's *The Selfish Gene,* which explores the notion of cooperation and collaboration as a genetically based predisposition. My cultural interests are more modest: I tend to read mostly business-oriented books; I like a good Broadway show; and my kids make sure that tunes inspired by Sandra Boynton's "Philadelphia Chickens" is the music heard most often in our home. As a result, Howard will periodically tweak me good-naturedly about cultural touchstones I don't recognize.

For example, I knew that the word *mentor* is both a noun (as in, "She's been a mentor throughout my career") and a verb (as in, "I've been asked to mentor a young analyst in our office")—but I didn't know where the word came from.

"It originated as the name of a specific person," Howard patiently explained one day, "a guy named Mentor, who is a character in Homer's ancient Greek tale *The Odyssey.* Mentor was an older man who guided and watched over the young son of the great King Odysseus—the guy who journeyed off to the Trojan War and had a hell of a time getting home again. In our times, the word *mentor* has come to mean a wise adviser and counselor, someone who offers guidance and insight to less experienced women and men."

But Howard believes the concept of the mentor has come to be misunderstood and undervalued—in a practical sense—by many people grappling with challenges in their life's work.

"And that's really unfortunate," he observed as we found ourselves on the topic one day. "There is often no more effective way to get information you don't have, work through problems you're not sure how to solve, recognize capacities you should build on, or find the best path to the place you're hoping to go than consulting a mentor."

"Why do you say that mentors are misunderstood and undervalued?" I asked him.

"For a few reasons," he replied. "First, a lot of people simply are disinclined to accept advice. For younger folks, it's just a natural tendency to reject what's come before. For highly competitive people, there's often a pride issue: they feel that asking for guidance shows a weakness. And, as you've heard me say before, really smart people are vulnerable to thinking they're equally smart in everything. Finally, there are folks who believe that if something isn't experienced directly, it doesn't count. But the bottom line is the same for all of them: they don't take advantage of a deep, abundant resource that could supplement their own intellectual and emotional energies.

"Second, our hyperlinked society makes it easy to overlook the benefits of getting knowledgeable, one-on-one personal guidance based on another person's concrete experience. In celebrating the world of information at our fingertips, we forget that information and real knowledge are very different things.

"And third, many people undervalue mentors because of the simplistic form of mentoring that pervades many workplaces today," he explained. "Almost every organization of consequence has some kind of program it calls 'mentoring,' whether to help acclimate new staff, coach rising stars, or provide a neutral sounding board for newly promoted executives. And I applaud the intent. But there are effective ways and ineffective ways to go about it—and most of the examples I've seen are simply not effective.

"The intent is noble, but the execution is weak," I suggested.

"Well put," he replied. "The wrong way—the pervasive way—is to throw mentors and mentees together based on superficial commonalities of their work and their relative places on the career ladder. It works in a narrow sense: any experienced industrial chemist is going to have valuable guidance for the young PhD adjusting to a business environment; and a veteran sports reporter will be able to teach a younger colleague how to get surly professional ballplayers to talk. But that narrow view ignores the broader, deeper contexts in which mentors can add value.

"Mentors—true, effective mentors—can't just be assigned based on a formula," Howard said emphatically. "There has to be more to it than just one person having relevant experience or deeper technical knowledge. And it's because so many organizations overlook this point that mentoring programs have middling success. They pair two people who may have superficial similarities but not necessarily a deeper affinity on goals, values, and priorities—on the fundamental things that underpin career satisfaction." He shook his head in wonder. "In that kind of situation, of course both parties are going to walk away feeling there's not much long-term value in this mentoring thing."

To make a mentoring relationship work, Howard explained, "there needs to be a fit between a mentor and mentee, because this is first and foremost a relationship between two human beings."

Fixing the state of corporate staff-development programs was not what Howard was aiming at in our conversation (although I'm sure he'd be happy to take on that subject with a group of HR executives some time). He believes that mentors can be powerfully beneficial—can be catalysts in your life's work—and that folks need to be proactive in identifying and cultivating their mentors. So I asked the practical question I knew he was working toward: "If we can't rely solely on formal mentoring programs, how do people develop their own really meaningful mentor relationships?"

"To begin with, we've got to step back and clear up one other common misunderstanding: mentors and role models are two very different things, and to confuse them—as many people do—is to court disappointment," Howard pointed out. "A role model may also happen to be a mentor, but they're not synonymous; they serve separate purposes and interact with you in different ways. A role model is an image that you'd like to emulate—you don't even need to have a direct relationship with someone you view as a role model. On the other hand, a mentor is someone who'll engage with you. It's someone who'll grab a shovel and dig into the complex causes and effects of events around you, helping you understand the consequences of your actions and choices."

"In other words," I suggested, "a mentor is invested in your life's work."

"That's a great way of putting the distinction between mentors and role models," Howard said. "But we need to make another distinction as well, because there are two different lenses to use in determining what you're actually looking for in a mentor. There are career mentors, who focus on helping you with the more tactical aspects of your career, whether in the short term at a specific organization or over an extended period and across employers. And there are legacy mentors, who bring a broader and more comprehensive perspective to the table, looking at your career in the context of your life. In my experience, most people who seek mentors focus on the career aspect—not recognizing the value of getting guidance and feedback on the big picture in which their career fits.

"Of course there's a certain amount of overlap in the two perspectives; however, it's a mistake to assume they are the same.

It's also a bad idea to expect that any one person is well prepared to offer both kinds of mentorship. Not everyone can see
you clearly through both lenses," he noted.

"Although," I interjected with mock seriousness, "I must say
that as a mentor for me you've been uncommonly bifocal."

"Be that as it may," he said, laughing at the pun and waving
away my compliment, "it's essential to be clear about the lens
you're using when seeking mentors—clear for yourself, so you
get the advice you need, and clear for the person whom you're
seeking as a mentor."

"Okay, then talk to me a little more about the focus that a
career mentor will have compared to a legacy mentor," I encouraged.

He thought about it for a moment, then laid out his view of
the two roles. The career mentor's focus, he explained, is more
short term and tactical—narrowly focused on your current job
and your anticipated professional track in coming years. Thus, a
career mentor will help you better understand two broad sets of
information.

The first concerns your context and path: how your goals and
interests fit within your current organization's mission, strategy, and culture and within those of your broader profession. A
career mentor can help you consider the best routes for moving
toward your near- and midterm career goals, and how to choose
among those routes. As you move along your chosen path, he
or she can help identify and develop responses to roadblocks
you encounter, and create strategies for skirting similar hurdles
down the road. Often, this mentor will know the inner workings of your employer—where the land mines are buried, and
which people to avoid and which to emulate. A career mentor
can also help assess whether you're advancing on your path at
an effective pace and if you're getting full value from each step
on that path. "In other words," Howard quipped, "a good career mentor will put your feet to the fire and ask, 'Over the last

year, have you gotten twelve months' experience or one month's experience repeated twelve times?'"

The second information set, Howard explained, concerns your competitive advantages and disadvantages. A career mentor can help you assess how well your skills and abilities match up with your goals within your existing professional context and can serve as an honest sounding board, providing feedback about how powerful your competitive advantages really are. With that information in hand, you can consider how best to leverage your strengths into sets of broader—and more powerful—capacities. "As important," Howard emphasized, "a good career mentor will also tell you whether you're cheating at solitaire on essential capacities for success on your chosen path."

Once I'd absorbed those ideas, we discussed the role of a legacy mentor. "These are folks who focus less on your individual career moves and competitive advantages, than on the overall pattern of your life's work," Howard said. "The fancy word for this overarching view is 'gestalt'—seeing your life's work as more than just a collection of individual facets labeled 'job,' 'career,' 'family,' and 'everything else.'" Thus, he explained, the kind of questions you'd consider with a legacy mentor are integrative ones. Many of them will be intuitive, like "How does my current job fit into the context of my legacy vision? Which path will maximize my chances of realizing that overall vision? And is there a more effective way for me to juggle competing goals or to sequence them in a manner that gives me a better chance of accomplishing them?'

"But a really good legacy mentor," Howard said, "will also ask some less intuitive questions, like, 'Is there a disconnect between the things that come most easily to you and the things that would bring you the most long-term satisfaction?' Or, in other words, 'Would leveraging particular strengths and competitive advantages actually move you away from your legacy vision?' Those unexpected questions are often the most important ones."

And legacy mentors are especially helpful when you're trying to respond to an inflection point, Howard pointed out. "There's nothing like having an experienced pair of eyes to help define a situation, parse out its short- and long-term implications, and develop a strategy for responding."

Clearly, Howard and I both feel deeply about the value of mentors. So as we sat in his office one rainy autumn day, I made a point of coming back to the topic and we talked about three important nuances he wanted to tease out.

"First, when I said that there needs to be a fit between mentor and mentee, I wasn't suggesting that it needs to be a hand-in-glove fit," he explained. "In fact, too much similarity could actually be counterproductive, since you want someone who can add to your perspective. So you shouldn't necessarily be seeking a mentor who is exactly your vision of the person you want to be in ten years.

"In this respect, a mentor doesn't need to have the exact same goals as yours; doesn't have to look or act like you; doesn't have to be the same race, religion, or personality type. Rather, you should look for a mentor with several fundamental characteristics," he said, ticking them off on his fingers. "Experience and insight to ask the right questions. Sincerity and genuine interest in your answers and the process you go through to get those answers. Ability to give objective, actionable, and constructive feedback. And, underpinning it all, willingness to invest time in understanding your values and your vision. When those four elements are present," he said, intertwining the fingers of his hands, "you'll find there's a natural fit—a personal chemistry that has a catalytic effect."

Howard's second nuance wasn't actually about the mentor; it was about the mentee. "You can't be passive. Good, effective mentors don't just come to you unbidden. You need to put real thought into what kind of person you're seeking and where you might find him or her. Then invest time and energy into building and maintaining those relationships."

"Based on my own experience," I offered, "I'd also say, don't be shy about asking for guidance from someone higher up the food chain. Too many people think, 'Why would the higher-ups be interested in me?' But that's where you'll find the richest veins of knowledge, experience, and broader perspective. And I've found that even if they don't get a substantive response, few people hurt themselves simply by reaching out for advice and to establish a relationship. I mean, I wouldn't suggest that a junior field adjuster jump through seven layers of management to cultivate the senior vice president for underwriting as a mentor. But seeking out a mentor a level or two above you in an organization's hierarchy is completely appropriate."

"That actually leads perfectly to the third nuance I want to offer," Howard replied. "There are any number of reasons that people become mentors. The core reason that I am a mentor for up-and-coming people is because I feel an obligation to give back. I think that giving money to a charity is one thing—and hugely important—but I believe that giving time and true care to those who come after you is the biggest contribution you can make.

"But that said, mentoring is not a one-way street. While the mentee clearly is getting the greater benefit, there needs to be some kind of personal value flowing the other way, too—a return of the sincerity, interest, and concern that the mentor offers. And a person who's serious about cultivating good mentors would do well to understand this."

"That's interesting," I said. "What's the value that you personally get from being a mentor—beyond the satisfaction of giving back?"

He thought about that a bit, smiled, and said, "There's certainly an intellectual value I get: an offering of new ideas in return, as well as the data from what you might call the 'field testing' of the ideas I offer. At the most basic level, the return I hope to get is an element of fun and energy from interacting with folks who aren't part of my day-to-day routine. It keeps me young and in tune with what's new in the world—which is a great help in trying to keep up with my kids and grandkids!"

I laughed when he said that, recalling that it was through a mentee that Howard learned about the wonders of his iPhone and iPad. And I vividly remembered the day that he "friended" me on Facebook, after a mentee helped him create an account.

Howard has been an amazing mentor for me. But I haven't let that stop me from building strong mentoring relationships with several other people who have been able and willing to provide valuable guidance. I believe that the only limit on how many mentors you have is the amount of time and energy you can invest in building and maintaining each relationship.

Kirk Posmantur, my business partner at Axcess, has been an incredible career mentor for me. What's interesting is how his mentoring role has evolved over the nearly twenty years I've known him. It started with me interning for him during my second year of college and continued early in my career, when he hired me to work for him in an interesting little corner of corporate America. His mentorship continued even as I explored other companies and fields after we both left that particular company. And it took another turn when we launched our own company, something we had spoken about almost since the time we first met. Today, although we are professional peers and dear friends, he is still a mentor, because I continue to learn from him. Interestingly, though, he's also learning a few things from me, too.

My relationship with Kirk demonstrates the idea that what you need from mentors evolves as you move through different stages of career and life. I've seen that play out in my relationship with Howard, too. When I was just out of graduate school, his career mentorship was hugely important and influential, especially during my time as a fund-raiser for Harvard. As the years have passed and my career has followed a new path, Howard's role as a career mentor has changed. Others are equally influential because they have deeper experience in my field than does Howard.

If Howard's career mentorship for me has decreased, his place as a legacy mentor is, if anything, more important. His observations on the complex challenges of running a business while raising a family while trying to maintain far-flung friendships while trying to be part of a community are amazing, and . . . well, let's just say that I steal a lot from the Stevenson playbook.

These evolving relationships with my own mentors represent just one arc of the mentoring circle. As I develop a body of experience that others find valuable, I get calls from people wanting guidance and advice. With some of those people—where I find a good fit—I make a conscious decision to continue the relationship, to become a mentor. Why do I spend the time? Why on a Saturday afternoon do I take a call from a young executive or give up a night with the family to speak to a college class? In part because it fulfills a sense of obligation to repay the debt I incurred with the people who did it for me, like Howard, Kirk, Chip Conley, Andrew Tisch, and many others. But I also know that there will be value coming back at me from the effort. In fact, one of the coolest things I've observed is that mentoring can become a continuous, multigenerational cycle; and multiple streams of mentoring relationships can intersect and be mutually reinforcing and beneficial.

I happen to be an intersecting point for a number of mentoring cycles that grew out of my experiences at Cornell, Harvard, and my previous jobs. One of those cycles involves at least four mentoring generations: Kirk mentored me early in my career.

Subsequently, I mentored Eric Brinker, now an Ohio-based entrepreneur who worked for me right out of college. A few years later, when "Brink" helped drive the marketing program for a new company called JetBlue, he mentored Brett Muney, whom Kirk and I hired years later based on Brink's recommendation. . . . And on it goes. I have no doubt that Brett will build on this mentoring cycle, and that he, Eric, Kirk, and I will all have gained intellectual, emotional, and practical benefits from the seeds each of us has planted.

I won't even begin to count the generations of planting and harvesting—and the untold benefits to thousands of people—for which Howard's mentoring has been the catalyst. Nor, I think, would he. That's because he views mentoring in the light of the biblical passage "Cast your bread upon the waters, for it will surely return to you." There's no reason to keep track of numbers when you're part of a continuous catalytic process.

Howard also would not keep count because he's not done, either as a mentor or as a mentee. "As long as I've got something to offer, I feel a sense of obligation to offer it," he told me soon after his retirement. "And as long as I can take in new experiences and face new challenges, I'll be able to benefit from someone who's further down a similar path."

RACHEL JACOBSON

Say the words *National Basketball Association* to the average person and here's an image that assuredly *won't* come to mind: a five-foot woman who totes around pictures of her twin toddlers. Nevertheless, my old college friend Rachel Jacobson is one of the most important people in the NBA. She doesn't play the game—she helps run the game.

Rachel is the NBA's senior vice president for marketing partnerships. Overseeing major sponsorship programs for the NBA and the WNBA, she's helped create some of the organizations' most important business and community relationships. Those include corporate partnerships with companies like Sony, T-Mobile, Foot Locker, Sanofi, and Under Armour—as well as many other groundbreaking partnerships in sports and entertainment. Just as important to Rachel, she's developed a series of major community-service collaborations with organizations like the American Red Cross, UNICEF, and nonprofit agencies in NBA cities. Most of these collaborations focus on keeping kids healthy through initiatives to combat conditions like asthma and diabetes and to prevent the spread of communicable diseases like meningitis and influenza.

But when I asked her to drop by my office recently, it wasn't to talk about the things she's doing in the world of professional basketball. (And it wasn't to look at pictures of her amazingly cute kids, although that's inevitably how we spent the first few minutes.) I wanted to learn more about a different kind of professional organization that she's been involved with for the past few years: a top-notch leadership training and mentoring program called W.O.M.E.N. in America. Rachel was part of the program's first cohort of mentees and is now "paying it forward" by helping other young professional women advance their careers. In other words—in sports-speak—she's helping other women get into the game and make it to the big leagues.

"W.O.M.E.N. in America was created about four years ago by a handful of accomplished female executives who met at the 2008 Fortune Most Powerful Women Summit," Rachel told me. "These were women like Ursula Burns, CEO of Xerox; Joan Amble, formerly a top executive at both American Express and GE Capital Services; Linda L. Addison, partner in charge at Fulbright & Jaworski; and one of my mentors, Carol Hochman, former CEO of Danskin. The mission they took on was to help women fulfill their highest potential, by providing an early-career "leg up"—through focused mentoring, sharpening of leadership skills, and the development of a cohort of professional colleagues who could provide support over the long term. Their goal has been to enable more women to fulfill their potential in the boardroom, as senior executives and as entrepreneurs starting new businesses—as leaders in whatever profession they choose."

A select group of twenty-five young "rising stars" is chosen to participate in the three-year program, Rachel explained. There are classes, meetings, workshops—a complete, defined curriculum that provides both content knowledge about professional fields and practical tips on managing day-to-day challenges in the workplace. "But the real catalyst in the program is the one-on-one mentoring relationship," Rachel noted. "Each person is assigned a dedicated mentor; someone who has reached the top of her profession; someone who has a real affinity for her mentee. We meet with our mentors every six to eight weeks. And it's in those conversations where the rubber really meets the road, because these women have been where we want to go. They've dealt with the challenges, sometimes well, sometimes not—but, in either case, they've come through, they've overcome. They are fabulous guides for those of us hitting the same challenges for the first time."

Each mentee in the program also becomes part of a cohort of eight or nine women who are interested in a similar professional niche—business and marketing, the public sector, or science and technology. "One of the pleasant surprises has been how close many of us have become through this process," Rachel noted, "not just as professional colleagues, but as good friends who have developed into a really close mutual-support network."

Why is a program like this so important for young, ambitious women? I asked Rachel. Hasn't the glass ceiling finally shattered?

"You know, Eric, I'd like to think that it has, and there certainly are a lot of cracks and some big holes in that ceiling. But it's still there in many, many organizations. Beyond that, there's the simple fact that in our society and others, the dynamics of family and marriage haven't fully adapted to the idea of powerful, accomplished women.

"For that reason, the mentoring program addresses a pretty wide range of 'hard' and 'soft' subjects. There are lots of discussions on practical issues, like how to handle business setbacks or the most effective way to drive a strategic planning process. Then there are questions that shade more toward interpersonal challenges: How do you deal with serious conflict between you and another executive? How do you negotiate through different visions of corporate mission?

"Finally, there are the hard personal questions: How do you handle the inevitably tough choices in balancing career and personal life? How do you handle some of the hard realities of marriage—like having two high-powered professionals in the marriage or a situation where the wife is more professionally successful than her husband?

"One of the things that's become clear to me over the

last few years is how important these subjects are for a large number of women," she observed.

Rachel and I go back a long way, so I knew I could ask her the tough question that was rattling around in my head. "This kind of program is fantastic for the very select group of women who get chosen every three years," I said, "but what if you're not one of the twenty-five?"

"Look, there's no question, W.O.M.E.N. in America can't single-handedly solve the problems that women face in fulfilling their professional potential," she replied, "and the organization's founders were under no illusion that it might. But I believe it has the potential to help change the landscape for an increasing number of women in both the business and public sectors. This organization can be a model for others around the country—around the world, in fact.

"And each of us who benefits from the program can become a catalyst. That's part of our responsibility as we graduate from mentees to mentors ourselves: helping to nurture succeeding generations and expanding groups of women who have the talent and the ambition to reach the top of their professions."

(If you're interested in seeing who's involved in W.O.M.E.N. in America and learning how its mentoring program works, you can check it out at www.wom eninamerica.net.)

CHAPTER TEN

Catalysts, Part Two: Rise of the IBOD

When you're stuck in a deep hole, you don't need a bunch of people debating how to get you out; you want someone to jump in with you and say, "I've been here before, and together we'll find the way out."

IF YOU GO TO DICTIONARY.COM and type in "catalyst," first you get a couple of scientific definitions. Then you get these two: "a person or thing that precipitates an event or change" and "a person whose talk, enthusiasm, or energy causes others to be more friendly, enthusiastic, or energetic."

Reading those definitions helped me understand a phenomenon I experienced on many of my walk-and-talks with Howard. To traverse the HBS campus on my own takes maybe ten minutes. To walk the same path with Howard on a sunny day can take an hour. Not because he walks slowly—he's got a tennis player's hustle and an entrepreneur's instinct for conserving the scarce resource of time. The difference when walking with Howard is that every third person we pass wants to stop and speak with him. Sometimes it's just a student's momentary, "Hey, Professor Stevenson. How you doing?" Other times it's a two-minute dialogue that starts with, "Howard, did you see that piece in the *Journal* today?" Too often it's somebody saying, "Listen, Howard, I'm really concerned about . . ." as they draw him off to the side for an extended ad hoc consultation. That's not even mentioning the times Howard is the initiator, grabbing a passing colleague to say, "Listen, I talked to the dean about your idea; he liked it, and our next steps should be . . ."

Howard is the walking personification of a catalyst. He makes things happen just sauntering down the street, through his personality, energy, ideas, and reputation. So I am amused and fascinated when he periodically talks about how challenging it can be for him to engage with new people, to begin the process of building a relationship. I pressed him on it one day, as we drove back from a meeting where he seemed to do just fine building a rapport with two donors he hadn't met before.

"I certainly understand the importance of building connections with people in all aspects of my life's work," he explained in response. "I've worked hard and learned to do it with moderate effectiveness. But at heart, I'm a bit of an introvert. Relationship building isn't a natural strength."

When we stopped at a red light, he turned toward me and said, "You, on the other hand, get this stuff intuitively. You're very good at bringing together people who can help each other. It's an area where you have a real competitive advantage over me."

I thought about that a bit, because it would certainly be the only place where I had any kind of advantage over him. (All right, maybe on the tennis court, too, but only because my legs are thirty years younger.) He was right in the sense that building relationships and collaborative partnerships is what I do for a living. In some ways, it's easy for me; I'm a natural extrovert. "Maybe," I replied, "but I have to say, for an introverted guy who doesn't think he builds relationships naturally, you have an amazing ability to attract people. You've got constellations of fascinating people orbiting around you."

"No, you're right, being introverted does not, itself, have to be a major impediment to building relationships—especially those connected to one's career. We introverts just have to devote more energy, and approach the task in a more focused way.

But, believe me, I'm not aiming for constellations in my orbit. The real value, for me, doesn't come in the quantity of my interactions with people. A few good friends and advisers are worth their weight in gold."

He stopped to think, seeking just the right metaphor to illustrate his point. "When you're stuck in a deep hole, you don't need a bunch of people debating how to get you out; you want someone to jump in with you and say, 'I've been here before, and together we'll find the way out.'"

"In other words," I said, picking up his thought, "the point is not how many people you've got milling around you, it's whether you have the *right* people around you. The ones with the perspective, experience, and expertise you need to help navigate past the challenges and setbacks you encounter."

"Yes, but having the right mix of people around you is important not just when you hit those tough points—when you're stuck in that deep hole—it's important day to day, too," he replied. "We all have natural blinders about our strengths and weaknesses; and we get so focused on tactical stuff that we miss the big picture. Nor are any of us as effective problem solvers as we think, because we're psychologically hardwired to focus on information that reinforces our previous decisions." He chuckled at a thought. "It's hard to see the whole chessboard when you're one of the pieces. That's why, in all these situations and more, we need others' views to help us see more clearly."

When we pulled into his driveway at home he said, "Come on in. I'll pour you a cold drink and we'll talk a little more." We went in and settled down at the kitchen table, I with an iced tea and Howard with a Diet Coke.

"We've talked a lot about mentors," Howard began, "but when I suggested that folks need to have flesh-and-blood catalysts in their lives, I obviously wasn't thinking *only* of mentors. You need a multifaceted web of people who connect with you in a variety of meaningful ways—a personal support system comprised of people who, individually and collectively, can help you define, pursue, and succeed in your life's work."

"Great," I said, grabbing a pad of paper from my briefcase. "Let's drill down on this a little."

"Not so fast," he said, giving me a Yoda-like smirk and sliding the pad of paper over to his side of the table. "This is a place where your thoughts are going to be especially relevant—perhaps more than mine." He put down his drink, took out a pen, and said, "So now it's your turn: start talking."

A couple of years ago, I went to a fancy event in Manhattan—a hospitality industry awards gala. Although I am passionate in my involvement in the hospitality and travel industries, I hadn't made many such events recently. So, when my schedule opened up for that evening, I decided to attend the gala.

Entering the majestic ballroom of the Waldorf-Astoria hotel, I saw beautifully arrayed buffet tables, well-stocked bars, and hundreds of people engrossed in the kind of business/social event that occurs every night in cities around the world. Ten or fifteen years ago I would have felt right in my element: adrenaline flowing and eager to make new contacts and build my professional network, I would have been one of the most active people in the room—hand extended, business cards at the ready, looking for new faces. This night, however, was different: I found myself looking for familiar faces; and within half an hour of arriving, I was feeling uncomfortable. I couldn't pin down why.

The reason became clear when Alexandra, who was a year behind me at Cornell, came over with a hearty, "Well, look who's here," shook my hand, and asked what I'd been up to recently. Barely thirty seconds into our conversation, her eyes started straying over my shoulder—she was already searching for the next person to connect with, the next node for her ever-expanding network of contacts. That's when the light went off in my head, when I understood the discomfort I'd felt increasingly at these kinds of events over the past few years. These weren't the kind of connections I wanted to pursue. These transactional, superficial "networking" interactions were not how I wanted to relate to people—personally or professionally. Soon, Alexandra headed off to corral an old classmate of hers, leaving in her wake an inauthentic promise to call to make a lunch date.

At that moment, I was pleasantly surprised to see my friend Christian Hempell across the room. He was standing in a group of people and had a kind of glazed look on his face. I walked toward him, caught his eye, and mimed, "Let's get outta here!" He nodded enthusiastically, and a couple minutes later we both scooted out of the Waldorf-Astoria in search of a local bar. I hadn't seen Christian face-to-face for months, and it was great to catch up with him. Eventually, we got to talking about why the gala had been so painful for both of us.

"As I've gotten older, I've realized how important it is to nurture my relationships with a core group of people—those in my work and private lives whom I care about and who reciprocate that feeling," Christian observed. "I remember, early in my career, my boss told me, 'I don't really need more contacts, more acquaintances; I can manufacture those. What I need is to connect more and better with the people who are at the core of my life and work.' I didn't fully understand him then. How could knowing more people be a bad thing? But now I understand that the time and energy involved in broadening my 'contacts' returns far less value than the same effort put into deepening key relationships. . . . We need to invest in relationships we care about. And that's not what these big networking events are for."

* * *

To understand why that story came immediately to mind, I
refer you to two definitions: "network" is a mechanism for providing information and services among a group of people, "relationship" is an emotional connection or involvement between
individuals. The difference between those two definitions is
significant. So, too, are the practical distinctions between the
terms "networking" and "relationship building." Far too many
people get the two confused, and I think that's more than just
a semantic mix-up. It's actually a big problem. And when
Howard told me to start talking about catalysts, he knew that's
where I'd focus.

Ask the average person about their "network" and they'll
likely tell you how many people they have in their Contacts list,
how many connections they have on LinkedIn, or how many
Facebook "friends" they have. Which is fine, because these and
myriad other digital connectors are highly efficient mechanisms
for putting you in touch with others. At the same time, however, most people's networks are impersonal, built around individuals whom they interact with briefly and infrequently—who
are usually acquaintances at best. (And that applies even if the
first introduction comes face-to-face at some networking event,
like the gala I attended.) The participants in this kind of network may or may not call you back when you need to hear from
them. Why? Because likely as not, they're not people who really
care about you as an individual. (As Howard once advised a colleague of mine: "Don't confuse acquaintances with friends, or
networking with knowledge.")

Don't mistake me: business networks are important tools.
Studies of successful people in all lines of work consistently
show that the wider a person's connections, the more effective
she is—especially when those connections represent a broad
diversity in background, capacities, and perspective. It is invaluable to be able to pick up the phone and call exactly the

right person to answer a question, handle an important task, or help solve a specific problem.

But the catalysts for your life's work will have a whole different level of engagement with you—one with a depth and value that aren't possible through networking, digital or personal. In that regard, what we're talking about is kind of the anti-Facebook: not an endlessly expanding mesh of connections from everyone to everyone else, but a carefully defined and deliberately constructed spiderweb where all the lines radiate from a central point—you. At the other end of those lines are a handful of people who are invested in your success and willing to commit time and energy on your behalf. They should be people who understand you as a professional and a human being and want to help you advance your life's work. People ready and able to provide support on issues large and small, from major inflection points to small juggling-and-balancing choices; on matters of career or family, of finance or philosophy.

"These are the folks who walk in your door when everyone else is walking out," Howard likes to say. "Folks who'll tell you the truth and hold you accountable for the choices you make."

You should have a conscious, deliberate approach to creating and maintaining this team of catalysts. Why? First, because you want them to be available when you need them. Second, because you don't want to rely on the first people through the door; they may be well-intentioned but lack the particular characteristics, experiences, and perspectives you really need. You should be proactive, even assertive, in identifying your catalysts: go get the people you need!

I've done exactly this. And to help me be crystal clear about the role these folks are supposed to play, I've come up with a specific title for them: they're my Individual Board of Directors—my IBOD. (And, no, this isn't a cute play on iPod. In fact, with its emphasis on personal connection, the IBOD is the polar opposite of a passive electronic device—as wonderful as the iPod is.)

I came up with the idea of an IBOD ten or twelve years ago, when I ran into some challenging and humbling early-career experiences. They were humbling in that they made clear how much I didn't know and how difficult it could be to reconcile knowledge I did have with real-world situations that seemed to directly contradict it.

I realized that if I was going to accomplish the most important personal and career goals I had set—if I was going to reach my legacy vision—I was going to need support from people whose knowledge complemented mine and whose perspectives would allow me to see past my own blind spots. Over time, the more I thought about this imperative, the more I saw the parallels with a business's board of directors.

In creating a board of directors, a corporation will seek out people with specific capacities. Collectively, the individual directors will represent the wide range of experience, knowledge, and perspectives that the organization needs to ensure its long-term success. While they may weigh in with specific guidance on crucially important matters or at inflection points, these aren't the people who will design or implement any specific aspect of the organization's efforts. Rather, they will gauge and guide the overall quality, direction, and value of those efforts at a strategic level. And, ideally, they'll provide unvarnished and unbiased feedback.

In this same way, for my IBOD I've drawn together a handful of people who help me step back and assess how I'm doing in the most important aspects of my life's work. These folks have assisted on a range of questions, problems, and choices: interrupting my career to get a master's degree after I thought I'd never go back to school; selling my KaBloom franchises quickly and cutting my losses; devoting a big chunk of my free time to co-founding Axcess; then, later, leaving a secure job at

Harvard—mid-recession—and jumping into the company with both feet. More generally, these catalysts have supported me in being the husband and father I aspire to be while pursuing the professional achievements I seek.

On draft day in major sports, you'll often hear the question asked, "Do we take the best all-around athlete or the best person available for the position we need to fill?" In building an IBOD, you go for the latter. Instead of just taking the generally smartest or most successful people around at a given time—or a few friends and relatives easily at hand—you identify the specific capacities you want and then, over time, draft people who have them.

That's why your IBOD, if you create one, won't look like mine or anyone else's. The mix of capacities will be driven by your specific concerns, challenges, and relative weaknesses—because, fundamentally, your IBOD is compensating for the knowledge, insight, experience, and strengths that you lack. However, there should be one commonality between your IBOD and mine: each member must have your trust; must have time and energy to invest in your life's work; and must care about you, professionally and personally.

Here are several of the most important "seats" on my IBOD and the kind of people who fill them.

Subject-matter experts—people with skills I need periodically and don't have. I've mentioned before that my friendship with Vikram Mansharamani is almost as old as we are—it started in pre-school. Since then, he's earned a PhD from MIT and become a respected guru on finance and money management. While I'm more than competent with money matters (especially for a "relationship guy"), Vikram's in a whole other league. In fact he's a major-league switch-hitter: superb at macroeconomics—he predicts movements in global financial markets, and his recent book, *Boombustology*, is based on the course he teaches at Yale—he's also translated that expertise into concrete financial advice for individuals. So Vikram is the one I call when I need unbiased, expert advice on equity positions my company secures; and he's my go-to guy when I'm making big decisions about my personal finances. Just knowing he's there—and knowing how much he knows that I don't—makes me less inclined to wing something on my own.

Travelers who've been down a path similar to mine—people who can help me anticipate problems around corners and over hills. Chip Conley, the eccentric and accomplished founder of Joie de Vivre hotels, has been a forward scout on the path I'm traveling. Like me, he opted to get off the traditional corporate ladder and instead became an entrepreneur in a relationship-building and service-oriented business. He's been a hugely successful entrepreneur for more than twenty-five years, an innovator in developing organizational culture, and a community leader and philanthropist in San Francisco. He's also had his share of disappointments and failures. Those experiences of hitting the heights and the depths, connected to his firsthand understanding of my capacities and interests—he offered me my first real job out of college—gives him a unique and valuable perspective on the professional challenges and hurdles I come across.

Spiritual and cultural connectors—people who understand my philosophical roots and can help me wrestle with spiritual challenges. The primary person filling this role on my IBOD is eighty-four-year old Henry Rosovsky, the scholar and iconic former Harvard dean, whom I've nicknamed Hawk. My relationship with him has nothing to do with my career and everything to do with my life's work. Hawk reminds me—physically and philosophically—of my grandfather, and his religious perspective and his roots in Eastern European Jewish culture help connect me to aspects of my background that are easily drowned out in my hectic life. He's got a perspective, wisdom, and depth of humanity that leaves me feeling spiritually richer every minute I spend with him. And I'm happy that every once in a while I'm able to reciprocate when he asks for my opinion about a particular company or business where I have expertise.

Personal historians—people who can offer a long perspective through shared history and experiences. While I go back a long way with both Vikram and Chip, the person who has been most continuously connected to my life's work is Phil Baugh, a Cornell classmate. Something about Phil's ability to understand me intuitively has made him the perfect counselor ever since our freshman year, when we founded a student organization together. We began our relationship working together and—in some sense—have been ever since. He's seen me mature professionally and personally, observing my reactions to situations good, bad, and indifferent for more than twenty years. As a result, he doesn't need a lot of detailed background on a situation to be able to offer substantive input. More important, he has an uncanny ability to predict what I will do—and to point out what I *should* have done when something goes off the rails. His ability to look backward with clarity is immensely helpful when I need to decide how to move forward.

Gymnastics coaches—experts in the art of juggling and balancing. Although there are many good things that Christian Hempell brings to my IBOD, I chose him for a very specific reason: he's one of the most balanced people I know, and he has a nuanced and insightful view on how to juggle the competing facets of his life. His ability to maintain a dynamic balance is due in part to his levelheaded and methodical personality. And in part it's due to his strong religious beliefs—he reads a selection from the Bible each morning. He brings an interesting mixture of pragmatism and spirituality to the difficult juggling-and-balancing choices he makes: on one hand, he knows that he's going to have to say "Nope, sorry, can't help" to someone every day; on the other hand, in thinking through the options, he often literally asks himself, "What would Jesus do?" During my family's "flat and fat" experience, when he called virtually every day to check in, I came to rely heavily on Christian's capacity for balance and his spiritual energy.

These five guys—along with Howard, who is that rare player who could play several positions on a person's team—form the core of my IBOD. It's unlikely that I'll "fire" them from the role any time soon. There are others who have seats, too, each filling a different and sometime short-term role. Why short term? Over time, as my needs change, I've taken some people off my board; sometimes they remove themselves, no longer able to offer the time or energy. It's sort of like the term limits that govern most corporate boards of directors—but, generally, I set those limits.

Unlike with a corporate board, there is never a "vote" on any issue before my IBOD. All the decisions are ultimately mine to make and to take responsibility for. Likewise, the people comprising my IBOD almost never come together as a group—most don't have any idea who the other members are—and all the consultations occur through a series of one-on-one conversations with me. (Remember: it's like a spiderweb, with me at the center.) The lack of a formal gathering makes it important that I have a disciplined, structured way to connect with them. So I keep a list of my IBOD members taped to my desk at work. And I try to touch base with them every couple of weeks, whether or not there is a specific reason—because, beyond nurturing the relationship, invariably I pick up something of value that I wasn't consciously seeking when I started the conversation.

Usually, the members of a corporate board will be investors

and will receive some kind of cash or equity compensation for their engagement. The people on my IBOD have made an investment, too—of their time, energy, thought, concern—but the return they receive is psychological and emotional, not financial. They get satisfaction from helping someone they care about and vicarious success when I succeed. (Howard describes this as natural reciprocity.)

They also get a bit of insurance: knowing that I will be there for them, ready to help in any way possible, should they ever need it. To use Howard's metaphor, they know that I'll jump into that deep hole with them, armed either with a map for the exit or a pair of sturdy shovels for us to dig ourselves out.

So I have to ask: How many of *your* LinkedIn connections and Facebook friends are ready to jump into that deep hole for you?

CARL BANKS

Back in 1988, the movie *Twins* paired tall, muscular Arnold Schwarzenegger with short, round Danny DeVito as fraternal twins who were separated at birth. The two find each other as adults, have some madcap adventures, then live happily ever after. It was kind of funny, kind of silly, light entertainment. I hadn't thought about it for years—probably not since the night I saw the movie on a date with my high school girlfriend.

But a recent conversation with former New York Giants All-Pro linebacker Carl Banks brought it back to me. Because, after talking about our careers, our business philosophies, and our goals, I was convinced that somehow we—a tall, athletic African American guy and a short, wiry Jewish guy—must share a lot of genetic material.

Like me, Carl is an entrepreneur through and through. He's the embodiment of Howard's definition of entrepreneurship: the pursuit of opportunity beyond the resources currently under one's control. Since leaving professional football in the mid-1990s, he's pursued a series of cool and interesting new business ideas—most notably, his line of sports apparel for women, GIII Sports by Carl Banks.

I assumed he'd begun his business career after retiring from the NFL, and I was surprised when he told me, "I actually started laying the groundwork for my business life after my second year in pro football. I was very interested in the apparel industry and began talking to talented people about their approach to design and marketing—really soaking up everything that I could learn from them, and identifying the kinds of people that I wanted to work with."

That explanation tipped me off to another piece of our shared genetic code: Carl's career has evolved in large part through connections to people who had aligned interests, shared values, and complementary skills and resources. Many of his business ventures today are built around collaborations and partnerships that emerged parallel to meaningful personal relationships. "Networking is fine, and I'm always happy to meet new people," he told me in one of our conversations. "But my businesses grow out of deep relationships I've developed with people who have a shared vision and similar approach to achieving that vision. To me there's a big difference between being in business with someone you are familiar with as a businessman or -woman, and having a business relationship develop with people who you know—and who know you—first as individuals.

"Friendship in business is very important to me, be-

cause I believe partners need to be authentically themselves in that relationship. There's too much at stake to
get tied up to people whose actions you can't anticipate.
You've got to know each other's strengths, values, and
goals."

"How much of that approach comes from instinct and
how much from your football experience?" I asked him.

"Some of both, I'd say. I've always naturally sought
out people to learn from and partner with. I'm also a
very analytical person and work hard at understanding
the people around me as individuals.

"But from football I learned how important it is having a group of people whose skills fit together—having
somebody's strength positioned to cover the place where
somebody else has a weakness. I learned about the need
for individual accountability to a group vision. I learned
that you need to know who you could count on in a difficult situation—plus who'd be counting on you and for
what.

"So I've been using those skills and experiences together to analyze the way that particular people—or
organizations—would interact as part of the team or
partnership. I analyze whether we can help one another
leverage our core competencies in a significant way. And
I assess where and when I need to go out and find people
who can fill holes—add a key piece of knowledge or
ability that I and my team don't already have."

"You know," I said, "I've got to introduce you to Howard Stevenson. He's more of a tennis guy than a football
guy, but in a whole lot of other ways, you two would
really click."

"I'd love that," Carl replied. "I would love to pick his
brain. And it would be interesting to talk about football
as preparation for a business career."

"Yeah, maybe business and grad schools should require that all students spend a month in an NFL summer training camp," I joked.

"Don't laugh. It's not all that far off. Professional sports helped me develop a core set of skills that I've relied on in making the transition from the field and the announcer's booth to the boardroom: a strong sense of discipline and focus, the ability to deal with adversity, the capacity to prepare for major challenges quickly and to make effective adjustments on the fly.

"You don't succeed—in football or in new business ventures—without those skills," he concluded.

I shook my head in wonder at how sharp this guy was and how much I might be able to learn from him. Then I said, only half joking, "Hey, Carl, can I draft you for my team?"

CHAPTER ELEVEN

The Calculus of Culture

*The difference between being in a culture that works for you and
one that doesn't? Well, that's like the difference between just having a job
and doing your life's work.*

THE SOUTHERN MASSACHUSETTS COASTLINE is a wonderful place to be in late summer. It's warm but kept comfortable by the ocean breeze. There's a relaxed summer culture that's an interesting mixture of year-round residents—many of whom are descended from nineteenth-century whalers and early-twentieth-century textile workers—and summer residents escaping offices in Boston, Providence, and Hartford. Despite the different backgrounds, somehow everyone blends into communities of straightforward people with few pretensions, regardless of whether they work in a shipyard or on a college campus.

When Howard and his wife, Fredi—seeing retirement not too far in the future—decided that it was time to buy a summer place, this is where they focused their attention. Of course, Howard being Howard, he couldn't just find a nice, ready-made place, buy it, and move in. That wouldn't have been any fun. Nor would it have served his very well-thought-out purposes. The property they chose had a house that needed to be expanded and have all its systems replaced; and it stood next to a big, abandoned old structure with a falling-down roof, rats, and piles of stray beer cans from long-ago teenage trysts. Nevertheless, Howard saw it all as perfect raw material for a summer home that matched his vision. And after many months of planning, project oversight, and hands-on effort, the vision was made real. The house quickly became Howard's favorite place to be.

The house is low-key and deceptively spacious—nothing like the "McMansions" that many people use to signal their financial success. Interestingly, the layout allows fluid movement from room to room, but in such a way that individual parts of the house seem like different living environments. That's deliberate, because Howard and Fredi had a specific goal in rebuilding the house. To understand that goal, you need to know that when the two married—a few years after Howard's divorce from his first wife—they created a pretty sizable blended family: Fredi had four daughters, Howard three sons. In the twenty years since, they've added daughters-in-law and sons-in-law and an expanding troop of grandkids. A full complement of family visitors on a summer weekend runs to two dozen. That doesn't include the many close friends who have open invitations to visit.

With those numbers in mind, Howard wanted to be sure there'd be plenty of beds and lots of space for the grandkids to run and play. He also wanted the visiting families to feel that they could retreat to a discrete space within the connected whole of the house—wanted to create an environment where everyone felt part of the family but could also find quiet and separation when needed. So the bedrooms are in different areas of the house, and each is connected to a quiet sitting area and close to a bathroom. They're all near the rooms where people gather—the den, the screened-in porch, the living room, the office/library that Howard and Fredi share—but they're separated. And in addition to a large open kitchen/dining room area, there is a small kitchen in another part of the house. That way, visitors have the choice of coming together for a big raucous breakfast or having a quiet cup of coffee and a bagel on their own.

Although it's funny when Howard boasts that he's tucked five dishwashers around the place (so that everyone can be self-sufficient in cleaning up after their meals), Howard is rightly proud of the house and how he's molded it to serve the connected-but-independent culture that best suits his family's visits. In essence, he's created a mutually supporting village in their home.

For many reasons, I am always happy to get an invitation to visit the Stevenson clan at this house, and I headed up there one weekend a couple of summers ago. Jennifer wasn't able to travel that weekend, but I'd had a really hectic few weeks and she encouraged me to go. I drove up on a Friday morning, getting an early start on some much-needed relaxation. Arriving at lunchtime, I had a wonderful meal with Howard and Fredi, sitting under blue skies on their patio. Immediately, I felt myself starting to unwind.

Unfortunately, my business world was not yet ready for me to relax. As we cleared away the lunch plates (placing them in dishwasher number one), my cell phone rang. I excused myself, spent fifteen minutes talking to my business partner, Kirk, about a staffing issue, then returned to the patio. Howard and I started chatting. Fredi brought out some homemade cookies and I enjoyed one as I stretched out on a lounge chair. But midway through my oatmeal raisin cookie, the cell phone rang again. More conversation on the staffing issue, this time with one of our vice presidents. Half an hour later, I returned to the patio to finish my no-longer-warm-from-the-oven cookie.

That's how it went throughout the afternoon. One call after another as this issue exploded into a full-blown crisis. Where I had expected some downtime, I was finding a series of tough conversations. During the first few hours of this, Howard had been perfectly understanding about being, essentially, ignored by his guest. Finally, though, he looked at me and said, "I think we'd both be happier if you turned off the phone for a while."

"I'm sorry; you're right," I said, powering down the phone and taking a deep breath of the salty air.

"What's going on that can't wait till Monday?" he asked.

I explained the gist of the situation. The brewing crisis related to a guy, Art, whom I'd hired a few months earlier. Back then, somebody had put Art's résumé in my hand and said, "I don't know much about this guy personally but he's got the background you're looking for." To that point, our company had grown on the energy and enthusiasm of a lean and very efficient staff. But now we were generating a lot more new business opportunities than we could handle with our current team; and many of these new opportunities required someone with experience and seniority. I saw Art, a seasoned fifty-year-old executive, as both a solution to our immediate problem and an experienced presence.

Kirk and I met with Art a few times to lay out a role and goals for him. Neither of us was completely bowled over by our conversations with him, but I looked at his skills and background and thought, "He could make us a lot of money." I told myself that the big financial upside outweighed the risks of hiring someone we hadn't worked with before and didn't know well. Kirk was less sure, but he left the decision in my hands. So I hired the guy.

"I wasn't completely confident in my decision," I told Howard. "But there was no obvious shortcoming I could put my finger on, and, I rationalized, the guy was ready to take on some very important deals that would really build the business. For a while, it seemed to be working okay. Now and then, a few negative blips on the radar, but nothing major. At least, that's what I thought. In reality, problems were bubbling under the surface, and in the last few days things started boiling over. One staff member after another—junior and senior people—has come to Kirk and me and said essentially the same thing: 'We've really tried, but we just can't work with this guy.' . . . And, Howard, none of these people are slackers; none are overly sensitive prima donnas."

"What specific problems are they having?" Howard asked.

"The senior staff are primarily concerned about the way he interacts with clients, and they don't want to be a party to it. They say he overpromises then is slow to deliver; that he seems to create problems just to be seen as the guy who then resolves them. They admit that he's bringing in business, but they're worried he'll undermine the company's ability to cement long-term relationships."

"And how about the more junior people—what are their concerns?" he asked.

"They're uncomfortable with how the guy treats *them*. They say he cuts them out of projects and dismisses their ideas. Apparently, he's even told a couple of the younger members of our team to clean up the coffee cups and stuff after his client meetings."

"The coffee cups—that's not part of their job?" Howard asked.

"Definitely not," I replied, standing up and pacing across the flagstones. "Listen, in our office, everybody's equal. You have a good idea, you offer it, whether you're a vice president or a junior account manager, and it gets considered on its merits. You invite people to the office and give them coffee, you clean up after; you need help with it, you ask—not demand. Vice presidents in our company get that title because of the skills they have; but the title doesn't make them better people or more deserving of basic respect than our IT coordinator or receptionist.

And beyond that—" I stopped myself, realizing that I'd gotten pretty worked up. I sat back down across from Howard. "Anyway, I'm not sure exactly what to do."

Howard raised an eyebrow and looked at me with some concern. Then he turned to gaze out at the tall pines and oaks surrounding the house. After a moment he said, "You seem pretty angry and frustrated at the situation." I just nodded. "Who are you angry with?"

I thought about that very good question for a while before answering. "Both of us," I finally admitted. "Him, for being the wrong guy. Me, for knowing in my gut that he'd be the wrong guy and hiring him anyway. . . . My greed got in the way of my judgment."

"Yeah, I think you both made a mistake," Howard said. "From what you've told me of his background, it sounds like he's acting exactly as he did in his previous jobs, where—for better or worse—he fit right into the culture. His mistake was in not recognizing that the environment in your company was different; or maybe he recognized it but doesn't have the capacity to adapt. Your mistake was, for expediency's sake, overlooking what his résumé said about the environments he thrived in and not explicitly talking with him about how your office's culture would likely differ. Painful as it might be for both of you, it seems to me you've got to swallow these mistakes and move on."

"Meaning I've just got to let this guy go and deal with the short-term consequences?" I asked the question, but he and I both knew it was only rhetorical.

Howard had helped me focus on the fact that Art was not just an outlier in our office culture. He was an active threat to that culture—and he had to go.

Anywhere you have two or more people interacting, there is a culture.

Like the air on a windless day, an organization's culture surrounds you, even if you forget it's there. Like gravity, culture is an intangible but very real force.

And culture is important. "Culture trumps strategy," Howard often says.

Culture can define an organization; define how its employees interact; and define its level of success. Research clearly shows that culture can be the decisive competitive advantage underpinning an organization's successful strategies and innovations. (Howard firmly believes that its strong culture was a decisive factor in the success of Baupost, the money management firm he co-founded.) Conversely, even great ideas fail in the wrong culture. "Culture is a huge contributor to the success of places like Google, Starbucks, and Teach For America, as well as organizations I know firsthand like HBS and the Baupast Group," Howard has observed. "But, on the other hand, it was also a big reason that the American auto industry fell off a cliff, because an arrogant culture blinded them to the competitive threat from small Japanese cars. And it was a culture of short-term profit versus long-term fiduciary responsibility that allowed the banking industry to drive the world economy into the last recession."

For us as individuals, understanding the culture in which we work—and the one in which we'd most like to work—is essential to achieving satisfaction. "The difference between being in a culture that works for you and one that doesn't?" Howard once said to me. "Well, that's like the difference between just having a job and doing your life's work."

Not matching up with the culture can have major consequences. Jeff Leopold—the successful executive recruiter who learned huge lessons from his own early-career mismatch with the Microsoft culture—spends a good chunk of time analyzing the reasons why corporate executives are fired; it helps him better identify candidates who *won't* fail. The top reason for those failures, he's found, is a mismatch between the executive and the organization's culture.

As an expert on entrepreneurship, Howard's well versed in the positive and negative effects of culture on a new organization's ability to thrive and grow. That's why he was so quick to pick up on the fundamental problem with Art. ("Culture is certainly more than the sum of the people in a group," he reminded me, "but the wrong people can ruin a good culture.") Howard has also had some tough personal experience: you'll recall that it was a fundamental mismatch with the old HBS culture that drove him away from Harvard thirty years ago, and a new culture that helped lure him back.

As early as my first real job out of college—when I worked for Chip Conley at Joie de Vivre—I saw the power of culture in action. I was lucky because that first experience was a very positive one: over the years, Joie de Vivre has won all kinds of awards for its culture and environment. With that as a standard to strive for, our Axcess leadership team has consciously nurtured an energizing and dependable culture—a culture that will be the cornerstone for the company's long-term growth and success. The principle that "everyone speaks up and carries their own coffee cup" is a pillar of that culture. But, clearly, there was more for me to learn about culture; if I'd mastered the subject, Art never would have gotten in the door.

That's why I took advantage of having that whole summer weekend with Howard to get a refresher course in culture. It started that first evening, after dinner, as we sat in the living room.

"There are lots of ways to think about workplace culture," Howard offered, "but let's come at it from the perspective of the individual employee—because, ultimately, that's where the proof is in the pudding. Any organization can talk about how good its culture is, but what matters is how the culture's seen and felt by the people who make the organization go day to day."

"All right," I replied, "if you're looking at an organization—whether coming for a first interview or starting your fifth year there—what should you focus on? What are the elements of culture you need to be most aware of?"

"Culture is multifaceted," Howard explained. "But no matter if the group is big, little, for-profit, or nonprofit, there are two fundamentals from which the other facets emerge: the alignment of the organization's mission and values and reward system; and the way that power and information are used and shared. In essence, everything grows from those fundamental elements. Just like there are zillions of things in this universe that start with carbon and hydrogen in one combination or another.

"By the way, it's useful to remember that these elements can combine in different ways to create distinct subcultures *within* an organization. It doesn't happen only in huge entities like GE, where the major divisions are like wholly distinct companies, or like Harvard, where each school is its own little universe. Smaller organizations experience it, too; your local high school probably has different subcultures in the guidance office, the history department, and the athletic department. Those internal cultural differences can be a hurdle for people moving around the organization. I've seen many situations where someone succeeds wildly in one subculture and is mediocre—or even fails—in another part of the same organization."

Fredi came over, handed Howard his not-quite-empty wineglass from dinner, and sat down to join us. Howard took the last sip of wine and twirled the glass slowly as he considered his next point. "It's interesting. When we're discussing a case study on business culture, a lot of students start with the assumption that there are inherently good and bad kinds of cultures, or inherently strong and weak ones. In my view, if you leave out the unacceptable extreme ends of the spectrum—complete anarchy on one hand and slavery on the other—there aren't any inherently right or wrong cultures. Different missions require different approaches. But cultures *can* be judged effective or not effective relative to the organization's mission and goals.

"In the same way, there's no generically good or bad cultural fit for any one individual. In that respect, it's a lot like marriage," he mused as he turned to look at Fredi. "For this fine woman, I am a good husband; there are several billion other women for whom I wouldn't be, including my first wife. That doesn't make me a bad husband—just not the right fit for all those other women."

"But how does someone find their own Fredi, culturally speaking?" I jokingly asked.

"There's but one Fredi, and I'm keeping her," he said, taking her hand in his. "But if you'll let me sleep on the question, I'll gladly offer some thoughts on that excellent question."

True to his word, over the course of the weekend Howard laid out a thoughtful framework for gauging an organization's culture. The framework was based on five big questions that extend naturally from the two fundamental elements of culture that Howard had noted. His five questions struck me as so straightforward and sensible that I've incorporated my Axcess-specific answers to them into the briefing material we give to new employees. The process of answering those questions for yourself will lead naturally to considering how well a particular culture fits you and your goals. (And the initial conclusions you come to on the rightness of that fit are perfect fodder for discussion with your mentors and the folks on your IBOD.)

In the real world, the answers to these five questions may be interconnected. However, you should try to tease them apart, examine each separately, and only then consider how they relate. Why? Because individual elements of culture will have a different significance for each person and should be weighed independently; and the unique way that these elements interact in a given organization can change—subtly or greatly—the way they affect you.

Here are Howard's questions and his thoughts on why they're worth answering.

QUESTION 1: *Is everyone singing the same hymn?*

"What's your mission and why are you here? That's what I want to know about any organization I get involved with. And I'm hoping I get a similar answer no matter who in the organization is responding," Howard explained. "I don't want to hear about the tasks the organization performs—'We sell widgets' or 'We design Web sites.' I want to hear, organizationally, who they are, why they exist, and what they most value."

Howard stopped, and a wistful smile crossed his face. "You remember Frank Batten, don't you?" he asked, recalling his good friend and role model. Frank, who died a few years ago, was a hugely accomplished news industry entrepreneur and pioneer in television and cable systems and programming. The creator of the Weather Channel and former chairman of the Associated Press, Frank was a smart, creative businessman. But most impressive to Howard was Frank's integrity and vision and the values he instilled in his companies—which Howard witnessed firsthand as a long-term member of the board of directors of Frank's company, Landmark Communications. "Frank believed that a company's primary goal was to serve customers and that profit was simply a constraint on that goal— but that if you served customers well, profit would follow. That sense of the company's purposes, and the values that grew from it, were cornerstones for the Landmark culture.

"Mission, purpose, values—these are core elements of a culture, and, obviously, a person not in synch with them will experience great friction with her surroundings. What's not as commonly recognized is the challenge of being part of a fragmented culture, where there's no commonly shared under-standing of the organization's purpose, values, and strategic goals. In fact, you could argue that if there is no common view of these things—if folks don't know how they fit into the larger, coherent picture—then the mission, strategies, and val-ues don't fully exist. The result is that everyone ends up pulling in a slightly different direction. Working in this kind of culture offers challenges to someone who is focused on pursuing a well-defined legacy vision—if only because they can't be com-pletely sure of the path the organization will lead them down.

"In my experience," Howard concluded, "the most effective cultures emerge from 'self-aware' organizations—organizations that explicitly, consistently, and energetically define their pur-pose and values to the people who work for them."

QUESTION 2: *How do leaders lead?*

"When I look at an organization—whether for my research, as an investor, or as a board member—I want to know how it's led," Howard explained. "I want to see how leaders from the top ech-elons to the smallest units of the organization conduct them-selves. There are many ways to assess the leadership's impact on culture, but you can learn a lot from three specific factors."

The first factor is whether leaders' actions match their words—especially what they say about values and goals—and whether they follow through on the commitments they make. Cultures are much more stable and easier to navigate when leaders do exactly what they say they'll do. "Sometimes, when I was a kid," Howard recalled, "my mother would say to me, 'Son, your actions speak so loudly I can't hear what you say.' Cultures can be confusing like that, too, when there is a disconnect between what the organization says is important and the 'informal rules' made clear through leaders' actions and decisions."

The second factor, Howard continued, is whether leaders hold themselves—individually and collectively—accountable for the performance of the people and units they lead. "Leadership accountability is inversely related to how political the culture is," he noted. "The greater the sense of accountability, the less political is the environment around individual employees. So I want to see who takes responsibility for disappointing outcomes or outright failures, and who gets credit for positive developments and major successes. I also want to see how much image management goes on—and whether 'cults of personality' have been created around the leaders, artificially shielding them from accountability. The cultural impact of leaders standing up to disappointments and failure—or, conversely, pointing fingers—is quickly translated across the organization."

The third and perhaps most important factor Howard cited is the leaders' use of power. "How power flows and is allocated in an organization is—excuse the obvious pun—a powerful influence on culture," he said. "I'm particularly interested in the balance between the two basic kinds of power: using authority to *compel* people to do something, and fostering responsibility that motivates them to *want* to do something. All other things being equal today, a culture of shared responsibility has a leg up on an authority culture: power exercised through collective responsibility leads to more high-quality thinking and more productive personal interactions; in an authority culture, it's too easy for people to say, 'I just did what I was told, so it's not my fault if it failed.' That's why, for most organizations, responsibility should be the meat and potatoes of how power is exercised, and authority should be the spices and condiments. Even in the military, where authority is so clearly a part of the culture, 'unit cohesion' depends on both strict discipline and mutual responsibility among fellow soldiers."

QUESTION 3: *Who gets to drink from the information reservoir?*

"Information is an essential organizational resource," Howard explained, "and culture is shaped substantially by how—and how much of—that resource is shared. Outside of organizations where there are very good reasons for limiting information flow—the CIA comes to mind—one of the most potent markers of an effective culture is fluid movement of information. In these cultures, there are no unnecessary barriers to information flow; in fact they have proactive mechanisms for getting information to all the places where it can benefit the organization. Conversely, ineffective cultures are frequently marked by information hoarding and by unnecessary constraints on information flow. That's why I shy away from any culture that treats information as a zero-sum commodity."

Another very important marker of an organization's culture, Howard observed, is how a particular kind of information is handled: bad news. "I want to see how problems are addressed and how people deal with bad news—from small mistakes or shortcomings in performance to disappointing results on a group project or the outright failure of a major initiative," he said. "For me, I want to be part of a culture that takes a problem-solving approach to things that don't go right. This means doing an open and objective analysis of all the factors that went into the situation. And when criticism is necessary—of an individual or a group—it is delivered in a forward-looking way, emphasizing lessons learned and constructive changes that are warranted. It does not focus on placing blame."

Howard believes that another key facet of an organization's "information culture" is how well diverse and divergent opinions are not just accepted but actively cultivated. "The British philosopher John Stuart Mill said, 'It is hardly possible to over-rate the value . . . of placing human beings in contact with persons dissimilar to themselves, and with modes of thought and action unlike those with which they are familiar. Such communication has always been, and is peculiarly in the present age, one of the primary sources of progress,'" Howard quoted. "He wrote that in the nineteenth century, and it's fascinating how in our present age his point is still fresh and on target. In almost any organizational context, 'mono-cultures'— places where fresh ideas are stifled—are generally short-lived entities. That's why the most successful organizations have a culture of honest feedback; and an environment where dissenting opinions and alternate ways of looking at things are encouraged. Those cultures are marked by a commonly held understanding that ideas are debated through civil dialogue despite disagreement, no matter the stakes involved. Leaders in these cultures encourage push-back, and they prize the ability to disagree without being disagreeable."

QUESTION 4: *Is this an organization of teams or of stars and satellites?*

"There's a widely held myth that the typical organization's success is built on a few stars surrounded by a supporting cast of people who are interchangeable," Howard observed with a bit of frustration. "It's based on the mistaken belief that the stars create enormous benefit for the organization solely through their own exceptional talents. That may be the case in sports, but it's rarely the case in most other organizations. It's not a good thing when we see investment managers, attorneys, bankers, and CEOs treated like winners of the NFL's Most Valuable Player Award or baseball's Cy Young Award.

"It skews the culture in really bad ways. And the graveyard of failed organizations is adorned by the bright images of 'stars' and 'irreplaceable' players. Nevertheless, this phenomenon persists, played out every day in organizations large and small— and not just at the senior executive level. It's happening also when the head of an office or a department manager decides that only his or her ideas or skills or experience are relevant— that everyone else's job is to advance that one agenda," Howard observed.

"The truth is that it's the cast of characters around an organization's 'stars'—whether real or self-imagined—that makes the difference between mediocrity and excellence. As good as any one person may be, there's rarely someone whose capacities exceed the collective abilities of the people around him or her. So in constraining employees' opportunities to exercise their abilities, the organization is hamstringing its own potential for solving problems and developing new ideas. It's creating a talent-constrained culture, and is wasting resources by employing people whose skills and energies are not fully leveraged.

When you've got this situation going on, Howard explained, the culture can be unhealthy. "Not only do individuals narrow their vision and dial back their commitment, an 'everyone for themselves ethos' develops—which, at its worst, evolves into an outright competitive culture. Even at its mildest, the 'all for none and none for all' atmosphere leads to a bunch of people working in silos and interpreting goals in ways that best serve them, rather than pursuing commonly held goals." Both the mild and harsher forms of noncollaboration undermine the organization's effectiveness, Howard suggested, creating a lonely culture of disconnection between employees, even those working in parallel and not at cross-purposes. And, it almost goes without saying, it's hugely difficult to create a culture of shared responsibility where a star-oriented ethos predominates.

"I find these kinds of cultures frustrating, because the whole point of organizations is to accomplish goals together that individuals can not accomplish alone," he said. "I suppose there are specific situations where it's not the case, but the most effective cultures are those that prize and nurture collaborative effort. Those that encourage people to believe they can succeed together—and help them recognize that they'll succeed better if they strive together.

"So it's important to consider a few questions: What kind of support do I want to have around me? What kind of support do I need if I'm going to continue moving on my chosen path? How does this culture expect me to interact with my colleagues?'" Howard suggested. "And that latter question should apply not just to the folks in your office, but to people in other areas of the organization and, in fact, to outsiders like customers, vendors, and partners.

"Finally, to understand the extent to which a culture is collaborative, parallel, or overtly competitive, it's useful to ask the kind of mission oriented questions I raised earlier: 'Do the folks working here understand why they're all there? Do they share a mission? And do they know how they fit into it?'" Howard said. "Because you can't be collaborative—or even parallel—if you're not all going down the same path."

QUESTION 5: *How does the organization evaluate employees' performance?*

Howard prizes cultures that are marked by transparency, predictability, progress, and trust. What does that mean when it comes to evaluation? "First," he explained, "I want to be assessed on clear goals and benchmarks and—to the extent possible given the nature of the organization's work—objective measures of performance. These measures don't necessarily have to be quantifiable, but they do need to be explicit and not simply a matter of one person's changeable interpretation. Next, I want to know that the points of evaluation are explicitly guided by the organization's mission, goals, and values. Finally, I want to know that the organization celebrates small wins and incremental progress toward shared goals—recognizing that major successes come from cumulative minor accomplishments," he continued.

"Research on organizational psychology shows that transparency, predictability, and progress are fundamental to an individual's sense of job satisfaction and personal achievement," he noted. "They are also essential to building trust, which is the foundation for a culture of shared responsibility.

"The flip side of a 'predictability and progress' culture, however, is where one's effort is judged based on seat-of-the-pants assessments tied to unclear and shifting set of objectives; where trust runs thin; where a person feels lucky to have succeeded. In this situation—rife with inconsistent goals and metrics and a sense that expectations change on the fly—employees are confused, on edge, and tentative. As a result, the culture is one where folks don't commit one hundred percent to any decision or effort because they need to be ready to shift direction, sometimes without warning or explanation. It certainly is not a culture of shared responsibility.

"And, from a personal perspective, it's hard to maximize your strengths, build on your competitive advantages, pursue a clear path, and make effective juggling-and-balancing choices when you're working in this kind of environment," Howard observed.

In considering how evaluation is done within an organization, Howard noted, it's particularly important to drill down on another key point: whether assessments are focused on performance or results. "Even where the organization conducts objective, strategically focused assessments, the distinction between performance-focus and results-focus is significant—because one is much more in your control than the other," he said, grabbing a pad of paper and a pen and scribbling two quasi-mathematical equations—$Performance = f$ (effort + skill) and $Results = f$ (performance + luck)—then turned the pad toward me.

"I hope that's not calculus—I kind of maxed out at algebra and statistics," I said.

He laughed. "Not technically, I suppose. But you could call it the calculus of workplace assessments. It means that 'performance' is a function of effort and skill, while 'result' is a function of performance and luck. You can control the amount of effort and skill you put into your work; you can't control luck. When an organization evaluates and rewards people based primarily on results, not performance, they're reducing predictability and transparency. That isn't a good thing, by itself. But it can also lead to a culture where long-term value—and the organization's supposed values—is secondary to short-term results. From a purely business perspective, that's a formula for failure. And from a personal perspective, it's bound to conflict with one's ability to pursue a legacy vision."

Howard reflected on an earlier part of our conversation. "Frank Batten believed that a company's primary goal was to serve customers, and that profit would come if the primary goal was achieved. He rewarded performance toward that goal, making results a secondary consideration. That's why he gave a bonus to a guy whose division lost money but performed well in a tough environment where the outcome could not be controlled. That's also why he fired an executive who made money but whose single-minded push for results undermined the broader organization's strategy, cohesiveness, and long-term success.

"Now, there's a culture that's transparent, predictable, self-aware, and mission-driven," Howard said with pride in his voice.

Calculus is a high-level form of mathematics that helps organize quantities of information to make predictions. The calculus of culture is a less precise discipline. Nevertheless, Howard's five questions yield information about the core elements of culture and the many permutations of how those elements work together. As important, the very act of asking and answering those questions makes explicit and evident many things we unconsciously sense about the environment around us but haven't quite put a finger on. In these ways, his questions provide a framework for making good predictions about the mix of cultural elements that works best for us as individuals.

However, for that framework to be really effective, you need to build upon it and personalize it by asking and answering inwardly focused questions. Some of those questions will have simple and intuitive answers (especially as they're applied to the culture that you are in now or have been part of), such as: Do I feel comfortable on a day-to-day basis in this culture? Do I feel secure—psychologically and professionally—in this culture? Am I able to navigate effectively in this culture, or do I find myself regularly tripping over "land mines" I didn't know were there?

Other questions will require some deep thought, such as: What mix of cultural elements will best enable me to use my strengths and competitive advantages? Which mix will best enable me to juggle and balance the most important of my selves and dimensions? What kind of culture best matches my definition of success and satisfaction and offers the types of rewards I seek?

Because the calculus of culture is imprecise, as you flesh out your framework, you very often can benefit from other people's perspectives. Your career mentors and IBOD can be particularly useful in helping with these calculations, especially in clarifying the kinds of culture where you have thrived in the past and would likely succeed going forward.

Identifying, selecting, and embracing an organizational culture that supports the professional component of your legacy vision requires time and effort. It isn't enough to simply look at a "Best Places to Work" list and go "eeny, meeny, miny, mo." In the end, though, the extra effort will return valuable rewards—denominated in the currency of satisfaction. Because what could be more rewarding and satisfying than being able to say, as Howard did of his experience with Frank Batten's company, "It was a distinctive place and a special culture to be part of"?

EMILY HUNTER

Emily Hunter grew up in Cincinnati, went to college in Athens, Georgia, and finds herself now, at age twenty-seven, a resident of Manhattan and a savvy navigator of the New York City subway system. Some people would have a severe case of cultural whiplash from that journey. But not Emily. She's found a great cultural match with where she lives and where she works.

"There was definitely some adjustment early on, like having to get used to the hustle of New York and the far different cost of living. But I'd experienced the Midwest and the South, and I knew that I wanted to try something different as I started my career," she explained one evening, just before she and her husband, Andrew, headed back to Ohio to celebrate Christmas with their families. "Since I'd studied fashion merchandising at the University of Georgia, I figured that New York would serve my purposes. I arranged to do a couple of internships in Manhattan right after I graduated, and they were great experiences. I loved the pace of the city and really enjoyed working in the fashion industry."

The whole transition felt right to Emily, so she started interviewing for jobs and, within a few months of her graduation, secured a position at J. Crew, one of the top names in apparel. "Going into the job, I had a sense that the company was a good place to work—it is on many 'Best Places to Work' lists—but it's only by experiencing the organization that I've come to understand why it's a good match for me," she observed.

"It's a young company, in the sense that a lot of the staff are in their twenties and thirties. The executive vice president of J.Crew is just thirty-nine. This makes it easier to relate to the people I work with every day," Emily said. "It's possible that when I'm forty I'll feel less comfortable working in an environment dominated by people younger than me; but for now, it's a good fit.

"I also like that the company is committed to identifying employees' skills and talents and nurturing their professional growth. They expose us to a variety of areas and responsibilities; we're encouraged to try new things; and people get promoted when they've demonstrated new skills," noted Emily, who's been promoted twice in the three-plus years she's been at J.Crew. "This has worked well for me particularly because I've had good managers, who've mentored me in new roles and helped me master new challenges."

Another important aspect of the J.Crew culture for Emily is the openness of communication and information sharing. "The managers and senior leadership want to hear our ideas and perspectives," she observed. "In fact, the CEO, Mickey Drexler, walks through the offices every day; he talks to everyone, seeks opinions, asks questions—and if someone gives an answer that doesn't work, he'll take the time to offer constructive criticism and explain where it's off target.

"What's great is that this openness in communication focuses outward, too—the people who run the company care about customers' opinions and feedback. It's a point of pride for Mickey that he replies to every e-mail he receives from a customer. Little things like that send a big signal to employees like me: it says that the company acts on its principles."

I suggested to Emily that even "Best Places to Work" organizations had some shortcomings and asked if there were things about the culture she didn't like.

She thought about it for a moment and said, "Yeah, I guess there are two. First is the flip side of having lots of professional development opportunities: you're on what seems like a continuous learning curve. Just when you're getting up to speed in one job—learning to do it well— you get moved into another area, with a whole new set of information and skills to learn. It can get frustrating.

"Second is the downside of being a new person in a relatively small and stable company: I found that there can be very tight social circles, and it can be hard to break into the social connections among staff who've been there a lot longer.

"But," she emphasized, "those are things I'll be able to work through over time, and they're pretty minor compared to the parts of the J.Crew culture that work for me."

CHAPTER TWELVE

The Light of Predictability

I've rarely met a successful entrepreneur who likes risk. They figure out how to manage their fear of risk, how to proceed in spite of risk.

I PICKED UP THE PHONE, dialed the number by heart, and—after he answered with his distinctive "Stevenson!"—said to Howard, "Boy, did I just have a really scary conversation."

"Is everyone okay—Jen and the kids?" he asked with concern in his voice.

"Oh, yeah, they're fine," I hurriedly replied. "Actually, I was referring to a kind of career counseling session I did with this young woman."

"What was so scary about her?"

"She's not a scary person herself, but her career situation is an existential nightmare," I said, adding, "Bet you didn't think I knew what *existential* meant, did you?" Howard laughed heartily, then I told him about my conversation with a very bright twenty-five-year-old woman named Lourdy. An office assistant in the corporate headquarters of a high-end jewelry company in Manhattan, Lourdy had been taking notes at a meeting where I'd been making a presentation. During the coffee break afterward, she'd sought me out and asked a lot of good questions about my work; then, overcoming her obvious hesitation, she asked if I could spare half an hour sometime to talk about careers. A few weeks later, we sat down in my office for that conversation.

She took charge of the conversation right away, and much of the discussion was driven by her increasingly detailed questions about my career. In particular, she wanted to know how I'd charted my general career path and how I made decisions on whether to move from one job to another. How did I know that it was the "right" move, that I wasn't precluding a better opportunity? What specific steps had I taken to be sure that I wasn't going down a dead-end path—to ensure that I wouldn't have to waste time retracing my steps? Were there times when I did, in fact, make a mistake, and how far did those situations set me back?

After answering these questions for about forty minutes, I was curious about what was driving her line of inquiry. Almost as soon as I turned the focus of the conversation around—to her background, how she enjoyed her current job, where she envisioned herself going—the reason became clear. Lourdy had grown up in an upper-middle-class family in Pittsburgh; her mom was the administrator for a multispecialty medical practice, and her dad was a corporate attorney. Having thought a lot about her career and deciding that she'd like to be a teacher, she'd gone to college in New York to study elementary education. All went well for four years of classes, until she did her senior-year student teaching experience—the first real opportunity to get in front of a classroom—and found herself dissatisfied by it. Still, she wanted to make the most of her undergraduate training and decided that the increased challenge of working with special-needs kids would be much more satisfying. So she went directly into a master's program in special education. Her boyfriend—a young engineer on the partnership track in a thriving consulting firm—was completely supportive of her decision; in fact, they decided to move in together when she started grad school. Two years later, she, her boyfriend-turned-fiancé, and her family celebrated her new master's degree, and she was looking forward to starting her first full-time teaching job.

Unfortunately, the woman who sat in my office two years after that high point was an unhappy and confused person. Her career as a special-education teacher had lasted less than a year. "I liked the kids, one-on-one, and felt that I was doing important work," she explained to me. "I put a lot of energy into it—and it left me completely drained. I felt no positive energy flowing back to me, even when my students were making positive steps. After just a few months—when I started getting stomachaches every Sunday night—I realized it wasn't going to work." So Lourdy left teaching behind. With great regret. Feeling like a failure at an important job. Feeling she'd wasted six years of education and a lot of tuition money.

I summed up for Howard, "She needed a job and—lacking any sense of direction—let a friend arrange an interview for her at the jewelry company. They offered her an entry-level position; she took it and has been there for the past year. Except it's a double dead end: she knows she doesn't want to make a career in high-end retail, and the company isn't interested in helping her build her skills or broaden her experience."

"Hmm. What's her plan now?" Howard asked.

"Well, that's where the scary part comes in," I replied. "There isn't one. She's frozen—a complete paralysis-by-analysis situation. She's talked to a dozen different people, just like me, gathering information and ideas; except it's clear that nothing's come from all of it: no plan, no planning process, not even a concrete next step. It's like all the information is getting dumped into this big machine that churns and churns but produces nothing.

"Lourdy's in limbo and she knows it. But she's afraid to make a definitive move in any direction. She fears failing; fears wasting time and money; fears disappointing her parents; fears not realizing her potential. And, to make the box around her complete, she fears getting caught in a career she doesn't want, driven by self-imposed pressure to get moving on her career path," I concluded. "What scares the hell out of me is her sense of complete paralysis—hating her situation and dreading what could happen if she changes it."

Howard was quiet for a moment, then he asked, "How did you leave it with her? I mean, you're not a guy to leave a damsel in distress—and she's clearly in distress."

"I told her that, at the root, what was freezing her in place was her worry about risk—the risk of making another career misstep being the big one, but not the only one," I said. "I told her that she should come back to talk with me in a few weeks; but first, I wanted to talk to somebody who knew a whole lot about assessing and mitigating risk." I paused. "So, coach, you want to help me help her get unstuck?"

"Sure. Why don't you tell me a little more about her situation and I'll think on it," he replied. "Are you coming back up this way anytime soon?" I was going to be in Connecticut about two weeks later, meeting with clients; so we agreed I'd take the train up afterward and have dinner with Howard and Fredi in Cambridge. "Will that be soon enough for you to get some thoughts back to Lourdy?" Howard asked.

"Yeah, I'm afraid so—she's not going anywhere any time soon."

I was sitting at the dining room table with Howard and Fredi, sipping a glass of wine and enjoying the afterglow of a tasty and pleasant dinner. Fredi, who was watching Howard's diet like a hawk, had prepared bluefish (full of heart-healthy fish oils) broiled with a dash of pepper and a splash of lemon, a salad, and several kinds of nicely seasoned vegetables. I put my dessert spoon down after finishing my last bite of warm poached pear, and said, "Fredi, don't tell my wife or my mother, but that may have been the best home-cooked meal I've ever had."

"Thank you, Eric," Fredi replied and nodded in Howard's direction. "I've got to keep on my culinary toes if I'm going to keep this guy in line." Howard smiled a little sheepishly because he knew she was right. He appreciated interesting, well-prepared food, and it was all too easy for him to succumb to the lure of a fat and cholesterol-laden dinner followed by a custard fruit tart for dessert. Earlier in their lives, when there was no obvious negative impact from Howard's food choices, Fredi was content to let him follow his appetite. But with the onset of Howard's heart problems in 2007, the risks of eating the wrong things far outweighed any crustiness he might display when she hemmed in his menu. She was both creative and steely in enforcing Howard's good nutrition.

"What do you boys have planned for the evening?" she asked as she began to gather the used dishes.

"We're going to talk about some really risky stuff," Howard said with a straight face. Fredi gave me a questioning look, as if to say, "What shenanigans are you dragging my husband into now?"

"Actually," I said, standing up and taking the dishes from her, "first, I'm going to clear up. Then, we're going to talk about the *concept* of risk—and how to approach risky decisions in your life's work."

"Eric's got a young friend who's in a bit of quandary," Howard elaborated as he walked into the kitchen. "She's afraid to take a risk—even a short-term, low-cost one—because all she sees are the imagined downsides waiting to fall on her."

"Have you given her either of Howard's books that deal with risk?" Fredi asked me. "That would be an excellent place to start."

"Ladies and gentlemen, meet my book publicist, Fredericka Stevenson," he quipped. "Let's see if we can give this young woman a primer before we have her dive into the deep waters of my research on entrepreneurial risk and predictive intelligence."

He and I took a few more minutes to clear the table and put away the leftovers. Then we excused ourselves to Howard's little office in the basement. I always get a chuckle when I walk into the room, because a foot-high Yoda doll stands watch on a shelf overlooking Howard's desk. (I spied it in FAO Schwarz one day, while buying a present for my son Daniel, and I couldn't resist getting it for Howard.) Most of the wall space surrounding Yoda is taken up with chock-full bookshelves. The mini library includes a few copies of each of Howard's own books. Pulling two of them off the shelf, I said to him, "You know, Fredi's got a good point. Either of these would give Lourdy lots of ideas and information to work with."

"Yes, that's true," he replied, "but from what you've told me, lack of information is not her problem right now. The challenge she's facing is how to organize the information she has, how to evaluate one idea versus another, and how to use all her information as the basis for a reasonable prediction of the result of any one choice."

"Fair enough," I said. "Where should we start?"

He thought for a moment, then said, "I laughed at you when you first described your conversation with Lourdy as scary. The more I think about it, however, I realize that what I find scary about your conversation is how many times I've had a version of it—with people of all ages. Granted, everyone's situation is unique; but the issues they're wrestling with are, qualitatively, very similar.

"With students, the conversation will often start with them saying something like, 'I want to do my own thing, be my own boss. But I'm really not a big risk taker. So I guess I can't be an entrepreneur, right?'" He shook his head and laughed. "When we launched the entrepreneurship program at HBS years ago, the common assumption was that entrepreneurs were just crazy people who thrived on risk. That's one reason there was so much resistance to introducing the subject in an academic setting. Even today, people think of entrepreneurs as big risk takers. The reality is that in forty years of research, I've rarely met a successful entrepreneur who likes risk. There are exceptions—natural daredevils who happen to be in business instead of some other risk-taking career—but the huge majority hate risk. They figure out how to manage their fear of risk, how to proceed in spite of risk, not because of it.

"The principle of proceeding despite risk is relevant not just for go-it-alone business entrepreneurs; it should be mastered by people who want to be entrepreneurial and innovative within any kind of organization. More to the point here, though, learning to proceed despite risk is extraordinarily important for anyone determined to be entrepreneurial and proactive in driving her own career. That's the first idea that Lourdy needs to understand and internalize."

I nodded in agreement and offered, "The reality is that we all do this every single day in ways that are less obvious—don't we? There's risk in crossing Fifth Avenue at rush hour; in eating sushi instead of grilled shrimp; in buying stocks versus putting money in a savings account."

"Exactly," Howard said, "but Lourdy doesn't have problems making decisions on those kinds of risks, and she needs to apply that day-to-day acceptance of risk to her career. One reason she's comfortable acting in the face of those risks is that she naturally—almost unconsciously—narrows the risk profile. She crosses Fifth Avenue at the light, instead of jaywalking; she eats at established sushi restaurants known for serving absolutely fresh fish. That's what entrepreneurially minded people do, regardless of their actual career path—they figure out how to reduce the range and potential magnitude of the risk. And that's the second idea that Lourdy needs to digest: she can be proactive in mitigating the potential impact of the risks she sees.

"Now, with those two ideas in mind, the reasonable question she might ask is—" Howard stopped and smiled broadly as Fredi appeared at the door carrying a tray with cups, a carafe of coffee, and a small pitcher filled with steamed milk for making lattes. "You read my mind," he said to her, "but why only two cups—aren't you going to sit with us?"

"I'd love to hear how you help this woman," she responded. "You know that I'm very interested in how young people deal with the risks around them. But, ironically, I have a Summer Search board meeting tonight." Fredi is one of the founders of Summer Search Boston, a nonprofit community organization that provides at-risk, low-income high school students with year-round mentoring, life-changing summer experiences, and college advising. The program helps them gain the skills to succeed in college and to dramatically improve their life prospects. Fredi is rightfully proud of Summer Search's amazing record with these kids: 100 percent of the students in the program graduate high school; 94 percent go to college; and 89 percent have graduated college or are on track to do so—a far higher percentage than their peers in the Boston schools. One of the reasons that Summer Search is successful is that they tackle head-on some of the biggest risk factors facing kids in poor, urban communities.

"I'll give you a complete debrief," Howard assured her, and I gave her a big hug and a kiss good-bye.

When we'd mixed our lattes, Howard picked up right where he'd left off. "Lourdy's question is going to be, 'How do I understand and mitigate the risks sufficiently to feel comfortable moving ahead?' And here's where you need to do a little foundation building with her."

"How so, foundation building?"

"You need to lay out for her, concisely, some of the very points that we've discussed for the book you're writing. Lourdy's hit a major inflection point in her life—and, after all, what are inflection points but situations laden with potential risk?—but she isn't recognizing it as a valuable opportunity. She hasn't developed a legacy vision; so she has no concrete orientation for her path and no consistent focus point as she negotiates the balance beam of her life. Finally, she clearly hasn't identified her competitive advantages—or else, at a minimum, she'd be looking for a job that lets her do what she does best, even if she's not sure to what end she's working."

Howard took a long drink of his latte. "With me so far?" he asked.

"I think so," I replied. "You're saying that the process of developing this foundational information will help her get unstuck and move forward."

"Indeed it will," he said, "because the results of that process—even if it's just a rudimentary sense of her legacy vision and competitive advantages—will give her benchmarks to use in analyzing where the risks lie and how significant they really are."

He gestured for me to hand him one of the books I'd taken off the shelf. "That's the basic point we made here," he said, paging through *Make Your Own Luck: 12 Practical Steps to Taking Smarter Risks in Business*—which he wrote with Eileen C. Shapiro. Written primarily for entrepreneurs—and those who want to be—the book offers a sophisticated framework for analyzing the potential risks and benefits of hewing to an existing entrepreneurial path. At the core of the framework is a series of twelve straightforward questions—"The Gambler's Dozen"—that help leaders of and investors in entrepreneurial businesses decide whether they're going to stay engaged or jump out of a venture. While *Make Your Own Luck* is aimed at businesspeople, its fundamental ideas are useful for anyone who simply wants to be entrepreneurial in his or her own career.

After a moment's reflection, Howard said, "Boiling down the Gambler's Dozen to its essence, Lourdy could use the results of her foundational thinking to consider three basic questions:

"First, how satisfied are you with the current situation and the results you're getting from it?

"Second, what specific results do you want to achieve in the next year or two?

"Third, if you take a risk but don't achieve those results, will you end up in a substantially different situation than you're currently in—and in what specific ways would that situation be better, worse, or the same as your current situation?

"Those questions would give her a concrete way of benchmarking risk," he noted.

Then he reached across the desk and picked up the second of the books I'd taken off the shelf, *Do Lunch or Be Lunch: The Power of Predictability in Creating Your Future*, a deeply researched statement on the importance of building predictability in business, society, and our personal lives. Paging slowly through it, Howard said, "You know, I have some pretty strong opinions on the subject of risk—beginning with the idea that the word *risk* is the wrong term to apply to . . . well, risk."

I laughed. "Maybe your next book should be called *Howard's Definitions*."

"Maybe so," he mused, then continued making his point. "I'd define risk simply as the combination of outcome and uncertainty—a simple mathematical formula. If you eliminate the uncertainty and the outcome is clear, the risk disappears. Now, the flip side of uncertainty is predictability, and it follows that the more confidently you can predict the outcome of a situation, the easier it is to decide whether to pursue it. So, the best way to reduce risk is to increase predictability." He handed me the copy of *Do Lunch or Be Lunch*. "Take away all the fancy academic language and detailed research findings, and that's the basic point of this book."

"Hey," I said, pointing to the book's cover, "I've always wondered: what's with the title? *Do Lunch or Be Lunch: The Power of*

Predictability in Creating Your Future. How the heck are lunch and predictability connected?"

Howard shook his head and chuckled. "Ironic, isn't it, that a book on predictability has a confusing title? The publisher thought that adding the 'or be lunch' part might make readers feel they were taking a big risk in *not* reading it. Actually, I think they just cluttered things up—thereby decreasing predictability and increasing their own publishing risk! And therein lies a great object lesson for me: even when you've literally 'written the book' on the subject, you can never completely eliminate uncertainty and ensure predictability. But"—he slapped the desk for emphasis—"clear away the clutter surrounding an opportunity, and you do begin to lift the veil of uncertainty.

"While we can't control the ultimate outcome of *any* choice," he continued, "we can shine the light of predictability on the outcome, through a deep and honest assessment of the options and their implications. The light of predictability also helps take regret out of the equation: when you make the best choice possible using all available information, you might be displeased by the ultimate outcome, but you have no reason to regret the decision itself."

As Howard and I talked further that evening, and then continued the conversation on the phone during the next week, he offered a series of practical, concrete steps that Lourdy—or any of us—might use to "shine the light of predictability" on the risks associated with specific paths, options, and decisions. These steps are most effective when based on the kind of foundational thought that he recommended for Lourdy. Here they are.

1. Deconstruct the risk. What many people view as a singular risk is often, actually, a variety of elements woven together. It's another example of "not being able to see the trees for the forest"—being overwhelmed by the whole and not seeing the distinct pieces. So it's useful to tease apart the "outcome" factors from the "uncertainty" factors, and to separate the factors requiring specific attention from those that don't. Then, deconstruct further: be explicit about the potential benefits and costs of each possible outcome, and about the drivers of each element of uncertainty. Untangling the myriad factors reduces an apparently huge and complicated bundle of risks to a series of distinct—and much more manageable—options and questions. It also helps avoid climbing up the "ladder of inference"— where a person infers or assumes something that may not be completely accurate, then uses that supposed "fact" to step up to the next level of evaluation, which will inevitably be skewed; and after just a few of these inaccurate inferential steps, the risk assessment is completely off track. Finally, deconstruction is a way to identify (and confront) any fears or other emotionally based reactions that are wrapped up in the "risk bundle" but that have nothing to do with the facts of the matter.

2. See past the short term. Among our many frailties, people tend to overemphasize the risk of losing something we have and minimize the potential for gaining something new. Likewise, it's human nature to give short-term impacts—both positive and negative—more weight than long-term impacts. But neither is the most effective approach to assessing risk. Recognize these natural inclinations, and dig deeper in your analysis whenever your initial reaction is to shy away from accepting short-term risk in exchange for mid- or long-term benefit. "A notable and frequent example of 'short-term vision' is when people are reluctant to take on new challenges at work—not because they worry that they won't eventually master the challenges, but because they might look less competent as they learn the necessary new skills," Howard noted. "In overweighting the short-term risk to their professional pride, they lose out on the long-term opportunities." Being willing to take on this risk can be key to achieving ambitious career goals; but it requires a certain kind of courage—what I call "emotional muscularity."

Emotional muscularity also comes into play when you consider accepting short-term salary risks in order to realize long-term career advancement—a trade-off that's often a bargain in disguise. My friend Mike Leven, who is now the hugely respected president of the Las Vegas Sands organization, attributes a big chunk of his professional success to the times when he "took a step down" to a less well paying or prestigious job in order to get valuable knowledge or experience. "I've always looked at the long term," Mike has explained to me, "and I never saw it as risky to take a job that made me better at what I did." Likewise, Lourdy is perfectly positioned to take a short-term salary risk that would help clarify her long-term path. "With a supportive family and fiancé, she's got a strong financial safety net," Howard noted. "In her situation, I'd ask myself, 'What kinds of activity could I pursue over the next year or two—regardless of how well or poorly they pay—that would let me test the career options available in areas that I feel really passionate about?' Of course, understanding the long-term financial implications of those options will be important data to collect; but the short-term financial risks will likely prove insignificant compared to the energy and sense of direction she'd gain."

(As I think about this particular piece of advice, I marvel at how it embodies so many of Howard's key beliefs: that we need to live life forward; that time is a personal resource to be actively managed; that career satisfaction is an important goal unto itself; that *any* new information we learn about ourselves—positive or negative—is beneficial, and is useful in identifying options and assessing risk. For all of these reasons, taking a short-term risk such as Howard suggests will almost definitely return greater long-term benefits for Lourdy—emotionally, for certain; and, in all probability, financially, too.)

3. Run the whole movie—forward and backward. Research shows that young people tend to be most worried about *doing* something that will go wrong, while older people tend to be most displeased with things they *didn't do*—an experience they didn't have or opportunity they didn't pursue. Similarly, studies suggest that people magnify their concerns about something that *might* go wrong in the future and how bad it will make them feel; but once that negative event has actually occurred, they realize they're much more comfortable with the outcome than they'd anticipated. For these reasons, it's important to consider how these human tendencies skews one's perception of risk. "Starting at the end," which is important for defining a legacy vision, is also an effective way to counter these skewed perceptions. "Play out the whole 'risk' scenario going forward," Howard suggested, "then roll it backward, from the vantage point of your funeral. Ask yourself, from that perspective, which choice actually appears more risky. And while you're doing that, keep in mind the words of the immortal comedienne Lucille Ball, 'I would rather regret the things I have done than the things I have not.'"

4. Separate reversible from irreversible decisions. Many perceived risks may be less significant than they seem at first blush if the underlying actions can be undone or at least partially walked back. Conversely, some risks that initially appear insignificant are more consequential precisely because they're irreversible. The risks involved in dropping out of law school may be reversible; the worst result may be that you have to reapply. The risks involved in taking a long hiatus from training for the Olympics may be irreversible; the window of opportunity is pretty small. Quitting your accounting job to try out for a Broadway show may or may not be smart, but it's probably a reversible risk; if you don't make the big-time, you go back to accounting. On the other hand, you're accepting an irreversible risk if in order to get fired by the accounting firm and collect unemployment insurance while you do auditions, you deliberately screw up an audit. "Frankly, there are a hell of a lot more career-oriented risks that are reversible than not. In fact, you could say that anything that isn't ethically wrong or doesn't harm someone else—physically, emotionally, or legally—is reversible to one extent or another," Howard observed. "So it's self-defeating to ignore reversibility as a factor in determining how risky a situation may be."

5. *Figure out how to spread the risk.* Once you clearly understand the risks and their magnitude, it's time to figure out how to spread it around. "A basic principle in entrepreneurial ventures is having multiple people share the risk," Howard noted. "The venture capitalist takes much of the financial risk off the shoulders of the people driving a start-up company; in return for assuming that risk, they get a piece of the long-term benefit. In turn, they spread their financial risk by investing in multiple projects and by bringing in a larger pool of investors." While it won't necessarily work for every situation and every person, you don't have to be a venture capitalist to share risk and reduce uncertainty. It's worth applying some creative thought to the task. Ask yourself: Can I cut the risk by spreading it over a longer period of time or taking action incrementally? Are there ways to run experiments before committing to a decision with uncertain implications? Are there 'partners' who might be willing to share the risk with me? Are there people who might feel that taking on a piece of my risk actually diversified their risk?

   Howard is a master at spreading risk and reducing uncertainty—in all kinds of situations. One of my favorite stories is about how he dealt with a valuable sculpture he bought while traveling in Europe. The challenge was to get it transported safely back to his home in Cambridge. He could have had it insured to protect his investment, but if the piece were damaged he'd have to put a lot of time and energy into getting it repaired, which would have been a further cost for him. So here's how he spread the risk: he bought the dealer a round-trip airline ticket to Boston and said, "You put the sculpture in my hands at Logan Airport, undamaged, and I'll hand you full payment for it." In the end, Howard risked the cost of an online ticket; the dealer risked the time required for the round-trip flight; and both parties got what they wanted by sharing the risk between them.

When I sat down with Lourdy again, I discussed each of these five suggestions. And, with Howard's encouragement, I added three caveats based on my own experiences.

First, I told her, "Don't accept someone else's definition of what's risky." If you ask me what kind of work environment I find risky, I'd say a big corporation, because putting myself in that environment means giving up any real sense of control over my own destiny. Ask that question of my close friend Mark Birtha and he'll tell you that it's risky to join a relatively small entrepreneurial venture, where the economics are dynamic and there's little room for mistakes—a place just like Axcess. Is either of us wrong? Nope. Is either of our personal definitions of risk directly applicable for Lourdy? No, again.

Second, I told her, "Don't worry until it's time to worry." As an example of what I meant, I recounted the time, ten years ago, when I was stressing about whether or not to apply to Harvard for grad school. I was trying to assess in minute detail what the risks might be for my career trajectory if I took a year or more away from my entrepreneurial focus; what the financial impact would be of not working and paying tuition; whether Jennifer would be comfortable picking up and moving to Boston—on and on and on with the questions. One day, I was rambling on to my friend Al Pizzica about my desire for almost-mathematical precision in assessing the various risks in my decision. Finally, he stopped me and said, "Knock it off, will you? You're worrying about options and risks that don't even exist yet. Get the option first. Get accepted to Harvard, then think about the potential implications." It's advice I find myself repeating—to others and to myself—at least once a week: get the option, then worry about exercising it. (And I shared Howard's corollary suggestion: Don't worry about stuff that's not your problem. Don't make your process of analyzing risk more difficult by dwelling on issues and concerns that belong to someone else.)

Third, I told her, "Don't not choose." It's almost a cliché to note that not choosing is, itself, a choice—except that so many people keep falling into this trap. In situations where you are dissatisfied, continuity is a risk, even if familiarity makes it seem less so. Accept that there are no risk-free options in your life or career. (Howard would quote Ralph Waldo Emerson on that point: "As soon as there's life, there's danger.") Recognize that managing risk is a skill you need to develop over time, sometimes through trial and error. Attempting to avoid risk by not making choices is a false defense. It just creates other kinds of risk. Beyond that, it's boring and unsatisfying.

MINDY GROSSMAN

From a certain vantage point, the steps in Mindy Grossman's career could look like a series of increasingly and unnecessarily risky leaps from one peak to another, higher peak. But her perspective is different. The extraordinarily successful and widely respected CEO of HSN, Inc. (formerly Home Shopping Network), sees accepting risk as a natural part of one's career development—and necessary to achieving satisfaction.

That's the perspective you might expect from someone who left college midway through her senior year, feeling it was actually *less* risky than continuing on the career track others had laid out for her. "I saw myself heading to graduation, then to law school, then . . . to somebody else's life," she told me one morning as we sat in HSN's New York office. "People said I was foolish. My parents were hugely disappointed; but they understood, eventually, that I needed to go in a different direction." That direction turned out to be the retail and apparel industry; once she figured it out, she never looked back. It appears that the lack of a bachelor's degree hasn't hurt her any: *Financial Times* named her one of the top fifty women in world business; *Forbes* magazine placed her among the world's one hundred most powerful women.

At each step in her journey from "dropout" to "most powerful," Mindy has recognized the power of taking well-considered career risks. Initially, those risks were low-key, personal ones that few other people had reason to notice. Then, about twenty years ago, she took a step that was visible in the business world. Having been part of the management team that grew the Tommy Hilfiger brand from sales of $38 million to $300 million in just four years, she took a risk and left to lead a smaller and weaker company, Chaps Ralph Lauren. The overwhelming reaction in the industry was that she'd made a huge mistake, wouldn't be successful, had probably derailed her career. But she believed that her future at Hilfiger was going to be less exciting than the past had been: fewer big challenges, fewer opportunities for learning. Where others saw only risk at Ralph Lauren, Mindy saw the opportunity to be one of the few female CEOs in the industry and to build a brand. And build she did, increasing revenues by about 1,000 percent in three years.

So imagine the reaction when, three years and two days after she started that job, she quit. "My company sat within a conglomerate—named Warnaco—that had the worst corporate culture I've ever experienced. It was a toxic, fear-based culture deliberately fostered by the CEO," Mindy recalled. "Even though I was being treated appropriately, I realized I was condoning that toxic culture by my presence, and I couldn't do it any longer. One day, I walked into the CEO's office, told her I was going to resign—and was escorted out of the building before the sun set." She had recognized going to the office that morning that she was taking a huge career and financial risk, but she knew that the bigger risk would have been to cast aside her personal values.

Fast-forward about twelve years—through several more risky leaps, each driven by a clear vision of who she wanted to be, personally and professionally—to 2006. Mindy was then global vice president of Nike, Inc., leading a $4 billion apparel business. Over the course of six years she had succeeded wildly in a job that, when her appointment was first announced, industry insiders predicted she'd lose in six months. "And then," she said, "I realized that it was time for me to change the balance in my life—to spend less time traveling the world and direct more energy to my daughter, my husband, and my parents. But I wanted to do it in a way that also let me take on some new professional challenges." How did she do it? By driving the know-it-alls crazy again, of course.

At the peak of her career, Mindy left Nike to do something she had absolutely no previous experience doing: running a media and e-commerce company, and then guiding the company through an initial public offering. That company is known today as HSN, Inc.—the corporate parent of HSN, HSN.com, and Cornerstone Brands—and is one of the most successful and respected companies in its industry.

"When I left Nike, once again the consensus was that I was either committing career suicide or had lost my mind—or both. And for a while in 2008, when the economy tanked and our stock nosedived, I thought they might be right," she noted with a rueful laugh. "I had more than a few sleepless nights, feeling responsible for the financial security of our six thousand employees and their families. Still, I knew that we were doing exactly what we needed to do—not just to weather the storm but to emerge as a much stronger company."

To talk with Mindy and experience her energy, passion, and intelligence is to understand why she has succeeded so well at each job she's taken on. But it wasn't until she said those words—"I knew that we were doing exactly what we needed to do"—that I felt I understood how she has been able to confidently pursue opportunities that most others saw as huge, fear-inducing risks. Mindy's risk-taking decisions are driven by a clear legacy vision, anchored in uncompromising values, and guided by a dynamic awareness of what is needed for her life to be in balance. She is doing exactly what she needs to be doing—and, for her, doing anything else would be the real risk.

And now, in retrospect, what did she think about all the others who thought they knew what she should be doing? She sighed when I asked the question, then said,

"I've learned that the unfortunate nature of many, many people is to bet against someone taking a risk. But I believe it diminishes you when you do that. So I have a very strict rule—I never bet against anyone. I bet on who's going to succeed.

"And I surround myself with creative thinkers—people who emanate positive energy, who think in three dimensions, who know that progress won't happen without breaking the rules. In other words, people who are willing to take intellectual and professional risks. Because nothing really new happens without vision, creativity, and smart risk-taking.

CHAPTER THIRTEEN

Failing Forward

What other people might call failures I simply see as situations laden with meaning—full of new data and new opportunities for assessing and recalibrating a strategy.

A FEW YEARS AGO, a group of Harvard faculty, students, and administrators sat down to talk about a subject that has been too little discussed: rejection and failure. The sponsors of the session, entitled Reflections on Rejections: An Exploration on Resilience in the Face of Failure, described their motivating question this way:

> *At some point in your life, you will experience rejection. You apply for a job, school, or grant, you audition or try to get something pub-lished, you seek some other dearly sought prize, and it just doesn't work out. In difficult circumstances or dark times, how do we turn ambiguity into opportunity, disaster into discovery, failure into for-tune, lemons into lemonade?*

At the session, participants talked honestly about their own stories of rejection and how those perceived failures had af-fected their lives over the long term. They considered the defi-nition of the words *success* and *failure* in light of what they'd learned since those tough experiences. A broad range of folks shared their stories, from lawyers and business school applicants to scientists and mathematicians to novelists and jewelry makers. For example, Harvard genetics professor George Church, now a highly respected researcher and innovator who wrote the first software for automated DNA sequencing, described some notable speed bumps he hit as a student, including repeating ninth grade and flunking out of a PhD program at Duke before successfully restarting his doctoral studies at Harvard.

Xiao-Li Meng, a witty and creative statistics professor, shared some of his own rejections and failures, and offered a whimsically logical "statistical theory of rejection" based on what he's learned from those experiences. It provided a reassuring dose of reality for those conditioned—by society, family, or their own internal compass—to believe that rejection and failure are marks of poor moral character or insufficient effort. "For any acceptance worth competing for," his theory stated, "the probability of a randomly selected applicant being rejected is higher than the probability of [his] being accepted." And the probability that any of us will be accepted for—or succeed at—everything is zero, he noted.

Like Meng's conclusion, the takeaway from the Reflections on Rejections conversations was straightforward: no one is immune to rejection and failure; even the most accomplished and successful among us don't win 100 percent of the time. But another conclusion was clear as well: failure need not be the end of a story. For many of the session participants, rejections and failure proved to be a big motivator. (In Howard-speak, they were Foe inflection points with tremendous latent motivational energy.) For others, they were a big wake-up call, helping them realize that they needed to reassess their goals, take another look at their legacy vision, and reevaluate what they viewed as competitive advantages.

I described the Reflections on Rejections session to Howard one spring day as we sat on a bench in the grassy square outside his office. "It really spurred some interesting conversations," I noted.

Howard responded to my comment with a nod and a sigh. "And we need to have a lot more of those kinds of discussions. Increasingly over the decades, there's been a disconcerting expectation of almost effortless success, and a supremely self-defeating sense that failure is somehow morally tainted," he said.

"You mean here?" I asked, gesturing to the students traversing the HBS campus on that sunny and crisp day.

"Here, sure," he said, "but well beyond, too. Harvard's got no monopoly on the tyranny of success."

"That's an interesting new bit of Howard-speak," I mused, "but pity the poor Cornell grad and define 'tyranny of success,' please."

He chuckled and explained, "Well, it's actually not 'Howard-speak' because the phrase has been around for at least a decade, in different contexts. It's been used to describe the tendency of corporate executives to manage for short-term profit rather than long-term growth; and some entrepreneurs use it to capture the challenge of moving past today's big thing to find tomorrow's new idea and better way of doing things.

"The word *tyranny* means arbitrary, complete, and oppressive control. And I use the phrase 'tyranny of success' to describe a deep sociological condition: too many of us are arbitrarily and completely ruled by an unconscious sense that success is everything; that it must be complete to count at all; and that the opposite of success is abject, irreversible failure. In that context, the tyranny of success is bound up with celebrity culture, where being anything but a complete and awe-inspiring success is a metaphorical death—you no longer count and no one cares about you. The tyranny of success also thrives on a certain degree of emotional laziness that we collectively accept as normal: it's easier to think in black-and-white terms—to accept the simplistic equation that success equals good, lack of success equals bad, and there's no middle ground—rather than to seek out more subtle patterns and shades of gray.

"The philosopher Hannah Arendt once observed that 'under conditions of tyranny it is far easier to act than to think.' And I believe that too many people submit to the tyranny of success by simply reacting to the positive and negative events around them, without thinking through their implications. They don't stop to understand that there is no such thing as unalloyed success and that the only unalloyed failure is death—and perhaps not even that, if you believe in heaven or eternal life of the soul."

I chewed on those weighty thoughts for a bit, then asked Howard a question that was, I assumed, pretty straightforward: "What were some of your most significant failures—the ones that really stick with you?"

Howard thought for a moment, started to answer, stopped, started again, then looked at me with a slightly bewildered expression. I don't think I'd ever seen him as stumped by a question before, even ones that seemed, to me, infinitely more complex than this one. "I don't know how to answer that," he finally said. "I don't think about my life that way."

Then he sat back and considered how to tease out the assumptions behind my question and respond to them instead. "I guess my inability to answer is tied up with my belief in the importance of 'living life forward.' That means a few different things. Let me try to explain.

"I prefer to expend my energy only on things that I can affect. What's past is only useful to me insofar as it offers information to use going forward. And since nothing that I've experienced has been a complete and total failure—totally lacking useful new data—I don't see disappointments as failures. I see them as situations comprising certain positive results, certain negative results, and others that are basically neutral. This is another example of why it's so important to be able to see both the forest—the big picture—and the individual trees that make up that picture. So, because any experience has both positive and negative aspects, what other people might call failures I simply see as situations laden with meaning—full of new data and new opportunities for assessing and recalibrating a strategy.

"Don't misunderstand, I've certainly had my share of disappointing situations and painful experiences. But were they failures? Not to me. Was my first marriage a failure? It wasn't successful, but it certainly wasn't a failure—at a minimum, I've got three great sons and a slew of grandkids to prove that. Was my first stint at HBS a failure? It wasn't successful, but it was by no means a failure—I taught well, did some very good research, and laid the groundwork for many of my future accomplishments.

"I guess the fundamental reason I can't answer the question as you asked it is that, for me, 'not accomplishing' something and 'failing' are wholly different ideas. My only failure will be when I no longer try to accomplish things that are important to me and that are in accord with my moral sense; when I no longer work on things that are integral to who I want to be—integral to realizing my legacy vision." He stopped and leaned in toward me. "That make sense?"

I nodded. "A wise friend of mine, Francois Bennahmias, once said, 'There can be no failure amidst the act of striving.' Sounds like you'd agree."

"Wholeheartedly," he replied, then raised a finger of caution. "As long as two conditions are met. First, that the striving is ethical and based on your true values. I honestly believe that, beyond the 'failure' of death, the only irrecoverable failure is a moral one. It's very hard to repair the damage done through a knowing ethical lapse—it is the kind of failure that sticks with you forever. It lessens your ability to recover from other failures: if, in striving upward, you step on people's hands to pass them on the ladder, few will be willing to catch you when you slip and fall. Nor is it effective, when a setback has put you in a difficult spot, to convince yourself that the normal, ethical rules don't apply; doing so, in my experience, only redoubles the negative impact and deepens the failure.

"The second condition is that the striving is rooted in intellectual and emotional honesty, that the goals you're pursuing are, indeed, your own." He paused to retrieve a thought from his memory. "Do you remember Arthur Ashe, a great tennis player and one of the first African-American men to break through the professional tennis world's 'polite' racial barriers? When asked how he dealt with the big hurdles he faced in his life, he said very simply: 'Start where you are. Use what you have. Do what you can.' And I try to follow the same approach. Each day, I try to look objectively at the picture I have in my mind for who I want to be and ask myself, 'What do I have to do today to move another step or two closer to that vision?' Frankly, it doesn't matter what 'success' or 'failure' I had yesterday. All that matters is where I am today, what I have to work with, and what I can do to live my life forward, toward my legacy vision."

I have often found myself mulling over the substance of that discussion with Howard; and the subject of success and failure has slipped, unbidden, into a number of recent conversations I've had with others. Three particular conversations—with friends and colleagues who have vastly different but quite extraordinary experiences—are worth recounting because of the interesting perspectives they offer.

The first was with Mike Leven, a guy who, like Howard, has vast experience, insight, and wisdom. For decades, Mike has been a major force in the American hotel and tourism industry, but he's never been more widely respected than he is as I write these words. That's because, at an age when most people would be satisfied enjoying the fruits of past success, he took on one of the biggest challenges of his life. At age seventy-one, he agreed to become president of the Las Vegas Sands—the world-famous hotel and casino business that was then on the brink of bankruptcy—and to try to save the company. Less than three years later, Mike and his team (with the support of the company's founder, Sheldon Adelson) had accomplished what's been described as the "largest and quickest turnaround in corporate history." What Mike accomplished at the Sands was a huge achievement—an indisputable win capping a distinguished fifty-year career in the hotel industry. Yet when I asked him about the professional achievements he most prizes, the Sands wasn't at the top of his list. "One of the things I'm most proud of is the fact that it took me twenty-five years to become an overnight sensation," Mike joked with me one afternoon, sitting in his den at home in Atlanta. "It was that long into my career that I landed my first really big job, as president of the Days Inn hotel chain—which, by the way, was also the first time that we weren't living paycheck-to-paycheck, when I could pay the mortgage a month ahead if I wanted.

"I'm proud because I recognized that the slow climb was the right pace for me and I stuck to what I felt was right, professionally and personally. The slow road gave me time to truly understand the business I was in and to develop the tools I needed to be an effective leader. Most important, it enabled me to focus on being a good husband and parent."

Given that perspective, it wasn't surprising to learn that many other experiences on his "success" list had nothing to do with fancy titles or financial wealth. He defines success as much by the wins he brought to others as by his own achievements. "I hope a large part of my final legacy is the people I've helped to realize major professional accomplishments of their own," he explained, "and I'm most proud of two initiatives that helped whole groups of people." One of those was a program providing opportunities for older workers who felt their careers had petered out and who saw no way forward; it won an award from the Thousand Points of Light Foundation. The second

initiative, which he feels may be his most important professional achievement, was founding a trade group called the Asian
American Hotel Association. On the surface an innocuous,
bureaucratic-sounding accomplishment, it actually had huge
impact. "For many years, there was tremendous discrimination
against people of East Asian and South Asian descent within
the hotel industry; they couldn't get business loans to operate
hotels, and few hotel companies would sell them franchises to
run," Mike recalled. "It was a huge barrier to people who simply wanted to pursue the American dream in the way that immigrant communities had for more than a century. But, by
creating the association and enabling these people to work together to overcome the hurdles thrown in front of them, I
helped open a path to success for, literally, thousands of entrepreneurs and their families."

While my conversation with Mike focused on interpretations
of success, my talk with Mark Lazarus—the relatively new
chairman of NBC Sports—dealt much more with the implications of failure. For a major corporate leader, Mark is amazingly modest and has few pretentions. One of the things I find
most interesting about him is that when you ask for the back
story to his professional accomplishments, he'll begin by explaining how he bombed out of his junior year of high school.

"I made some bad choices in high school—the typical teenage stuff, just more so—and I had to re-do an entire year at a
new school. But, in retrospect, that experience turned out to be
a huge inflection point that set the path for much of the life and
career that followed in the next thirty years," he told me. "I've
thought about this a lot, and if I hadn't had that setback, I'm
pretty sure I would have had a much less interesting, fulfilling
career. And in the last year or so, I've become very conscious of
the connection between some of my biggest failures and my
subsequent successes."

A few years prior to our conversation, Mark was dealing with the fallout of what felt to him like a big failure: after six years as president of Turner Entertainment Group (and seventeen overall at Turner), Mark found himself suddenly out of a job as a group of very senior managers were dismissed. While the reasons behind the move are still not completely clear, believers in fate might conclude that Mark's firing took place just so that he could be perfectly positioned when another opportunity rang his cell phone.

After Turner, Mark spent a few years with CSE, an Atlanta-based marketing and production company, when Dick Ebersol (the iconic leader of NBC Sports for decades) recruited him to lead NBC's new sports cable group. And just months later, sitting in a corporate meeting in upstate New York, Mark got an unexpected call from Dick's boss, the CEO of NBC Universal. "He asked where I was and how quickly I could get back to Manhattan," Mark recalled. "I asked him why—what was going on? And he said, 'Dick Ebersol is retiring. Today. And you're taking over his job. Now. Get back here.'"

At that moment, he entered a whirlwind. Beyond the challenge of succeeding a living legend (which Dick Ebersol is), in his first eight months on the job Mark was responsible for managing the integration of the Versus network into NBC Sports and for closing six major sports broadcasting agreements valued at nearly $15 billion. For the first of them—NBC's blockbuster deal for the Olympics—the team had three weeks to completely reshape the primary presentation. Somehow, they managed it all. In retrospect, it would be hard for an objective observer to conclude that he wasn't exactly the right person for a hugely challenging situation. Nevertheless, in many ways, Mark is still processing the psychological, personal, and professional implications of his abrupt departure from Turner—an experience that still feels like a failure to him. But he's already taken some lessons from that inflection point, and they've made him a better manager and leader today.

"One of the first lessons I've taken from the Turner experience is on the nature of people and relationships," he observed. "More than before, I've learned to measure people by how they respond to others in time of need. I will never forget those who reached out to me—especially those who unexpectedly offered their friendship and support. And I feel an even stronger sense of responsibility to the people throughout our organization whose livelihoods depend on how well I do my job."

The third significant conversation—also about the interesting relationship between success and failure—was with a business partner and good friend, Ken Austin. Beyond being a wonderful, smart, and funny guy, Ken is a lifelong entrepreneur who started his first business in grade school and whose last couple of ventures have been especially big wins: he helped launch Marquis Jet in 2001 and shepherded its acquisition by Warren Buffett's NetJets; then in 2010 he launched a new premium liquor, Tequila Avion, that is one of the hottest new entries in the spirits industry. At one point in our conversation, I said to him, jokingly, "You're not one for failure, are you?" Ken's reply echoed Howard.

"I don't do failure," he said, shaking his head. Then he hurried to add, "I don't mean that arrogantly. I'm as susceptible to failure as anyone else, and there are situations where I've not had success. But I haven't had any crash-and-burn experiences. More than that, I've found that even the least successful experiences have given me some real, tangible takeaways—knowledge, skills, or connections—that I've put to use to make other ventures successful.

"Remember, I've been learning business lessons since the time, as a kid, I bought some snowblowers for my neighborhood snow-clearing business. So those takeaways have added up over the years. They've sharpened my eye for weak ideas, for the pitfalls under the seemingly solid surface of a business opportunity. To use a sports analogy, they've helped me see the whole game developing around me and enabled me to anticipate—pretty early in the process—what the final score might be. A big reason that I haven't really experienced failure in the commonly defined sense is that I've been able to spot losing propositions before I got really dug in," he explained.

"Sounds like not only were you able to spot them, but you were honest enough with yourself to acknowledge that you'd be developing a weak idea," I observed. "And confident enough to say, 'Nope, I'm not going to continue down a fruitless road.' A lot of people end up failing at something just because they lack the courage to get off a bad path."

"Yeah, I guess you could say I've been willing to acknowledge and accept small, short-term setbacks as a way to avoid outright failure."

"So, in the broad sense, you don't worry about failure," I concluded.

Ken responded with a half smile, half grimace, and said, "Actually, I worry about failure a lot—especially in situations like Tequila Avion, where a lot of people are depending on me. I feel a big sense of responsibility to the women and men working with me; to my partners and our investors; and to my family. Failing would let all these people down. In that sense, I fear failure. Except, it's not a paralyzing, weighing-me-down kind of fear. It sounds funny, but for me it has mostly positive effects: it motivates me, makes me more creative, gives me energy; it makes me much more willing to analyze things objectively and honestly, and fix problems right away, rather than waiting."

Subsequently recounting the essence of those three conversations to Howard, I observed, "One of the really interesting things was the nature of the relationship between success and failure for these guys—the far-from-simple connections between 'wins' and 'losses.' And the various ways that perceived failure can beget success."

"You know, people throw around words like *success* and *failure* assuming they mean exactly the same thing to everyone—and they don't," Howard replied. "There is no standard metric for evaluating success or failure, in large part because our assessments are heavily affected by the expectations we bring into a situation. In *Paradise Lost,* John Milton wrote, 'The mind is its own place, and in itself can make a heaven of hell, a hell of heaven.' He perfectly captures the degree to which expectations can color our perceptions of success and failure—and of their impact on our lives.

"More than that, our definitions of success and failure change based on personal circumstance; they're colored by what's happening around us. Do you consider yourself a successful or unsuccessful investor if you earn a two percent return? Depends if you're investing during an up or down market. Do you consider yourself more successful getting a B-minus in an honors class or an A-plus in a gut class? Do you feel like a failure if you haven't mastered a piano sonata after a year's effort—even if your hectic life permits you just an hour a week to practice and you enjoy every minute of it? Context is hugely important.

"It matters what comparisons you're making. I knew a guy who felt poor because he only had wealth equal to one percent of Bill Gates's net worth—which means he had millions of dollars!" Howard exclaimed.

"Weighing success and failure is further complicated by the fact that they're often two sides of same coin—it's difficult to define one without some reference to the other. I suppose that, theoretically, you could define them in pure terms. But in the real world, success doesn't require the complete absence of failure, and failure isn't marked by a total lack of success.

"Given all those confusing factors, it's not surprising that people are motivated by success and failure in what can seem to be contradictory ways; nor that success and failure can each have unexpected, contradictory long-term impacts. That's why, even though I have a clear perspective of what success or failure means to me, I think we get into trouble by making—or accepting— blanket prescriptions about which is a better or more appropriate motivator. For me, the bottom line is: don't put yourself in a definitional straitjacket, and don't allow others to do it to you, either.

"It's important to define success and failure in your own terms," he concluded.

What Howard meant by "in your own terms" will be clear to anyone who has read this book from the beginning: success isn't, if it's based on someone else's definition; failure isn't, if it's connected to something you really didn't want in the first place. Success and failure should be defined primarily in terms of *your* legacy vision. They should be measured, on a tactical level, in relation to the juggling-and-balancing decisions *you've* made and where you've chosen to invest your personal resources of time, energy, and emotional commitment. Those metrics should be informed by how *you* view your skills, passions, and competitive advantages; by which ones you've chosen to pursue, and with what expectations in mind. And you should periodically test those definitions and measurements against the experiences and track record of your personal catalysts—role models, mentors, individual board of directors—whose goals, paths, and perspectives parallel or complement yours.

Notably, for Howard, success and failure "in your own terms" are present and future oriented. Defining them begins from the perspective of where you are today and where you want to be tomorrow and next week. They are continuously redefined as your life changes, as you attain some goals and set new ones. They are recalibrated as your value weightings shift among the different facets and dimensions of your life.

Finally, he would suggest, defining success and failure in your own terms requires answers to several potent questions:

▓ *What investment did I have to make to achieve this success, and what opportunities did I have to give up? In other words: was the juice worth the squeeze?*

▓ *Conversely, did I fail simply because I did not invest enough of my personal resources? If so, was that underinvestment a conscious miscalculation or a subconscious statement that I wasn't really committed to the effort in the first place?*

▓ *Perhaps most significant, when will I have succeeded enough—made enough money, gained enough status, helped enough in my community, learned enough, et cetera—so that I feel satisfied in my life's work?*

When a terminally ill Steve Jobs resigned from Apple in August 2011, the *Boston Globe* ran a fascinating article. Headlined "Failing Forward," its opening lines read, "Nobody's better at failure than Steve Jobs. . . . [He] has failed time and again, occasionally in spectacular fashion. He's introduced products that bombed. He sent his companies in directions that went nowhere." Jobs's career demonstrated, the *Globe* said, "how failure can be a constant companion, even for winners." His experiences also showed how often failure holds the seeds of future success: the famously unsuccessful Lisa computer was the inspiration for hugely successful Macintosh (which spurred the creation of desktop publishing); Jobs's NeXT computer failed in the marketplace, but today's popular Mac software grew from NeXT's operating system; and the ROKR ("rocker") phone/music player hybrid was a flop—but the concept evolved into the iPhone.

That article hints at an important lesson that Howard has tried to instill in his students and his family. It's a lesson essential for everyone who hopes to make a career as an entrepreneur (or simply be entrepreneurial in their career): failure carries the seeds of future success, and success carries the seeds of failure.

Jobs's experiences perfectly exemplify the first part of that statement. And both Howard and I have met many people whose experiences bear out the truth of the second part. Those people had phenomenal success in one area of their lives, and that success sowed the seeds of unhappiness and failure in other areas. There are any number of reasons why those seeds took root and grew. Some people misunderstood the full nature of the success they experienced and the price it would require— like my friend Jan, who reveled in the prestige and pay that came with being named president of one of the biggest philan-thropic organizations in the country but quickly grew to hate the pressure of being in demand and under a microscope all day, every day.

Others simply let success run through their fingers like so much sand on a beach, assuming there would always be plenty for the taking. Musician-turned-businessman Jesse Itzler had that experience. Today Jesse is a successful serial entrepreneur: he is one of the co-founders of Marquis Jets and the guy behind what was one of the strongest consumer product launches in 2011: Sheets Energy Strips. But, Jesse, who counts LeBron James among his partners, started his working career as a rap musician, parlaying talents for musical composition and promo-tion into a recording contract right out of college. Performing as "Jesse Jaymes," he had success with his debut album: the first single hit the *Billboard* Hot 100 and was featured in a 2004 film; and his music video was featured on MTV. That latter mark of success, ironically, was the pivotal point for the failure of his career as a singer. "I'd been doing the whole thing on gut in-stinct, hadn't really thought through my goals, hadn't thought about what came next," he explained to me one day, sitting in an office surrounded by huge likenesses of LeBron and Amar'e Stoudamire holding boxes of Sheets. "When I got onto MTV, I thought that was the top of the mountain—and I just sat down and enjoyed the view. Unfortunately, I sat there so long, the music industry passed me by." Of course, it didn't take Jesse long to get himself going full speed on another career track, and he's been enjoying success since. But his MTV experience still serves as a great lesson in how easy it can be to "boldly rescue failure from the arms of success," as he laughingly described the summary of his rap career.

Success in one area can also mask the development of significant problems—and potential failure—in another aspect of our lives. "Some kinds of success shine a light so bright that it blinds you to the things outside the circle of light," Howard once observed. "Perhaps the most common instance is when phenomenal financial success blinds people to problems in their marriage or with their children." Sometimes it is, indeed, their own blindness. But sometimes their vision is unwittingly blocked by someone else trying to "protect" them or "support" them or "keep them from having to worry." Howard has a classic story of how this phenomenon—on a macro level—helped bring down an entire industry. "In the seventies and eighties, as a perk of their jobs, Detroit auto executives' company cars were brought into the shop each day and checked out," he explained. "Any problems the mechanics found were fixed before the executives drove home that night. As a result, the leaders of the industry never experienced a single one of the ongoing quality issues that were driving their customers crazy and pushing them away from American-made cars."

Regardless of how you define success and failure, notable success and significant failure can both be potent experiences. They're both inflection points in their own rights; and both can have the effect of nudging you off the path to your legacy vision, without your even realizing it's happened. Success can have momentum all its own, and sometimes that momentum carries you in an unintended direction. You get a new job, and you excel; you're promoted and make more money and begin to work longer hours; the competition at the top becomes fierce, so you push that much harder to maintain your success—and one day you wake up and success has led you down the path of becoming a workaholic, spending less time with your family than you'd promised and doing things that in other circumstances you'd find completely unacceptable. In many respects, this was Carter Cast's experience: the urge for success took on a life of its own—became self-justifying, instead of serving a broader purpose in his life—until, finally, he had to just sit down, take a few deep breaths, and get his bearings again.

In a similar way, success can lead you off your intended path and into what Howard calls a velvet-lined rut. "If you are good at something, find it comes easily, and are well rewarded for doing it, there can be a temptation to keep doing it even if you stop enjoying it. The danger is that one day you look around and realize you're so deep in this comfortable rut that you can no longer see the sun or breathe fresh air; the sides of the rut have become so steep and slippery that it would take a super-human effort to climb out; and, effectively, you're stuck. This was essentially the experience of many of my older colleagues in my early days at HBS," Howard recalled. "And it's a situation that many working people worry they're in now. The poor employment market has left them feeling pinned down in what may be a secure, or even well-paying—but ultimately unsatisfying—job."

More frequently, of course, we find failure knocking us off our path. A big—and often unrecognized—reason is that we've attributed the failure to the wrong cause and taken the wrong lessons from it. "When you boil it all down," Howard once explained, "there are just three kinds of failure: failure caused by something external, over which we have limited control; failure caused by something within us, over which we have more control; and moral failure, which may actually be disguised as success. The first key to managing failure effectively is to recognize which kind you're dealing with.

"This requires a mixture of objectivity, honesty, and courage to own up to shortcomings. On the other side, however, you need enough self-confidence to be able to say—when it's true—'This wasn't my fault; there was nothing I could do about it, and I shouldn't be changing my direction because of it.'"

I recently met a fairly senior health-care executive, named Meghan, who'd spent a lot of time wrestling with this dichotomy between external and internal factors. After two decades of steady success—attending a good college and grad school, then holding a series of increasingly responsible roles in big health-care organizations—she had hit a rough patch. In less than five years, she'd been fired from three different jobs. Looking at those three situations objectively, it seemed clear to me that each was a "right person in the wrong place at the wrong time" problem: in the first, her boss was fired and the department was restructured; in the second, the company was acquired and a whole layer of management cut; and the third was a variation of the first—a new boss deciding he wanted somebody with a different mix of skills than Meghan's. But the weight of frustration and confusion that Meghan felt made her wonder if, in fact, those three strikes meant that she deserved to be out because of some flaw in her character or skills. For a while, she considered going back to school to become a physical therapist and was about to head off on that new path when a call from a former colleague—hoping to recruit her for a top job requiring her exact set of skills—helped her put a more objective lens on her "failures." The story has a happy ending, because Meghan's loving the new job in a very stable company. But it was a tough psychological slog for a while.

In the midst of her agonizing self-reappraisal, Howard might have told Meghan, "You haven't lost your skill, just your nerve. Take a deep breath, clear your head—and instead of questioning your professional skills, figure out how to get better at the one thing you seem not to do well: assessing the stability of potential employers."

I've had plenty of occasions to reflect on Howard's thoughts on the tyranny of success, on the relative nature of failure, and on the importance of striving. Working where I do—in the heart of Manhattan, a center of the "culture of success"—and working with the kind of financially and professionally accomplished people I have as clients, there have been times when I've felt pressure to tally up wins and losses, and to divide outcomes into those that feel like successes and those that feel like failures. It is easy to get philosophically and emotionally out of balance. So I've really benefited from Howard's guidance, and I've tried to base my responses to notable "successes" and "failures" on the lessons I have picked up from him.

The infinitely quotable Ralph Waldo Emerson once said, "Bad times have a scientific value. These are the occasions a good learner would not miss." And my dear friend Michelle Wilson added a much less scientific but equally valuable thought to the sentiment: "Sorrow," she told me once, "creates an intense appreciation of joy." So I've tried to be a good learner, to absorb the pain when I haven't succeeded and revel in the times when I have. I've tried to dig beyond the surface of things that seem on their face to be "failures"—for myself, my colleagues, and my friends. What Howard has helped me understand is that the very act of questioning failure (and questioning success, as well) creates a kind of forward motion. It provides, in Howard-speak, latent motivational energy—it propels me toward the person I hope to be. He's taught me that "failing forward" is a positive action, one that balances out human beings' unique capacity to "succeed backward."

MELINDA LOPEZ

All the world's a stage,
And all the men and women merely players:
They have their exits and their entrances;
And one man in his time plays many parts. . . .

These iconic lines are from Shakespeare's play *As You Like It*. And at certain moments in our lives, all of us have felt a bit like characters on a stage: following a path another person has laid out for us; allowing ourselves to pursue goals set by others; substituting someone else's interpretation of success or failure for our own.

If it's any consolation, even playwrights can feel like they're following someone else's script, being guided by someone else's definition of success. They may even feel it more acutely because, for them, it's often literally true: other people get to pass judgment on their life's work. In talking with friends who are playwrights, I've gleaned some interesting perspectives on success and failure that are useful to those of us whose careers don't involve creating imaginary universes.

"The idea of achieving success can be confusing and challenging for a playwright. In part because there are so many uncontrollable factors; and in part because success for an artist can have as many bad implications as good ones," observed Melinda Lopez, an extraordinarily talented writer whose plays—including *Caroline in Jersey, Gary,* and the award-winning *Sonia Flew*—have been produced by major theaters across the United States.

"To begin with," she noted, "a playwright must willingly give up control over the actual performance of her work. We entrust a script to directors, actors, set and lighting designers, and costumers, and hope that they will bring out all of its strengths. And, ultimately, we leave it to audiences and theater critics to decide if we've been successful or not in writing a good play. So, a playwright needs to learn to trust the other people in the process—or you drive yourself crazy."

While, so far, many of those others have deemed Melinda's work very successful—she was the first recipient of the Kennedy Center's prestigious Charlotte Woolard Award for promising new voices in American theater, and has taught or been writer-in-residence at Wellesley College, Boston University, Harvard, the Sundance Center, and the New York Theatre Workshop—success has its own complications and downsides.

"Success can be double-edged," Melinda explained. "The writing process itself demands this strange balance of complete humility and the belief that my ideas are worth gold. I've got to be humble enough to let the characters' true voices come through; but confident enough to know that what they're saying is worth being heard by an audience. So I find myself worrying about success, because it's easy to lose that necessary humility; and on the other hand I worry that failure will make me lose that necessary confidence."

I recalled Tennessee Williams's observation that, for him, "Success and failure are equally disastrous."

"Sometimes that's exactly how it can feel. Although, one saving grace for me is that I often don't know where I'm going with a play when I start writing it. So I'm not hung up by a starting definition of success for that particular play. In that respect, while it's being written the play defines its own success—and that provides a temporary shelter from worrying about failure."

As those familiar with her work know, mere day-to-day

questions of success and failure aren't the only ones that
Melinda weighs; history is in the balance, too. As the
daughter of refugees from Fidel Castro's revolution, the
plight of the Cuban people and culture is never very far
from her consciousness. Her best-known play, *Sonia Flew,*
captures the heartrending experiences of families torn
apart in the aftermath of the Cuban revolution. And the
play she is shaping now, *Becoming Cuba,* explores the challenges and responsibilities of freedom through the lens of
Cuba's birth as an independent nation in the late 1890s.
"I'm not able to be there, in the country, to help defend
the culture and people from what's been happening there
for decades, from what's happening still," she said with
emotional pain in her voice. "This is how I try to help.
Although there are times when I wonder if writing is
enough—if maybe I've failed because I haven't become a
surgeon who goes out and helps people there directly. It's
an internal battle I may never outgrow."

With so many swirling factors coming into play in
defining success and failure in her career, Melinda has
had to develop a simpler, personal way of determining
whether she feels on the right path at any given point. It
is an almost physical sense—one not subject to others'
interpretations and that is not weighed down by the feeling of history looking over her shoulder. "Ultimately, I
think that success is when you're doing what your body
and spirit were made to do. When you just know, intuitively, that you're completely and fully using all the gifts
you have. That kind of success feels like a runner's high—
and that's how I feel when I know I've gotten it exactly
right with a play. That kind of high can move you past a
lot of uncertainty and worries about failure."

★　★　★

When I told Howard about my conversation with Melinda, he nodded approvingly and said, "I'm glad you had a chance to speak with her. Her experiences echo many of my own—even though we come from very different places, professionally and personally.

"Whether you're a playwright, a businessman, a nurse, or a systems analyst, success and failure are not just about you; they are the results of an interchange between you and the world around you," he observed.

"Determining success and failure is a matter of perspective and analysis; it is a complicated dance where we strive to pursue our passions and put forth our best efforts, then step back to assess the outcome relative to our goal—and begin again.

"And, no matter what professional path one pursues, success grows as much from the right balance of self-honesty and self-confidence as from any other individual factor," Howard concluded. "Or to use the words of another famous writer—Marcus Aurelius—'The first rule is to keep an untroubled spirit. The second is to look things in the face and know them for what they are.'"

CHAPTER FOURTEEN

Live the Ripple

ONE NIGHT NOT TOO LONG AGO, my wife, Jennifer, and I were sitting on the couch in our den. We'd moved into a new house just weeks before, and a few partially emptied boxes were still scattered around the room, but neither of us was up for even simple manual labor. What physical energy we each had left after a long day had been fully expended with the boys: playing tag through the house in a desperate effort to get our four-year-old tired enough for bed, and carrying our seven-month-old on long circular walks from bedroom to kitchen and back, helping him settle a rumbly tummy.

Now the exhausted parents vegged out together, enjoying the relative quiet and the lack of physical motion. Jennifer was reading the last few pages of a novel; I was cleaning up a few remaining e-mails from the day's accumulation. "Howard and Fredi send their love," I told her, "and they're looking forward to seeing you next week." The Stevensons were coming down to New York for a few days, and we planned to have dinner and see a Broadway show with them.

In reply, Jennifer smiled and nodded; then, a moment later, she closed her book and turned to me with a quizzical look. "I've been meaning to ask you: why *Howard's Gift*?" she said.

"What do you mean? You know why I'm working on this book," I replied.

"No—I know why the book," she said. "I meant, why are you calling it *Howard's Gift*? You've actually never told me."

"Oh," I said, realizing, sheepishly, that she was right. I'd chosen the title pretty early on, but in all the months since, apparently, I hadn't told Jennifer. "Sorry, that's pretty stupid of me," I said, shaking my head in frustration. It was a little thing, sure, but it made me angry at myself; it went right to one of my hot buttons, triggering one of those worries that I seem particularly susceptible to: whether I was making good choices about where I invested my time and energy. Was the fact that she needed to ask this question a sign that I had been so distracted by my job, the craziness with the new house, and this book that I was shortchanging her?

And then a little voice crept into my head: "Hey, fool—have you learned nothing from all that Howard's taught you?" Then the voice morphed into Howard's gruff baritone: "We can't get an A on every facet of life every single day. Stop worrying backward and keep living forward." I took a deep breath, let go of that twinge of regret I was feeling, and explained to Jennifer why I'd chosen the book's title: because, for me, *Howard's Gift* is about a variety of gifts given and received.

First and foremost is the gift that Howard received: the gift of life bestowed on him by that quick-thinking person who ran to get the portable defibrillator and the others who performed CPR when he collapsed in cardiac arrest that January day in 2007. Then there's the idea that this book itself is intended, in part, as a gift of love and thanks to Howard. (And when Fredi—having read the draft manuscript—said to me, "This is a wonderful gift to us, because it captures Howard so well for the kids and grandkids," I felt satisfied with the results of my labors, even without knowing if anyone not named Stevenson or Sinoway would ever buy the book.) In another respect, Howard's natural gifts—given to him by his parents and the folks who helped shape his way of thinking—are the ones that we are benefiting from: his intelligence, humor, warmth, and caring; his unique insight on individuals' capacities and motivations; his ability to ask incisive, to-the-heart-of-the-matter questions; and his great strategic vision for individuals and organizations.

But the gifts that are probably most important to you, the reader, are the ones Howard has given to us, collectively, and that I've tried my best to convey in these pages: the pearls of wisdom, the counterintuitive insights, and the practical guidance born of decades of experience. Taken all together, these gifts from Howard are catalytic. They invest us with a sense of inspiration and empowerment. They spur us to action on behalf of a goal that only we can accomplish: defining and fulfilling our unique, individual visions of who we are and what we want to achieve in our lives.

Actually, to represent Howard's perspective fully, I should say that his gifts spur us to *more* than just action. They urge us to engage in an ongoing cycle of thinking, acting, and learning and re-acting (as in "acting again"). Because just as Howard hopes we view "balance" as a dynamic quest in our day-to-day lives, he wants us to be continuously proactive in pursuing satisfaction in our life's work.

I don't like final chapters that simply rehash what the rest of the book already said. So let me conclude by sharing one final pearl of Howard's wisdom: As you pursue your life's work, plan for the ripple, not just the splash.

What does that mean? Like many of Howard's thoughts, it is a simple, direct idea wrapped around a more complex set of notions that become apparent as you tease them apart. If you drop a stone into a pool of water, the most obvious result is a splash that subsides relatively quickly; what lasts longer and has a broader effect are the ripples flowing out in all directions from the point of impact. Many of us, in making decisions about our careers or about how we invest time and energy in other facets of our lives, focus rather narrowly and hone in on near-term implications—that is, the splash. Howard urges us to broaden and lengthen our focus; to anticipate and observe where the ripples go and how big they are. And, more important, to pay attention to how they interact with the ripples sent out by events in the lives of the people around us.

"Plan for the ripple, not just the splash" means recognizing that choices, actions, and events have both short-term and long-term implications. However, it doesn't automatically privilege one over the other: in plenty of situations the immediate impact of the splash—whether positive or negative—is so significant that the longer-term ripples almost don't matter; in many others, the downstream effect will be strongest and most enduring. The key, Howard would suggest, is to be thoughtful in assessing both; and to be proactive in anticipating and addressing their effects on your career and life.

But Howard's ripple/splash advice is about more than just chronology; it is also about interconnection. It is a reminder that while we each must define and advance toward a unique legacy vision, in practical terms we will pursue much of our life's work in interdependence with others—family, colleagues, friends, and catalysts of many shapes and sizes. Our splashes and ripples intersect, overlap, flow into one another and create amazing patterns on the waters of our lives. But because we are human—because we see first and foremost through our own eyes and through the lenses of our own needs and wants—it is very easy to ignore those multifaceted, interconnected patterns. It is a form of tunnel vision that is both natural and to be guarded against. "Inconvenient, even challenging and painful as they may be at times, ultimately it's those intersections that truly make life worth living," Howard believes.

* * *

One early-summer evening, when I was visiting the Stevensons' place on the Massachusetts coast, Howard and I went for a walk along the harbor. He and I both love the water—seeing the warm setting sun reflected in it; watching its slow ebb and flow, its surface periodically bent by the slow-rolling wake of a sailboat or punctuated by a seagull swooping in for a morsel.

A few weeks earlier, Howard had stepped down from the Harvard faculty. However, as he told me about the projects and meetings he had on his schedule for the coming days, it was obvious that if he was technically retired, he certainly wasn't slowing down much: he was finishing a book on fund-raising and making arrangements for its publication and distribution; guiding negotiations for a nine-figure gift to the university's science and engineering program; reviewing plans for Harvard Business Publishing, where he remained chairman; speaking with several former students about strategic decisions they were weighing for their respective companies; overseeing remodeling work on the family's place in Maine; and engaged in half a dozen other activities that I don't remember.

On one hand, this level of activity is remarkable for someone entering retirement. On the other, it was far less remarkable than what he had accomplished in the previous four and a half years—the years after his brush with death. Still, on the third hand (to steal the quintessential joke about economists' advice), neither is surprising for a man who has had a crystal-clear sense of who he wants to be and the direction in which he is going, and whose motto is "Live life forward."

"So," I said to him as we strolled along, "it seems that the big retirement splash hasn't created huge ripples in your life."

Howard thought about that for a moment, then replied, "Not immediately, I guess. For me, it's likely that the ripples will have increasing size and impact over time." He stopped to look out over the water ablaze with the setting sun, and a Yoda-like grin crept over his face. "It won't take all that long for people at HBS or NPR to start saying, 'Howard Stevenson? Vaguely remember the name. Wasn't he the guy who . . . ?'"

Maybe it was my sentimental frame of mind at the time—or even a bit of naïveté—but that scenario seemed impossible to me. I blurted out, "Come on, you don't really think that folks at Harvard are going forget what you've meant to the place? You were there for forty years. Taught thousands of students. There's a professorship in your name."

Howard laughed, smiled indulgently, and put his hand on my shoulder. "Thanks for defending my memory, Eric—I could have no better knight-errant fighting my cause. Listen, I'm not saying the Stevenson name will be struck from their memories overnight; but eventually they'll know me simply as the guy the professorship is named for, and not as someone to call if they have a decision to make or a problem to solve. And that's okay, because I'm going to keep living forward, creating a whole new set of ripples for myself."

That conversation returned to me as I was readying this book for the publisher. Replaying it in my mind, I came on the perfect phrase to close with. It's a phrase that—lesson within lesson; meaning within meaning—encapsulates so much of what Howard has taught me. I offer it to you to mull over, tease apart, and use as you will:

Live the ripple.

ACKNOWLEDGMENTS

Howard's Gift has benefited immeasurably from conversations with many smart people, those included in the final text and those who contributed ideas and feedback during its creation. We have benefited from the encouragement, counsel, and contributions of Megan Adams, Andreas Beroutsos, Mark Birtha, Eric Brinker, Roxanne Cason, Colin Cowie, Jeff Diskin, David Ellwood, Rena Fonseca, Jan Freitag, Alan Fuerstman, Gary Garberg, Rob Goldstein, Henry Kesner, Kathy McCartney, Josh Macht, Josh Merrow, Michael O'Mahoney, Elaine Papoulias, Kevin Parke, Steve Reifenberg, Jan Rivkin, Arthur Rock, Henry Rosovsky, Adam Sandow, Tom Shapiro, Andy Sheldon, Prescott Stewart, Bonnie Subramanian, Ellen Sullivan, Bernie Steinberg, Jan Svendsen, Andrew Tisch, David Wan, Mike Wargotz, and Audrey Wong.

We also appreciate the time, thought, and trust offered us by the people whose experiences—good and bad, happy and painful—we profiled: Wendy Kopp, Arvind Raghunathan, Lori Schor, Soledad O'Brien, Carter Cast, Jeff Leopold, Bob Pittman, Nancy Brinker, Rachel Jacobson, Carl Banks, Emily Hunter, Mindy Grossman, and Melinda Lopez; as well as Tom Eisenmann, Christian Hempell, Jesse Itzler, Mike Leven, Mark Lazarus, and Ken Austin.

We owe a debt of gratitude to Joe Tessitore, a caring and insightful man whose contributions would be unfairly minimized by simply calling him our agent; he was the first to believe in this project and has been our champion, friend, and guide from day one.

We have been overwhelmed by the enthusiastic support from the entire team at St. Martin's Press, led by Jeff Dodes, Laura Clark, Stephen Lee, Matt Baldacci, John Murphy, Lisa Senz, and our editor George Witte—who has shepherded *Howard's Gift* with intelligence and commitment.

Of a more personal nature, we offer our gratitude to the people who—through their love, nurturing, and support—provided us with the many opportunities in life that have brought us to this point and enabled us to undertake this project.

From Eric:
When I began writing this book almost six years ago in the days following Howard's heart attack, it was because I felt compelled to capture the voice and wisdom of the dear friend who I had almost lost. As I write these words—quite literally the last page to be submitted to the publisher—I find myself reflecting not only on my relationship with Howard and the path that brought me to our first meeting that cold winter morning, but also on the innumerable mentors, role models, friends, and family members who have meant so much to me as I pursue my life's work.

I think of the many mentors who have provided me with guidance and inspiration as I move toward my own legacy vision, including my grandfather Daniel Davis, whose strength, honesty, humor, and heart built the foundation of our family and for whom my son Daniel is named; Don Ferrara and Danny Bottona, who believed in me and without whom I would not have attended Cornell; the family at the Cornell Hotel School, especially Don Bishop, Jan deRoos, Chekitan Dev, David Dittman, Cathy Enz, Neal Geller, Tim Hinkin, Giuseppe Pezzotti, Michael Redlin, Craig Snow, Bruce Tracey, and so many other current and former members of this remarkable institution;

Bonnie Reiss, who inspired me by her commitment to the public good to enroll at Harvard's Kennedy School; Lawrence Groffman, who educated and guided me and Jennifer with spirituality and care; Sarina Steinmetz, who served as an adopted member of our family during our time in Boston; Larry Davis, whose kindness and perspective proved invaluable when I needed them most; Jeff Altman, Phil Baugh, Lenny Lustig, Al Pizzica, and Josh and Carin Silverman who jumped in a ditch with me to help me get out; Todd Wagner, who taught me much and made it possible for me to learn more; Mike Leven, a mensch, coach, and friend from whom I learned much about business and life during the deal of the decade; and Holly Taylor Sargent, who first opened my eyes to opportunities at Harvard's Development Office—and who introduced me to Howard Stevenson when I was a graduate student.

I am thankful to Kirk Posmantur, whose friendship and love are deep and whose business acumen is pure genius; Mike Wargotz, whose perspective is wise, experience is broad, and friendship is lasting; and to the current and former members of the Axcess Worldwide family who have assisted—through direct contribution or the sharing of their personal wisdom and experience—with this project: Amanda Armstrong, Andrew Black, Andi Cross, Katelyn Delaney, Amanda Healy, Brian Holcomb, Bryan Johnson, Scott McCullers, Brett Muney, Ilan Perline, Molly Malgieri Schiff, Donna Simonelli, Andrew Taylor, and Taylor Yunker. A special thanks to Jaclyn Tarica and Thomas Barguirdjian, who dedicated early mornings and late evenings with good spirit, and to Alexandra Bastian for her passion, commitment, and uncanny skill at managing me with humor and class.

The writing of *Howard's Gift* overlapped with one of the grand inflection points in my life: the sixty-one harrowing days that Jennifer and I spent at Morristown Medical Center prior to our son Michael's arrival, a period when time stood still and our patience, faith, and strength were tested. During this time, I experienced firsthand the kindness and skill of Dr. Russell Hoffman and the remarkable men and women at Morristown Medical Center, including Roseanne, Olga, Shirley, and Paulette and the teams of perinatologists and neonatologists who cared for our family with compassion and skill while we waited out the clock and tried to proceed with some sense of normalcy. While we did, our dear friends Michelle Wilson; Albert and Meghan Pizzica; Josh and Carin Silverman; Phil and Becky Baugh; Christian, Morgan, and Brooke Hempell; John and Jen Prior; Jeanine Schoen; and Jennifer's sister Dr. Michelle Mele provided invaluable support and love.

I am thankful for Daniel and Michael, my children, from whom I've learned my own capacity for love, a capacity that may in fact be limitless; and for the three mothers in my life: my wife, Jennifer, who performed a miracle of her own during sixty-one magical days, and with whom I've been in love since the moment we met our first day of high school; my mother-in-law, Pat Mele, whose strength and accomplishments in life define true success; and my mother, Madeline Sinoway, without whose sacrifice and support nothing I've accomplished would be possible. Thank you, too, to the extended Sinoway and Mele families, who provide the love and laughter for which Jennifer, Daniel, Michael, and I are so appreciative.

And a final piece of recognition: to Merrill Meadow, a prince among men, an individual whose extraordinary writing talent is exceeded only by his compassion, intellectual curiosity, balance, and kindness. A mentor, role model, and member of my IBOD. I'm humbled that he is my partner on this project and grateful he is my friend.

From Merrill:
Working on this book has given me a renewed, deep appreciation for the people who played a role in the key inflection points

in my life and career, including Adam Freedman, Michelle Gorenberg, Barry Kramer, Lori Schor, and Robin Hummel; Robert Turtil, Renae Klee, and the late Astere E. Claeyssens; Geoffrey M. Cohen and Deborah Mackey Cohen; Margot Walsh; Owen Edmonston, Russ Lavery, and Patricia Baldridge; Michael O'Mahoney, Jeffrey Hauk, and Bruce Flynn; Joanna Bakule, Sarah Branstrator, Geoffrey Movius, and Lisa Schwarz; and Sal Jones, Gary and Mollie Garberg, and Tom Griffiths and Jane Trudeau.

I am most grateful for the continuing support and encouragement of my friends and colleagues at Harvard—especially my comrades and fellow writers Neil Angis, Justin Call, Christine Frost, Henry Kesner, Joe Raposo, and Frank White; and the entire UDO team, led by Tamara Rogers, Bob Cashion, and Mary Beth Pearlberg.

I offer a different kind of thanks to the connectors with the past: Charlotte Weiss, Jordan and Eva Choper, Bobby and Rona Parker, and May H. Kalkstein. And to four who cannot accept my thanks: David Kalkstein, Estelle Meadow, and Raphael and June Meadow. And to the extended Meadow/Brandenburg/Mintz family—Craig, Gale, Eliot, Stephanie, Wendy, Michael, Jaki, and all the nieces and nephews—for their continuing support.

But my broadest and deepest gratitude goes to my smart, funny, lovely wife, Cheryl, and to my children, Gabe and Zoe, who make me proud each day. From you all good things flow. This book is for you.